# REACHING
# OLYMPUS

## TEACHING MYTHOLOGY THROUGH
## READER'S THEATER SCRIPT·STORIES

# REACHING OLYMPUS

# THE GREEK MYTHS
## HEROES, BEASTS, AND MONSTERS

WRITTEN AND ILLUSTRATED BY ZACHARY HAMBY
EDITED BY RACHEL HAMBY

## DEDICATION
*For Luke*

"Whoever neglects learning in his youth loses his past and is dead for the future."
—Euripides—

ISBN-10:  0-9827049-0-9
ISBN-13:  978-0-9827049-0-5
LCCN:  2010936569

Reaching Olympus, The Greek Myths: Heroes, Beasts, and Monsters
Written and Illustrated by Zachary Hamby
Edited by Rachel Hamby
Published by Hamby Publishing in the United States of America

# TABLE OF CONTENTS

## INTRODUCTORY MATERIALS

Introduction to the Series     7

Using This Book in the Classroom     11

## SCRIPT-STORIES: HEROES, BEASTS, AND MONSTERS

The Tale of Perseus     13

Atalanta the Female Warrior     29

Oedipus the Cursed King     43

Narcissus and Echo     59

Orpheus and Eurydice     69

The Golden Fleece: Jason and the Argonauts I     79

Aboard the Argo: Jason and the Argonauts II     95

Medea the Witch: Jason and the Argonauts III     109

The Inventor's Apprentice     121

Daedalus and Icarus     127

The Winged Horse     135

## EXTRA STORIES, GAMES, AND PUZZLES

The Contest for Athens     151

The Adventures of Apollo                   153

Underworld Find-It Puzzle                  155

Underworld Find-It Puzzle Key             157

Temple Trouble Game                       159

## APPENDICES

Glossary of Important Names               165

Pronunciation Guide                       171

About the Author                          175

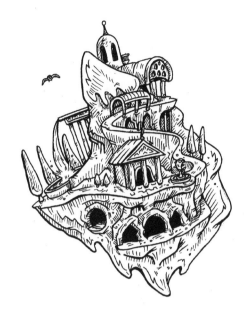

# REACHING OLYMPUS:
## AN INTRODUCTION TO THE SERIES

The faces of the souls of the Underworld could not have been more death-like. It was years ago, but I remember it well. In a matter of weeks, I had gone from inexperienced student to full-time teacher. Smack dab in the midst of my student teaching experience, I was asked to take over as the classroom teacher. Even more startling:  Four long years of college had not prepared me for the subject matter I would be required to teach—a class called World Short Stories and (gulp) Mythology. I remembered a few short stories from my survey literature courses, but with mythology, I was drawing a blank. In my cobwebbed memory there stood a woman with snake-hair and a psychedelic image of a wingéd horse—but that was it. Not to worry though. I had two whole weeks to prepare. After that I needed to fill a whole semester with mythological learning.

As any competent educator would, I turned to my textbook for aid. At first things looked promising. The book had a classy cover—black with the before-mentioned wingéd horse on it. Bold gold letters tastefully titled it *Mythology*. Edith Hamilton—in the same lettering—was apparently the author. Yes, my judgment of the cover was encouraging, but what I found inside was anything but.

When I opened the text to read, I quickly realized I was doomed. Edith Hamilton had written her book in code. It was the same indecipherable language used by those who write literary criticism or owner manuals for electronic devices. Every sentence was a labyrinth, curving back in on itself, confusing the reader with many a subordinate clause and cutting him off completely from context with an outdated aphorism. If she wasn't randomly quoting Milton or Shakespeare, she was spending a paragraph differentiating between the poetic styles of Pindar and Ovid. It was as if Edith Hamilton was annoyed at having been born in the twentieth century and was using her writing style as some kind of literary time travel. Originally published in 1942, *Mythology* reflects the writing style of the day—a style that has grown increasingly more difficult for modern readers to comprehend. I knew if I could barely understand Hamilton's language, my students were going to be even more lost than I was.

Designed for average learners, Mythology was a junior-senior elective—the kind of class that was supposed to be entertaining and somewhat interesting. With Edith Hamilton tied around my neck, I was going down—and going down fast. It was at this point that the stupidly optimistic part of my brain cut in. "Maybe it won't be so bad," it said. "Don't underestimate your students." My ambitions renewed thanks to this still, small voice, and I laid Hamilton to the side, somehow sure that everything would turn out all right in the end. This was still more proof that I knew nothing about mythology.

Before I continue to tell how my tragic flaw of youthful optimism led to my ultimate downfall, I should take a minute to say a kind word about Edith Hamilton. In a time when interest in the classical writings of Greece and Rome was waning, Edith Hamilton revitalized this interest by writing several works that attempted to capture the creativity and majesty of Greco-Roman civilization. Hamilton's *Mythology* was one of the first books to take a comprehensive look at the Greco-Roman myths. The popularity of mythology today owes a great deal of debt to this book and its author. Fifty years after its publication, it is still the most commonly used mythology textbook in high school classrooms. Ironically, *Mythology* is no longer on an average high-schooler's reading level. As I mentioned earlier, Hamilton's writing style, with its ponderous vocabulary and sphinx-worthy inscrutability, further alienates any but the most intrepid of readers.

My first semester of teaching Mythology was a disaster. If I hadn't been so idealistic and gung-ho, I probably would have given up. Instead the new teacher within me stood up and said, "No! I'm going to do this, and we're going to make it fun! After all, Mythology is filled with all kinds of teenage interests: family murder, bestiality, incest, etc. It'll be just like watching television for them."

Utilizing every creative project idea under the sun, I threw myself into making the class work. We drew pictures, read aloud, watched related videos, wrote alternate endings to the stories—yet every time I kept coming up against the same brick wall: the text. It did not matter how enjoyable the activities were. Whenever we turned to the actual stories and cracked open that dreaded book, the life was sucked out of my students, and I was staring at their Underworld faces once again.

My last resort was boiling the stories down to outlines and writing these out on the whiteboard. Even that was better than actually reading them. At least the students would get the basic facts of the story. One student, possibly sensing I was seconds away from the breaking point, made the comment, "I didn't know this class would be a bunch of notes. I thought it would be fun."

Then I gave up.

When I look back on that semester, I realize that I failed a whole batch of students. They came and went thinking that studying mythology was a brainless exercise in rote memorization. Perhaps the failure of that first experience would not have been so stark if a success hadn't come along the next year.

The second time through the class, I was determined not to repeat the mistakes of the past. There must be some way of avoiding the text—somehow relating the stories without actually reading them. But then I thought, "Isn't this supposed to be an English class? If we don't actually read, can it be called English? What has this outdated text driven me to?"

When I looked into the stories, I could see excellent tales trapped behind stuffy prose. How could I get the students to see what I saw? How could I set those good stories free?

On a whim I decided to try my hand at rewriting one of the myths. I had dabbled in creative writing in college, so surely I could spin one of these tales better than Edith Hamilton had. The idea of dividing the story into parts struck me as a good one. Maybe that would foster more student involvement. A few hours later, I had created my first Reader's Theater script-story. (At the time I had no idea that there was an actual term for this type of thing or that there was sound educational research behind reading aloud.) Part of me was excited. The other part was skeptical. "These kids are high-schoolers," I said to myself. "They'll never go for this." I looked at some of the elements I had included in my script: overly-dramatic dialogue, sound effects, cheesy jokes. What was I thinking? Since I had already spent the time and energy, I decided to give it a shot.

There are those grand moments in education when something clicks, and those moments are the reason that teachers teach. My script clicked. It clicked quite well, in fact. The students loved reading aloud. They were thrilled beyond belief not to be reading silently or taking notes or even watching a video. They performed better than I ever dreamed possible. They did funny voices. They laughed at the cheesy jokes. They inhabited the characters. They even did the sound effects.

As I looked around the room, I noticed something that was a rarity: My students were having fun. Not only that, but they were getting all the information that Edith Hamilton could have offered them. When the script was done, I encountered a barrage of questions: "Why did Zeus act like that to Hera? What is an heir? Why did Aphrodite choose to marry Hephaestus? Did the Greeks have *any* respect for marriage?" Did my ears deceive me? Intelligent questions— questions about character motivation, vocabulary, and even historical context? I couldn't believe it.

I was also struck by another startling fact: The students were asking about these characters as if they were real people. They were able to treat the characters as real people because real people had inhabited their roles. Zeus was not some dusty god from 3,000 years ago. He was Joe in the second row doing a funny voice. Something

had come from the abstract world of mythology and become real. And as for the quiz scores, my students might not remember the difference between Perseus and Theseus, but they definitely remembered the difference between Josh and Eric, the two students who played those roles. On top of all this, the class had changed from a group of isolated learners to a team that experiences, laughs, and learns together.

After the success of that first script, I realized I had created some kind of teaching drug. It was an incredible experience, one that I wanted to recreate over and over again. I wouldn't and couldn't go back to the old world of bland reading. So I didn't.

The great moments of Greek mythology flew from my keyboard, and I created script after script. Despite my overweening enthusiasm, I knew that too much of a good thing could definitely be bad, so I chose stories that would spread out the read-aloud experience. We would still use Edith Hamilton in moderation. After all, a few vegetables make you enjoy the sweet stuff all the more.

Over the course of that semester, I discovered a new enthusiasm in the students and myself. They enjoyed learning, and I enjoyed teaching. I had students arguing over who would read which parts—an unbelievable sight for juniors and seniors. Laughter was a constant in the classroom. As the Greeks would say, it was a golden age of learning.

Now I have the chance to share this technique with other teachers. With these script-stories, I hope my experiences will be recreated in other classrooms. Mythology should not be an old dead thing of the past, but a living, breathing, exciting experience.

# USING THIS BOOK IN THE CLASSROOM

Script-stories (also known as Reader's Theater) are a highly motivational learning strategy that blends oral reading, literature, and drama. Unlike traditional theater, script-stories do not require costumes, make-up, props, stage sets, or memorization. Only the script and a healthy imagination are needed. As students read the script aloud, they interpret the emotions, beliefs, attitudes, and motives of the characters. A narrator conveys the story's setting and action and provides the commentary necessary for the transitions between scenes.

While Reader's Theater has been enormously successful with lower grade-levels, it is also a great fit for older learners as well. Students of any age enjoy and appreciate the chance to *experience* a story rather than having it read to them. For years now script-stories have been the tool that I use to teach mythology to high-schoolers. I wouldn't have it any other way. Below are the answers to some of the most frequently asked questions concerning the use of script-stories in the classroom.

**How do you stage these stories in the classroom?** Hand out photocopies of the particular script for that day. (Note: It is perfectly legal for you to photocopy pages from this book. That is what it was designed for!) Certain copies of the scripts should be highlighted for particular characters, so that whichever students you pick to read parts will have their lines readily available. (This is not necessary, but it does make things run more smoothly.) Some teachers who use script-stories require their students to stand when reading their lines or even incorporate physical acting. As for the sound effects in the scripts *(fanfare)*, noisemakers can be distributed to the students and used when prompted. Otherwise, students can make the noises with their own voices.

**How do you structure a class around script-stories? How often do you use them?** Too much of a good thing can be bad. In my own classroom I do employ the script-stories frequently—in some units we read a story every day of the week—but I do supplement with other notes, texts, activities, and self-created worksheets. Some of these activities are included in the back of the book. For other examples of these activities, check out my website *www.mythologyteacher.com.*

**How do you assess script-stories?** A quick reading quiz after the completion of a script is an easy way to assess comprehension. In my own classroom I ask five questions that hit the high-points of the story. I never make students recall difficult names such as Agamemnon or Polydectes. Each script-story in this book comes with five recall questions for quiz purposes.

Another form of assessment is fostering as much post-story discussion as possible. How well students discuss will tell you how well they have comprehended the story. The discussion questions included in this book have been successful in my own classroom.

I hope you find this book to be a great resource. It was designed with the intent of helping a much wider audience experience the timeless tales of world mythology in a new manner. Below I have listed some further notes concerning the script-stories. Thanks for serpent. Perseus slays the sea serpent and takes Andromeda back to his home with him. Perseus uses the head of Medusa to turn King Polydectes (and all the nobles gathered in his hall) to stone. He then gives the head to Athena, who places it on her shield.

The tale of Perseus ends when he returns to Argos with his family and fulfills the original prophecy: He accidentally kills his grandfather, Acrisius, with a stray discus toss.

## ESSENTIAL QUESTIONS

- What does it mean to be a hero?
- What is justice?
- Is there such a thing as fate?

## CONNECTIONS

*Percy Jackson and the Lightning Thief* **(novel and film, 2010)** Percy (short for Perseus) is a modern version of a Greek hero. Like Perseus he is the son of a god. Many Greek gods and monsters make cameos in this story.

*Clash of the Titans* **(1981 & 2010)** These films retell the myth of Perseus and feature elements from other Greek myths (i.e. Pegasus).

*The Hero with a Thousand Faces* **by Joseph Campbell** This groundbreaking work analyzes the many elements hero stories from various cultures have in common. Campbell calls this common hero-story framework the *monomyth*, a pattern that can be used to explore many different hero myths from around the world.

## ANTICIPATORY QUESTIONS

- Who was Perseus?
- Who was Medusa?

- Who or what is Atlas?
- What is the definition of a hero?
- What people in our society are heroes?
- What are the qualifications for a hero?
- Is it possible to tell the future?

## TEACHABLE TERMS

- **Cause and Effect** Ask these questions: How did Perseus's decision to accept his quest affect the lives of those around him? How would it have been different if he hadn't accepted the quest?
- **Humor** Ask these questions: How is humor involved in the telling of this story? What does humor add to the story?
- **Onomatopoeia/Allusion** The word *snicker-snack* on pg. 24 an example of onomatopoeia. It is also an allusion to the Lewis Carroll poem "Jabberwocky."
- **Point of View** Ask these questions: From what point of view is the story told? 1st person, 2nd person, 3rd person limited, or 3rd person omniscient? What would be changed about the story if the point of view were changed?
- **Situational Irony** The death of King Acrisius on pg. 26 is an example of this term because he dies in a strange, unexpected way.

## RECALL QUESTIONS

1. What form does the god Zeus take when he appears to Perseus's mother?
2. How does the old king, Acrisius, try to kill Perseus and his mother?
3. What are three items that the gods Athena and Hermes give to Perseus in order to aid him on his journey?
4. How does the titan Atlas help Perseus?
5. How does Perseus kill his grandfather?

# THE TALE OF PERSEUS

## CAST

| | |
|---|---|
| **PERSEUS** | *Young Hero from Argos* |
| **ACRISIUS** | *Elderly King of Argos* |
| **DANAË** | *Daughter of Acrisius* |
| **DICTYS** | *Kindly Fisherman* |
| **WIFE** | *Wife of Dictys* |
| **ZEUS** | *Ruler of the Gods* |
| **ATHENA** | *Goddess of Wisdom* |
| **HERMES** | *Messenger God* |
| **MEDUSA** | *Evil Monster* |
| **GORGON** | *Another Evil Monster* |
| **SISTER ONE** | *One of the Gray Sisters* |
| **SISTER TWO** | *One of the Gray Sisters* |
| **SISTER THREE** | *One of the Gray Sisters* |
| **ATLAS** | *Punished Titan* |
| **POLYDECTES** | *Evil King* |
| **ANDROMEDA** | *Beautiful Princess* |
| **LOVER** | *Lover of Medusa* |
| **ORACLE** | *Prophetess of Delphi* |
| **MAN** | *Man in the Crowd* |

**NARRATOR:** Among all the Greek heroes one stands out above the rest—one that was not known for strength or speed or the crude abilities of war. His name was Perseus, and he was pure of heart and used his mind, an often forgotten muscle, to overpower the most terrifying monster the earth has ever seen.

Medusa was the name of this beast, a terrible gorgon. For hair, she had writhing snakes, her skin was made of the hardest scales, and her eyes—those eyes could turn any creature into stone if they met their gaze. Perhaps it is with her that the story should begin, for she was not always hideous and evil. Once she was a radiant maiden—a maiden in love.

**LOVER:** *(whispering)* Medusa! Medusa!

**MEDUSA:** *(whispering)* What are you doing? Father will kill you if he finds you here!

**LOVER:** Meet me! Meet me at the temple of Athena—at midnight!

**MEDUSA:** But…

**LOVER:** *(fading away)* Midnight, my love!

**NARRATOR:** Love proved more powerful than fear of any goddess for the young Medusa, and in the darkness, she crept forth from her abode and met her young love at the temple of Athena, a place where no mortal would think to look for two in a passion.

**LOVER:** Medusa! You made it. Let me take you in my arms!

**MEDUSA:** Oh, my love!

**NARRATOR:** But all did not bode well for them. It was Athena's temple. And being a virgin goddess, she did not take kindly to lovers using her sacred grounds for their secret meetings.

*(clap of thunder)*

**MEDUSA:** *(gasp)*

**ATHENA:** *(booming)* Foolish mortals! How dare you misuse my temple for your love!

**LOVER:** It was my fault! I asked her to come here! It was all—

**NARRATOR:** Medusa's lover was struck down before he could finish. The goddess of wisdom has little pity for men.

**MEDUSA:** Nooo! *(weeping)* Spare me, great one! I will have nothing to do with men the rest of my days! I swear!

**ATHENA:** *(slyly)* No, you will not. I will see to that. The punishment I have reserved for you will leave you begging for the same fate as your lover! Medusa, you are cursed!

**MEDUSA:** *(crazy)* No! No!

**ATHENA:** Where golden locks once stood, snakes will curl and slither. No adoring man will look upon you now—lest he wish to be made of stone.

**MEDUSA:** Noooooooooooooo… *(screams and hissing)*

**NARRATOR:** And so was the judgment of Athena. Medusa was banished to the far corner of the Earth. Envy and hate consumed her, and she became a horrific fiend. All that looked on her face became as hard as stone— as her heart had long ago.

Many years later, Acrisius, king of Argos, traveled afar to the Oracle of Delphi seeking knowledge of the future. He had a beautiful daughter, Danaë, but, as all kings do, he desired a son. Since he was heavy with age and had no wife, he traveled to the oracle to ask it how he might procure a great heir to his throne.

**ORACLE:** *(distantly)* Enter…

**ACRISIUS:** Oracle of Apollo, it is said that you speak the word of the God of Truth. I have come begging a question of you. Please hear me, and answer me my riddle.

**ORACLE:** You may speak, old man. But you may not find happiness in the answer.

**ACRISIUS:** *(pausing)* I have no son to receive my throne. If I do not produce a successor, my kingdom will fall into ruin. My wife has died many years before now. Tell me, oracle, what must I do?

**NARRATOR:** At this, the oracle's eyes grew white, and her voice became low, yet filled with the power of the gods.

**ORACLE:** *(deeply)* Your daughter shall have a son. He will be a great man, known by all of Greece.

**ACRISIUS:** *(relieved)* Thank you, oh, thank you. That is excellent news.

**ORACLE:** Halt! That is not all. This son of your daughter comes for a price. It will be at his hands that you will die.

**ACRISIUS:** *(shocked)* That cannot be.

**ORACLE:** I have spoken.

**NARRATOR:** King Acrisius returned to his home Argos in a stupor. What could he do? He desperately needed an heir, but in his heart he feared death more than anything. He therefore resolved to make sure his daughter would have no son.

**DANAË:** *(surprised)* Father? You've returned so soon?

**ACRISIUS:** *(coldly)* Danaë, come with me.

**DANAË:** Where are we going? What's going on?

**ACRISIUS:** Guards, lock her below.

**DANAË:** Father! *(weeping)* What have I done to deserve this?

**ACRISIUS:** *(to himself)* I will put her where no man can touch her.

**NARRATOR:** So the cowardly Acrisius had a house built for his royal daughter—a house that the light of the sun would never touch–hidden underground. And there she dwelt, weeping day after day in her subterranean prison. It was there that Zeus, looking down from Olympus, saw her one day.

**ZEUS:** *(amorously)* What a beautiful maiden! Why does she weep? I must comfort her.

**NARRATOR:** Under the earth, Danaë looked up and saw sparkling pieces of gold falling into her prison from nothingness. It was the form of Zeus.

**DANAË:** A shower of gold!

**NARRATOR:** She ran forward and let the gold fall upon her.

**ZEUS:** I am in the gold, Danaë. It is I, Zeus, lord of the sky.

**DANAË:** I don't understand.

**ZEUS:** Do not be sad. You will bear a great son from me—a son who will set you free.

**NARRATOR:** At this, Danaë grew silent, and the gold continued to fall.

Many months later, she found herself with child. She did not tell the guards who brought her food. She kept it hidden. And when the day came to give birth, she did so as quietly as possible, for she feared her father's wrath. And so was Perseus born.

**DANAË:** Perseus I will name you. Zeus is your father, little one. You shall do great things in this world.

**NARRATOR:** Danaë kept the baby a secret longer than any would imagine. He grew into a golden-haired toddler in the confines of the underground room. He learned to play quietly and to hide when the guards came with food. Danaë took little for herself, instead giving Perseus most. But it could not stay a secret forever. The guards heard laughing one day and reported it immediately to the king. Acrisius's worst fears had come true. The son of prophecy had been born—right below his very nose.

**ACRISIUS:** *(madly)* Fool girl! Is this the respect I receive? Raising you from a babe? I should stick you with my own sword!

**DANAË:** Father! No! *(weeping)*

**ACRISIUS:** Harlot! Who is the father? I was so careful! I sealed you in! No one could have reached you.

**DANAË:** Zeus reached me, Father.

**ACRISIUS:** *(quietly)* Zeus…

**NARRATOR:** Acrisius could no longer put the boy to death as he had planned. This child was a son of Zeus. The king knew he would be struck down before he removed his sword from the scabbard. But if the brat were to meet with an untimely accident, no one would be the wiser. Accidents happen after all—even to princes. So Acrisius made a great wooden trunk and placed Danaë and the boy inside.

**ACRISIUS:**  Go to a watery grave! I curse you!

**NARRATOR:**  He set the chest out to sea, sure that Poseidon, lord of the depths, would claim his human sacrifice. But Poseidon was no fool and knew Zeus's wishes, so he guided the wooden trunk safely through the turbulent waters to a faraway shore where he knew it would be found by the kind fisherfolk that lived there.

**DICTYS:**  Look! There in the surf!

**WIFE:**  A bit of driftwood perhaps?

**DICTYS:**  I will bring it in with the net.

*(scuffling sound, sound of door opening)*

**DICTYS:**  Ahhh!

**DANAË:**  Ahhh!

**WIFE:**  A woman?

**DICTYS:**  And her child!

**NARRATOR:**  Danaë and Perseus were found by the kind fisherman Dictys and his wife. Having no children of their own, the poor pair took them in as their daughter and grandson. It was a happy time for mother and son, when they were able to forget the past, and over the years Perseus grew to be a handsome young man with the glory of his immortal father shining in his eyes. Danaë, free of her prison, had become more beautiful than ever, and word of her famed looks spread throughout the land.

News of it even reached the ear of Dictys's brother, Polydectes. Now, Polydectes had much more ambition than his kind-hearted brother and through cunning and force had become ruler of the tiny island kingdom. He was ruthless, and his greed knew no bounds. Upon hearing of Danaë, he came to claim this beauty for himself.

**POLYDECTES:**  *(imperiously)* Hello, brother. How goes it down here in the filth?

**DICTYS:**  *(angrily)* What do you want? Have you come to gloat?

**POLYDECTES:**  You have been keeping secrets from me, Dictys. I hear you have a certain…treasure that you have hidden from my sight.

**DICTYS:**  I assume you speak of our daughter.

**POLYDECTES:**  You have no daughter, fool. Who is this woman you keep? I must see her for myself.

*(sounds of footsteps and Perseus laughing)*

**NARRATOR:**  As the two brothers spoke, the young mother and son ran into view up the narrow beach.

**DANAË:**  *(huffing/puffing)* You always beat me, Perseus! What a fast son I have!

**PERSEUS:**  Oh, Mother, I was even lagging behind. I didn't want to beat you *too badly.*

**DICTYS:**  Danaë! Perseus!

**DANAË:** Oh, I am sorry. I didn't know we had a visitor. Hello, sir. I am Danaë.

**POLYDECTES:** Beautiful—I am Polydectes, ruler of this realm.

**DANAË:** Your majesty, this is my son—

**POLYDECTES:** *(interrupting)* I have never before seen a woman as dazzling as you.

**PERSEUS:** *(forcefully)* And I am Perseus

**POLYDECTES:** Surely, my sweet, you will come to my palace with me and be my wife.

**DICTYS:** *(angrily)* Polydectes!

**DANAË:** I have no need for a husband. My boy is my only love.

**POLYDECTES:** *(pause)* I see. *(under his breath)* An obstacle that can be easily removed.

**NARRATOR:** His advances thwarted, Polydectes left in a huff. After he was gone, Dictys and his wife stared at Danaë in shock.

**DICTYS:** You should not have refused him, Danaë.

**WIFE:** He is an evil man. He will try to harm you and Perseus.

**DANAË:** Why should he want to do that?

**DICTYS:** He wishes to have you as a trophy, and you, my dear, have rejected him. His anger is legendary. He has sent many men to their deaths for his vanity.

**PERSEUS:** I'm not afraid of him.

**WIFE:** But you should be. His greatest desire has been to have the head of the vile monster, Medusa—a trophy, another jewel in his crown.

**DICTYS:** He has sent man after man to retrieve it. All because of his lust for power. Now, you seem to be the desire of his black heart. He will kill many men to get to you as well.

**NARRATOR:** Danaë pondered these things in her heart. She loved nothing more than her Perseus. She would do anything to ensure his safety. What was marriage to a man she didn't love? Little when compared to the life of her son. In the dark of night, Danaë made her way to Polydectes's palace and pledged herself to him.

The next day, it was declared that a royal wedding was to occur immediately. All the kingdom was in attendance. Perseus could not bring himself to go inside and brooded outside the great hall.

**DANAË:** Perseus, what are you doing out here?

**PERSEUS:** How can you marry that man?

**DANAË:** It must be done. We must give him what he wants.

**PERSEUS:** I refuse.

**DANAË:** It is not your choice to make. I have made mine.

**POLYDECTES:** *(walking up)* Ah, my queen-to-be, what are you doing out here with the riff-raff? You no longer have to associate with such people. You are a queen.

**PERSEUS:** *(seething)* And what am I?

**POLYDECTES:** Ah, Persiun, I'm glad you could make it. You were extended a special invitation after all—from the high to the lowly. It was such a select guest list—not even my poor brother was able to make it. Nothing disgusts me like the smell of fish.

**PERSEUS:** He's too good for you!

**POLYDECTES:** *(laugh)* Certainly. Now, tell me, what have you brought as a present? Surely, you did not bring shame upon your mother by offering her nothing on her wedding day?

**PERSEUS:** I—I—

**POLYDECTES:** Some fish-heads perhaps? A gown made from a bit of old net? Poor, poor Persiun, you look as if you could cry.

**PERSEUS:** *(determined)* I will bring a present, you snake, one that you have always desired! The head of the gorgon!

**DANAË:** Perseus! No!

**POLYDECTES:** *(laughing)* Medusa? How will you catch her, boy? With one of your nets?

**PERSEUS:** I will bring it back, and you shall look into her eyes and see your own demise.

**POLYDECTES:** *(not laughing anymore)* A strong promise, boy. I will be sure to inform all present. That way when you return empty-handed, I will declare myself shamed and have you put to death.

**DANAË:** No! Perseus, take it back!

**PERSEUS:** Goodbye, Mother. I will return. I will come back for you.

**POLYDECTES:** *(laughing)* Fly, fool. Hurry home. I await you with open arms.

**NARRATOR:** Perseus fled the palace, his mother in tears. He had no idea how he was going to accomplish such a task. In despair, he sat on the beach in despair. The sound of soft footsteps raised his eyes from the sands. A tall, powerful woman—one he had never seen before—was standing in front of him.

**ATHENA:** I heard your promise back there. Do not despair, Perseus.

**PERSEUS:** Why shouldn't I?

**ATHENA:** Because you are a child of Zeus. Just like me.

**NARRATOR:** Then he met her gaze and saw beyond her human disguise. It was Athena, goddess of war—his sister.

**ATHENA:** I have come to tell you to take heart. Your quest is not as impossible as you may feel it to be.

**PERSEUS:** That's easy for you to say. You're a goddess. I'm just a boy. It doesn't matter who my father is.

**ATHENA:** It was I who turned Medusa into the creature she is today. Do not doubt that I know how to defeat her. On top of hope, I also give you this.

**NARRATOR:** She pulled forth a shining shield. Perseus gaped at its beauty. There in its golden form, he saw himself reflected back.

**ATHENA:** You will use this to kill Medusa. No man may look on her face and live, but her reflection causes no pain.

**PERSEUS:** Thank you, but I have no way to kill a gorgon.

NARRATOR:  At that moment, there was a slight crackling sound in the air, and a young man stood beside Athena. On his cap and on his sandals fluttered four tiny wings. In his hand, he carried a golden staff.

HERMES:  *(cough)* Sorry I'm late—trouble in the Underworld.

ATHENA:  *(sighing)* This is Hermes. He has come to lead you to the gorgon's lair. And, unless I am mistaken, he also has some gifts to bestow upon you.

HERMES:  *(pause)* Of course, of course…

NARRATOR:  The god rummaged in a sack slung at his side. The first thing he pulled forth was a mighty sword.

HERMES:  *(proudly)* This…is from me. A sword powerful enough to pierce the hide of the gorgon.

PERSEUS:  *(mesmerized)* Thank you.

ATHENA:  And?

HERMES:  And what? *(pause)* Oh, yes, gifts from the Hyperboreans—the happiest people on earth that is.

ATHENA:  They have heard of your quest and wish to help.

PERSEUS:  How did—?

HERMES:  Here we go! A magical cap to make you invisible. You'll need that. And some winged sandals—just like mine. And this wonderful magical wallet. No matter how much you put into it, there's always more room.

NARRATOR:  Perseus stood speechless.

HERMES:  It's mainly for when you cut her head off. Y'know, you can put the head in there. It's a mess otherwise.

PERSEUS:  All I can say is, thank you.

ATHENA:  No, thank you. Medusa has been at large for many years. She has become more evil than I ever imagined. If it were my place, I would have taken care of her myself, but it is *your* destiny. Now, put on your sandals and your cap, take your shield and your satchel, and Hermes will guide you where you need to go. *(pause)* Hermes…

HERMES:  Yes?

ATHENA:  Guide him.

HERMES:  Who?

ATHENA:  *(annoyed)* Perseus!

HERMES:  Where is he?

ATHENA:  *(through her teeth)* He—put—the—cap—on…

HERMES:  Oh, right. *(cheerily)* Come along, Perseus.

*(sounds of beating wings)*

ATHENA:  Farewell, brother Perseus. You shall succeed. Have faith.

NARRATOR:  And with that, they were off. With his new sandals, Perseus flew beside the golden god, Hermes. The world spread out below them. They flew over great fields, churning seas, and high mountains, but no sign came from the messenger god as to where they were headed. Finally, Perseus gathered the courage to ask…

PERSEUS:  Are we there yet?

HERMES:  Ah! Forgot you were there for a second.

PERSEUS:  Over here.

HERMES:  Yes, right. *(cough)* Well, I don't know exactly where we're going.

PERSEUS:  What do you mean?

HERMES:  Well, what I mean is: We have to stop and ask for directions.

PERSEUS:  To find Medusa?

HERMES:  *(slowly)* No, actually to find the people who know where Medusa lives. It's complicated.

NARRATOR:  Perseus grew a little worried. Sure, Hermes was a god, but did he know what he was doing? Below the earth was growing flat and barren. Soon, Perseus feared it would end completely, falling off into the black nothingness of night.

HERMES:  There he is!

PERSEUS:  Who?

HERMES:  Atlas, of course.

NARRATOR:  And there he was, the titan who holds up the skies, groaning forever under the great weight. Perseus and Hermes flew close, and Perseus balked at Atlas's size—as big as a mountain.

ATLAS:  What now, Hermes? Another curse from Zeus?

HERMES:  Nah. Just some directions. This is Perseus.

ATLAS:  *(grunts)* Where to?

HERMES:  We seek the Gray Women. They alone know where the gorgons live.

ATLAS:  You seek the gorgon's head, eh? Good luck to you. *(grunts)* I will tell you where to find the Gray Women, but you must make me one promise.

HERMES:  *(to Perseus)* Are you getting this?

ATLAS:  When you pass back this way, let me look on the face of the Cursed One. I have borne this burden for an eternity, and I desire rest—even if it means my own destruction.

PERSEUS:  I promise.

ATLAS:  *(relieved)* Thank you. You can't believe how much this thing weighs.

NARRATOR:  Atlas told them how to find the Gray Women, three old sisters who all shared one eye. They lived at the edge of dreams on a dark, desolate plain. And they did not give information lightly. Since they lacked sight themselves, they loved to take it from trespassers. As Hermes and Perseus saw the first signs of that dark land, he felt fear rising up in his heart.

HERMES:  Here's the trick. All three sisters share an eye. They take turns sticking it into their empty sockets. They fight over it quite a bit. They are all three jealous of each other, and their greed will be their undoing.

PERSEUS:  What must I do?

HERMES:  You have on a cap of invisibility. Sneak into their midst and steal the eye. Once you have it, they will tell you whatever you wish to know.

**PERSEUS:** What if I fail?

**HERMES:** Well, let's not think about that. Just make sure you don't.

**NARRATOR:** Before too long, they saw the black plain where the three sisters lived. They sat in a circle around a bubbling cauldron. Perseus saw one remove the eye and hand it to her sister. He shuddered.

**HERMES:** (whispering) Go on. I'll stay here. Don't mess up.

**NARRATOR:** Perseus nodded and walked forward into the midst of the three gray sisters.

**SISTER ONE:** (cackling) Tell me, sister. What became of that delicious young man who came to our realm yesterday?

**SISTER TWO:** (witchily) Ah, yes, I remember him well.

**SISTER THREE:** We made a stew of him, did we not?

**SISTER ONE:** Yes, yes, I remember now—a fine stew. (pause) Give us the eye, love, I wish to see what creature I feel walking our way.

**SISTER TWO:** Certainly, sister. I will give you the eye when it is your time. I have just received it. I see no creature.

**SISTER ONE:** I feel it. A large creature. Give us the eye, so that I might spring upon it.

**SISTER TWO:** (growling) No, it is mine.

**SISTER THREE:** Sisters, give me the eye. I will see for us all.

**SISTER ONE:** (shrieking) No, give it to me!

(sounds of old women squabbling)

**SISTER TWO:** Where is it? You took it! I have it no longer!

**SISTER ONE:** You lie! I did not take it! I will cut out your tongue!

**SISTER THREE:** You both lie, and you keep it from *me*!

**PERSEUS:** (loudly) I have it.

**SISTERS 1-3:** (gasps) Who are you?

**PERSEUS:** My name does not matter. Just know that if you do not tell what I wish, I will squish this eye in my hand.

**SISTER ONE:** The eye! No!

**SISTER TWO:** Tell it what it wants to know!

**SISTER THREE:** We must!

**PERSEUS:** I wish to know where to find Medusa, the gorgon.

**SISTER ONE:** To the east, the east.

**SISTER TWO:** Past the Mountains of Fire.

**SISTER THREE:** Yes, yes, that is where you will find her. Now, give us the eye.

**PERSEUS:** Here! I throw it upon the ground. You can fight for it among yourselves!

**SISTER ONE:** It's mine!

**SISTER TWO:** It was mine first!

**SISTER THREE:** Miiiiiiine!

(sounds of old women squabbling)

**HERMES:** Nicely done.

**PERSEUS:** Thank you.

**HERMES:** I guess you won't need my help any longer. Follow the directions they gave you. You will be able to tell by the stench when you are near.

**PERSEUS:** But...

**HERMES:** Remember, Medusa is not the only gorgon. Her sisters have suffered the same fate as her. Do not attempt to kill them. They are immortal, yet they do not possess her power. Remember your shield, and you can't go wrong.

**PERSEUS:** I'm glad you have faith in me.

**HERMES:** Ah, you're a resourceful lad. You'll make it. Well, I have to be off. I've loved adventuring with you, but the dead have been piling up. Farewell!

**NARRATOR:** And with his golden staff spinning in his hand, Hermes disappeared. Perseus was on his own.

He followed the directions that the three, weird sisters had given him. Soon he smelled the stench of decaying bodies, and a black mountain rose up before his view. There on the peak, he saw the three gorgons sleeping. They were all fearsome creatures, but Medusa stood out above the others.

He was careful to only look at the reflection in his shield. Snakes writhed where hair should be. The terrifying scales of her skin rose and fell with her shallow breathing. She was a monster.

**PERSEUS:** I have to get in close.

**NARRATOR:** Perseus flew in, landed, and quietly crept toward the sleeping sisters.

Before he had taken three steps, he saw the reflection of Medusa rise.

**MEDUSA:** *(hissing)* Foolish creature! I cannot see you, but I can smell you. Now, I send you to Hades.

**NARRATOR:** He was shaking. In his shield, he saw her charge. He felt the sword heavy and still in his hand. He waited. With all his might, he swung his weapon.

*(snicker-snack of the blade)*

**MEDUSA:** Ahhhhhhhhhh...

**NARRATOR:** He felt its sharpness pierce her neck, and he realized that he had succeeded. But Medusa's dying cry had awoken her two immortal sisters. They rose up on their haunches and hissed.

**GORGON:** *(beastlike)* Murderer!

**NARRATOR:** Quickly, Perseus gripped the severed head of Medusa. The snakes still writhed and bit his hand. His grip did not falter. Careful not to meet its gaze, he slipped it into his satchel, and, just as Hermes said it would, it engulfed the head then shrank back to its original size.

**GORGON:** *(roaring like a lion)*

**NARRATOR:** He took to the air as the gorgons ran to their dead sister's body. He heard them wailing behind him as he flew away. He had done it.

**PERSEUS:** I have to thank Atlas for his help.

**NARRATOR:** As he passed the great titan, Perseus removed his magical cap and hailed him.

**PERSEUS:** Atlas!

**ATLAS:** *(grumbling)* Who is it?

**PERSEUS:** It is I, Perseus. I have returned with the head of the gorgon like I promised.

**ATLAS:** *(excitedly)* Have you? The weight of the skies has grown so heavy. I can stand it no longer. Please, show it to me.

**NARRATOR:** Perseus brought the head of Medusa forth from his satchel, and Atlas met its gaze. He turned to stone with these final words on his lips:

**ATLAS:** *(fading away)* Thank you…

**PERSEUS:** I've got to get back to Mother.

**NARRATOR:** And back he flew, as fast as the winged sandals could carry him—back over the barren fields, the high mountains, and the roaring seas—but as he crossed the sea, he heard a cry.

**ANDROMEDA:** *(screaming)* Heeeeelp! Help me!

**NARRATOR:** A beautiful young woman tied to a stake in the ground was alone on an island. Perseus landed and ran to her.

**PERSEUS:** What's the matter?

**ANDROMEDA:** *(crazily)* A serpent! A serpent is coming for me! Quickly!

**NARRATOR:** Her name was Andromeda. A terrible sea serpent had been terrorizing the people of her country. An oracle had told them in order to stop the beast, they must sacrifice Princess Andromeda. But Perseus knew none of this yet. He only saw a beautiful woman in need of his help.

**PERSEUS:** There. You're free.

**ANDROMEDA:** Too late. Here it comes!

**NARRATOR:** Perseus turned to face the giant snake. He was no longer the Perseus of before, self-doubting and weak. He was the slayer of Medusa, the son of Zeus.

The great beast of Poseidon rose from the brine—red eyes, scales dripping salt water, and a pink mouth, yawning wide, full of tiny teeth. Once again, he felt the blade swing from his side. It tore through flesh. *(snicker-snack)* Through half-closed eyes, he saw the limp body fall back into the water.

**ANDROMEDA:** *(stunned)* I can't believe it! Who are you?

**PERSEUS:** Perseus—but we must go—quickly! Let me take you back to your family.

**ANDROMEDA:** My family? No. They were the ones who put me out here to die. Take me with you.

**NARRATOR:** With this, Perseus smiled. He took the princess into his arms and flew back to the kingdom of Polydectes as quickly he could.

He and Andromeda found Dictys's hut abandoned. Neighbors told Perseus that after he had left on his quest, his mother had fled the palace, rejecting the king's proposal. The king in a fury had sent his guards after her. Dictys had helped hide Danaë, and they had fled to a faraway temple where they were allowed sanctuary. Polydectes had been furious.

Perseus knew what he now must do. He left Andromeda at the hut, kissing her before he left. He had a meeting with the king.

**POLYDECTES:** Men, I have called you here today for a great purpose. My pride has been scorned. A woman has made a mockery of me. I have spent these last weeks preparing an army to march on the land that hides her from me. You are here for that purpose.

*(sound of door opening)*

**POLYDECTES:** *(in shock)* Perseus? It can't be!

**PERSEUS:** I have come back, and I have brought what I promised.

**POLYDECTES:** No! I won't let this happen.

**PERSEUS:** You can do nothing to stop it. Die now.

**POLYDECTES:** Seize—

**NARRATOR:** Polydectes froze in mid-speech, his arm thrown forward in anger. So had the rest of the men in the hall stopped—forever turned to stone. At the door, Perseus stood, averting his gaze, holding the writhing head of Medusa aloft one final time. He had fulfilled his promise.

News spread quickly that the king had died. Danaë, Dictys, and his wife were sent for. They rejoiced when they saw the noble Perseus again and showered him with kisses and handshakes.

Athena was there as well, visible only to Perseus, and she took the head of Medusa from him and placed it on her shield. To this day, it still stares forth from her mighty armor. Dictys, once a poor fisherman, was made king of Polydectes's realm. Perseus and Andromeda were married on the very shore where he and his mother once washed up.

After the ceremony, Danaë stood apart from the rest, crying to herself.

**PERSEUS:** Mother, this is a happy occasion! What's the matter?

**DANAË:** Oh, Perseus. I miss my home. Even though my father was driven to madness, I miss my family. Argos is where I belong.

**PERSEUS:** Well, we have righted things here. Why shouldn't we return there?

**DANAË:** *(crying)* Perseus, you are the best boy a mother could ask for.

**NARRATOR:** Danaë, Perseus, and his new bride returned to Argos to seek out Acrisius the king. There was a great celebration going on—a great bout of games. They stopped and asked the people if they knew of Acrisius the king.

**MAN:** Don't you know? He is the king no longer. He was driven mad and fled the palace. No one knows where he is.

**DANAË:** Perhaps, Perseus, it is better this way.

**NARRATOR:** So, they resolved to make their home in Argos. As they walked through the festival, Danaë felt her spirits rising. She was home.

Perseus and Andromeda were deliriously happy. They had found each other. Feeling like a young boy again, Perseus entered the discus contest. Andromeda laughed at his antics as he joked inside the ring. *(laughing)* With his swift arm, the same arm that had slain the gorgon and the great sea serpent, he let the discus sail. *(whistling sound)* There was a commotion among the crowd. The discus had gone awry, into the bystanders, and had killed a man. It was the mad king, Acrisius, killed by Perseus's discus. Oracles never lie.

## DISCUSSION QUESTIONS

1. Even though she is a monster, do you feel sorry for Medusa? Explain.

2. Is it foolish to try to avoid a prophecy? How did this backfire on King Acrisius?
3. Why is Perseus a hero? Explain.
4. How is Perseus similar to a modern superhero? Explain.
5. Perseus has plenty of magical items to help him on his quest. Could he have succeeded without them? Explain

Importance of family; Fate, be brave and do not be so cowardly.

## ATALANTA THE FEMALE WARRIOR
## TEACHER GUIDE

### BACKGROUND

The myth of Atalanta captures many of the prevalent attitudes toward women in ancient Greece. Just as Atalanta is abandoned by her kingly father, many Greeks abandoned female babies—either in the wilderness or sometimes in the public market. Poor families could not afford an abundance of children, and a boy would be able to work a trade and carry on the family name.

Atalanta engages in many practices that were considered inappropriate for women living during the golden age of Greece. To us her actions seem normal, but the Greeks probably viewed her more as a wild woman—one completely separated from her domestic obligations. (The tellers of Atalanta's myth were undoubtedly male.) Just as Athena and Artemis, two Greek goddesses who take on more masculine roles, Atalanta has no desire to be married. It is only through a trick, one inspired by the gods, that she eventually marries.

After the events of this story, Atalanta is tricked into marriage by a young man named Hippomenes. Since her speed has never been matched, Atalanta vows that the only man she will marry is the one who can beat her in a footrace. Hippomenes prays to Aphrodite, who gives him her golden apples—apples that no woman can resist. The suitor uses these to distract Atalanta during their race and wins. The two are married and live happily until many years later when they offend Zeus by profaning his sacred grove by making love within it. Since Atalanta is a hero, Zeus does not strike her and her husband down with a thunderbolt. Instead he transforms them into a pair of lions. This may

seem like an odd punishment, but the Greeks believed that lions lacked the ability to mate.

### SUMMARY

The story begins with a nameless king anxiously awaiting the birth of a son. When he finds that his "son" is in actuality a daughter, he orders that the girl-child be abandoned in the wilderness. His orders are followed, and the infant is saved from death by a passing mother bear. The bear raises the girl as an animal and teaches her the ways of wild. One day the bear is mortally wounded by hunters and orders her daughter to go with the hunters and join the human world. The hunters adopt the girl, and the chief of their tribe names her Atalanta, which means "equal." Atalanta grows up to be a formidable huntress.

One day men from the region of Calydon come to the hunting tribe for help. The goddess Artemis, protector of wild beasts, has set a giant, man-eating boar loose in their country. They need the hunters' help to slay the beast. Among the men is the prince of Calydon, Meleager. When he meets Atalanta, he is taken by her beauty and impressed by the fact that she has killed two centaurs single-handedly. Atalanta has no interest in a romantic relationship with the handsome prince. She values her independence too much. In spite of her frosty treatment of him, Meleager continues to pursue her. In an attempt to soften her resolve, he tells her his darkest secret. His life has been cursed since the day of his birth. The Fates appeared to his mother on that day prophesying that he would die when the log burning on the fire was completely consumed. Frantically, his mother took the log from the fire and kept it guarded ever since. Because of this, the prince's very life is linked to a simple log.

The hunters agree to help kill the Calydonian Boar, and they accompany Meleager and his two vain uncles back to Calydon. There they encounter the boar, which kills several of the men. Atalanta wounds the boar in the back, and Meleager finishes it off. Their victory is short-lived as Meleager's uncles reveal their plan to murder Atalanta and the hunters. Defending Atalanta against his own countrymen, Meleager kills his uncles in the process. Some of the survivors of the skirmish run to the Calydonian palace and tell Meleager's mother how her son has killed his uncles. Thinking that Meleager has betrayed his family, his mother retrieves the magical log and throws it on the fire. Back in the wilderness Meleager begins to die and declares his love for Atalanta, who can only watch sadly as he crumbles into dust.

## ESSENTIAL QUESTIONS

- Why should men and women have the same rights?
- When can pride become *too much* pride?
- What rules does society place on certain groups of people?

## CONNECTIONS

*Xena: Warrior Princess* (1995-2001) In this popular television series loosely based on Greek mythology, the main character Xena strongly resembles Atalanta as she is a powerful, independent warrior woman.

## ANTICIPATORY QUESTIONS

- What activities are commonly associated with girls?

- What activities are commonly associated with boys?
- Can you name a female hero from mythology or popular culture?
- What do you expect will be different about a female hero versus a male hero?

## TEACHABLE TERMS

- **Compare/Contrast** Compare and contrast the characters of Atalanta and Meleager. How are their lives similar?
- **Culture** What does this story have to say about ancient Greek culture?
- **Alliteration, Imagery** The phrase "slap the silvery fish from the swift-flowing stream" on pg. 32 contains examples of both these terms.
- **Flashback** When Meleager tells of his curse on pg. 38, this is an example of a flashback.
- **Inner Conflict** Atalanta has a strong inner conflict brewing, which accounts for her standoffish personality. Have the students theorize what the root of her inner conflict is and use examples from the story to back up their claim.

## RECALL QUESTIONS

1. How is Atalanta wronged by her kingly father?
2. What type of creature raises Atalanta?
3. Atalanta gains acclaim by killing two of what violent creature?
4. What type of supernatural creature is terrorizing the people of Calydon?
5. How does Meleager die?

# ATALANTA
## THE FEMALE WARRIOR

**CAST**

| | |
|---|---|
| **ATALANTA** | *Female Huntress* |
| **MELEAGER** | *Prince of Calydon* |
| **KING** | *Atalanta's Father* |
| **SHE-BEAR** | *Wild Mother Bear* |
| **CHIEF** | *Leader of the Hunters* |
| **HUNTER** | *Hunter* |
| **CENTAUR ONE** | *Half-Horse, Half-Man* |
| **CENTAUR TWO** | *Half-Horse, Half-Man* |
| **WOMAN** | *Servant of the King* |
| **UNCLE ONE** | *Meleager's Uncle* |
| **UNCLE TWO** | *Meleager's Uncle* |
| **BOAR** | *Supernatural Beast* |

**NARRATOR:** A very long time ago in ancient Greece, women were not treated as they are today. Women never dreamed of holding power or seeing far off lands—and especially never dreamed of doing heroic deeds. Their realm was the home, and it was there they were told to stay, tending the children. But there was one girl who became a hero for all, flying in the face of tradition and standing tall among the ranks of men. Her name was Atalanta.

Her beginnings were humble. She was an unwanted child born to an elderly king.

**WOMAN:** Sire, your wife has delivered her baby.

**KING:** *(excitedly)* Excellent news! What is *he* like?

**WOMAN:** Sire, your baby is no boy. The queen has had a girl child.

**KING:** *(infuriated)* No!

**NARRATOR:** At this news, the king tore his beard and cursed the gods. Even at his great age, he had never been a father, and this baby was to be his heir—the child to whom his kingdom would be left.

**KING:** I will *not* have a girl as my heir!

**NARRATOR:** In his anger, he ordered that the child be taken into the wilderness and left there—prey for the wild things. And so was the babe abandoned on the cold slope of a fir-covered mountain.

It was here that she was found by the most unlikely of nursemaids. A passing she-bear, mourning the loss of her young cub, came upon the infant girl.

**SHE-BEAR:** *(surprised)* A man-child? Here in the forest? It will rain soon, and this child shall surely die of cold.

**NARRATOR:** The baby stirred something inside the beast, and she nuzzled the child with her warm snout and licked the dirt from its face.

**SHE-BEAR:** The humans have abandoned you. They are cruel and barbaric creatures, but I will take you for my own, young one, and I will raise you to have a nobler heart than those from which you came.

**NARRATOR:** The mother bear made good on her word and took the girl back to her den and raised the child as her own offspring. The she-bear gave her a name in the language of the animals that meant "equal" because the girl would be raised to be as much a bear as one had ever been.

When the time came for the girl to walk, the she-bear showed her how to run on all fours and how to stand up tall to intimidate an opponent. She showed her how to find grubs and how these might sustain one. She showed her how to slap the silvery fish out of the swift-flowing stream. And so the girl grew and grew.

**ATALANTA:** *(young-sounding voice)* Mother, why do I look nothing like you? Why do I not look like other bears?

**SHE-BEAR:** *(laughs)* Because you are not a bear. You are a human child.

**NARRATOR:** The girl's face wrinkled in disgust.

**ATALANTA:** Humans are cowards. They're the ones that come into the forests with their spears. What weaklings! They don't even have claws like us, Mother.

**SHE-BEAR:** No, they do not, but neither will you.

**ATALANTA:** *(disappointed)* Awwwww. I was hoping they might grow in.

**SHE-BEAR:** No, you will be as unprotected as any other man. But man's strength is not in his body. It's in his mind. He is tricky.

**ATALANTA:** I want to be strong!

**SHE-BEAR:** You will be, dear. You will be.

**NARRATOR:** One day while mother and cub were drinking from a cool stream, the she-bear froze.

**SHE-BEAR:** *(whispering)* Daughter, you must be still. There are men there on the other side of the stream. Can you smell them?

**ATALANTA:** *(whispering)* Yes.

**SHE-BEAR:** When I tell you, you must run.

**ATALANTA:** *(frightened)* No, Mother!

**NARRATOR:** But before either could move, a shrill cry came from the far bushes, and like a stinging fly, a spear shot forth and into the side of the she-bear. She roared and fell upon the shivering girl.

**SHE-BEAR:** *(badly hurt)* Be still. Be still.

**ATALANTA:** *(crying)* Mother, Mother…

**SHE-BEAR:** *(weakly)* The men are coming, my dear. You must go with them.

**ATALANTA:** No, Mother, I'm not one of them!

**SHE-BEAR:** Oh, you are. I was wrong to keep you from your kind. You must join them, but you must show them. You must be better. You must be kind and noble and fair…

**ATALANTA:**   But you—I won't ever leave you.

**SHE-BEAR:**   *(whispering)* Goodbye.

**NARRATOR:**   When the hunters rolled over the carcass of their latest kill, they were greeted by quite a shock. Curled into a weeping ball beneath it was a spindly little girl—naked, her hair a tattered mess.

**HUNTER:**   *(surprised)* What's this?

**NARRATOR:**   The little creature's eyes flicked open, and she lunged at them—sinking her teeth into the nearest man's leg.

**HUNTER:**   *(screaming)* Ahhh! Get it off!

**NARRATOR:**   It took two men to finally corral her. She kicked and scratched and cried like a wild thing. They finally pinned her to the ground, and her rasping breaths slowly started to subside.

**HUNTER:**   *(angrily)* We should take no chances. Let us drown this evil thing at once!

**CHIEF:**   *(laughs)* Evil thing? It is just a little girl.

**HUNTER:**   Look what she did to my leg!

**CHIEF:**   Is that why you are so quick to condemn her? She is alone out here—raised up by this bear. Now, *we* must raise her.

**HUNTER:**   What? She will tear out our throats in the middle of the night!

**CHIEF:**   Did you see her speed? Her agility? We will make her one of us.

**NARRATOR:**   And so the hunters took her back to their nomadic camp. She fought them

the whole way—crying like the Furies—but they did not let go of her.

**CHIEF:**   First thing she needs is a bath. Take her down to the river. Nikos, find her some clothes.

**NARRATOR:**   For a time the young girl resisted. She would be no human. She would not serve the men who killed her mother—but then the final words of the she-bear came back to her little mind. She softened and allowed the hunters to adopt her into their tribe.

**ATALANTA:**   I must live in their world, but I shall never be a part of it.

**NARRATOR:**   The leader of the hunters saw this change in her. He noticed that she listened when he and the hunters spoke, and after time, he perceived that she understood their words. One day, he took her by surprise and spoke directly to her.

**CHIEF:**   I am sorry that we killed the one that you love.

**ATALANTA:**   *(sadly)* She was my mother.

**CHIEF:**   What name did she give you?

**ATALANTA:**   She called me "equal."

**CHIEF:**   Then that is what we shall call you as well, little one. Atalanta is what you will be named, for it means "equal."

**NARRATOR:**   And so the wild girl grew up in the camp of the hunters. She learned to kill the animals with which she had once shared the forests—but did it with respect, never for sport. In time, her scrawniness dropped away, and she became tall and proud—the fastest, the smartest, and the fairest among the hunting tribes.

**CHIEF:** You know, I think our little Atalanta is growing up.

**HUNTER:** Why do you say that?

**CHIEF:** The men from the other tribes let their eyes linger upon her. They no longer think of her as our wild brat, but as a grown woman—one they desire.

**HUNTER:** I will kill them if they look at her in such a way!

**CHIEF:** *(laughs)* I remember how many years ago, you wished her dead.

**HUNTER:** I was a fool. She is one of us now—our daughter and our sister.

**CHIEF:** True. She is even the best among us. She can throw farther and run quicker than any man here. Soon, she shall leave us, I fear.

**NARRATOR:** As the two spoke, the radiant form of Atalanta burst forth from the underbrush. Her hair had grown free and hung like a golden shower upon her shoulders. Her skin was tanned from the constant sight of the sun.

**ATALANTA:** Brothers! I have killed a boar!

**CHIEF:** Very good, Atalanta. Where did it fall?

**ATALANTA:** Not far. I will drag him here soon.

**HUNTER:** All by yourself?

**ATALANTA:** *(defensively)* I can do it.

**CHIEF:** You should never be ashamed to ask for help, Atalanta, or pride shall become a weakness.

**NARRATOR:** The young girl snorted and disappeared back into the thicket.

**CHIEF:** She is independent to be sure.

**NARRATOR:** A far away cry was sounded, and the two nomads' attention was turned. Three men on horseback came riding through the forest and into the village—two old men in traveling coats and a dark-haired young man.

**UNCLE ONE:** *(shouting)* Who is the leader here?

**CHIEF:** I am. What do you lords want with us? We are humble hunters.

**UNCLE TWO:** We come to offer you riches—in turn for your help.

**CHIEF:** We do not pledge our help to strangers. Tell us who asks.

**MELEAGER:** I do.

**NARRATOR:** The young man rode boldly forward.

**MELEAGER:** I come in the name of my father, King Oeneus. A savage beast has been ravaging our land. A giant boar. It has killed our livestock, many travelers, and any who try to hunt it.

**CHIEF:** Powerful beasts do not just appear for no reason. Your father must have angered the gods.

**MELEAGER:** It is true. We have been cursed by Artemis. My father has forgotten her in his sacrifices.

**CHIEF:** We respect the will of Artemis, but I will admit we are poor, and our people want for the things your riches could provide.

**UNCLE ONE:** Then you will help us?

**CHIEF:** I will think on it. You may stay in our camp tonight.

**UNCLE TWO:** (*laughs*) Stay here? No, thank you.

**MELEAGER:** Uncle, there is nothing wrong with staying here.

**UNCLE ONE:** Sire, you are a prince. A prince should not sleep with such dogs.

**MELEAGER:** I will stay, and I will not be ordered around by you. *You* may do what you will.

**CHIEF:** Come, young prince. We shall show you our simple ways.

**NARRATOR:** The young man dismounted. The chief shook his hand warmly and led him away. The two uncles stared sourly at one another.

Through a faraway clearing, Atalanta was running—searching for her kill—and at that moment, it was eluding her.

**ATALANTA:** (*angrily*) It was there before! What has happened to it?

**NARRATOR:** At once, she stopped—and sniffed. Two creatures were in the thicket to the south. Two loud, uncouth beings. Creeping on all fours, she inched toward them and peered out from a low-lying bush.

**ATALANTA:** (*whispering*) Centaurs.

**NARRATOR:** There were the two great beasts—nine feet tall, half-man, half-horse. She had found her dead boar as well. They were making a quick meal of its red flesh. In one single movement, Atalanta sprang up, drew her bow, and nocked an arrow into the string. The heads of the centaurs flicked up.

**ATALANTA:** (*gritted teeth*) Leave it alone or die!

**CENTAUR ONE:** (*beastlike*) What do we have here? A pretty little huntress!

**CENTAUR TWO:** (*beastlike*) It seems so!

**ATALANTA:** I have given you your warning. You leave me no choice.

**CENTAUR ONE:** Perhaps we should teach her some manners.

**CENTAUR TWO:** She *is* a pretty thing.

**NARRATOR:** The centaurs raised their red, blood-wet lips into a howl and rearing their front legs started to charge. Two swift arrows split the air and found their marks in each of the beasts' necks.

**CENTAUR 1-2:** (*dying, coughing*)

**NARRATOR:** With a thump, the two huge bodies fell to the ground. Atalanta crept cautiously closer. She peered down at the decimated cadaver of her kill and wrinkled her nose.

**ATALANTA:** Beasts! (*spits*)

**NARRATOR:** Seeing that her prey had been ruined, she turned and ran quickly back through the wood. She smelled the strange scent of horses in the village before she saw them. It was growing dark when she arrived. The hunters and some strange men were gathered around a campfire. They all stopped their talking when she walked up.

**ATALANTA:** Who are these strangers?

**HUNTER:** Ambassadors from Calydon. The chief is talking with their prince.

**ATALANTA:** *(spitefully)* What do such great ones want with us lowly hunters?

**UNCLE ONE:** Those are our sentiments exactly, but our impetuous nephew sees it otherwise. What are you? The village wife?

**ATALANTA:** *(hatefully)* I would watch my tongue if I were you, white-head. I will bear no man to be the master of me.

**UNCLE TWO:** *(laughs)* What man would want to? Where is your chief? What is taking so long?

**NARRATOR:** Atalanta gave the newcomers a vicious glance, but looked up to see the chief coming forth from his hut—his arm around a handsome, young man.

**CHIEF:** Ah, Atalanta! You have returned!

**NARRATOR:** The prince stopped short, and he found a lump lodged in his throat. Before him was the most beautiful woman he had ever seen—the appearance of a goddess in earthly form—Artemis come to life.

**ATALANTA:** Why is he looking at me like that?

**CHIEF:** Ah, it seems that our young prince has noticed what you have failed to, Atalanta.

**MELEAGER:** No—I—just— *(cough)*

**CHIEF:** This is our sister-daughter, Atalanta. We have raised her from a child.

**MELEAGER:** *(nervously)* It is a pleasure to meet you.

**NARRATOR:** The fumbling boy stuck out his hand, but the huntress only looked at it in anger.

**ATALANTA:** *(angrily)* Is this what I think it is? Have you decided to marry me off to this weakling? Look at him! He probably couldn't throw a spear two meters!

**MELEAGER:** *(insulted)* I don't think—

**CHIEF:** Atalanta! Be silent! We have not arranged a marriage. The prince has come to recruit hunters to take back with him to Calydon.

**ATALANTA:** Oh. I see. Well, then, boy, you have met the very best.

**CHIEF:** She is ever-so-humble, my lord. Tell me, Atalanta, where is the boar that you have killed?

**MELEAGER:** A wild boar? That is a mighty kill.

**ATALANTA:** That is nothing, princeling! I have just slain two centaurs as well.

**CHIEF:** My girl! That is most wonderful—and most dangerous! You could have easily been killed.

**ATALANTA:** No, I could not have.

**CHIEF:** *(chuckles)* Very well. I know you are tired, but take the prince and show him some lodging.

**ATALANTA:** But—I—

**CHIEF:** Do as I say.

**NARRATOR:** Turning with a huff, Atalanta stalked away into the darkness.

**CHIEF:** There she goes, your highness. None of us may tame her. Perhaps you will have better luck.

**NARRATOR:** Meleager grinned and trotted off behind the girl. Like almost any man would, he was already falling quickly in love with the fiery, young maiden.

**MELEAGER:** My name is Meleager.

**ATALANTA:** *(angrily)* I hope you don't think that I have to be nice to you. I have no intentions of doing so.

**MELEAGER:** Well, that's to be expected.

**ATALANTA:** I'm a fierce huntress—savage and brutal. You really should be afraid of me, you know.

**MELEAGER:** I am. I am. But you're not always savage and brutal, are you?

**NARRATOR:** The girl stopped and stared him down.

**ATALANTA:** Always.

**NARRATOR:** She stalked ahead. Meleager struggled to keep up.

**MELEAGER:** I think deep down you are probably kind and compassionate—

**ATALANTA:** I killed two centaurs today, boy. I am no princess. I was raised as a man.

**MELEAGER:** Yes, but you are a woman. Perhaps you should start acting like it.

**NARRATOR:** Atalanta spun on her heel and grabbed the startled prince by the throat.

**ATALANTA:** Should I squeeze? I think so. Don't tell me what I should be.

**MELEAGER:** *(hoarsely)* All right! All right!

**NARRATOR:** The huntress released him and began walking again.

**MELEAGER:** They say that you were raised by bears.

**ATALANTA:** Not *bears*—a bear.

**MELEAGER:** I think that that's fascinating.

**ATALANTA:** Do you, princeling? Do you know what it's like to have your mother murdered before your very eyes? Do you know what it's like to be raised as the only woman in a group of men? Do you know what it's like to have people trying to tell you what to do and who to be?

**MELEAGER:** *(softly)* Yes. Actually, I do.

**ATALANTA:** Ha!

**NARRATOR:** They had reached a large hut. Atalanta angrily pulled open the flap and motioned for him to enter.

**ATALANTA:** Here you are, princeling—your palace.

**MELEAGER:** Thank you—and I understand.

**NARRATOR:** Meleager ducked into the hut, but Atalanta was soon behind.

**ATALANTA:** What do you mean *you understand?*

**MELEAGER:** What you've gone through.

**ATALANTA:** You couldn't understand—

**MELEAGER:** Will you let me speak? How will you ever know anything if you don't listen? You're angry at the world because you feel all alone. Well, I'm angry at the world for the same reason—only there are hundreds of people all around me.

**ATALANTA:** I don't understand.

**MELEAGER:** It's a long story, but I was cursed on the day I was born. The three Fates came to my mother a week after my birth and prophesied my death. They told her that I would be dead when the log on the fire had been consumed.

**ATALANTA:** Obviously, they were wrong.

**MELEAGER:** Thanks to my mother. As soon as the vision of the Fates disappeared, she ran to the fireplace and put out the fire. Then she took the log—the one that symbolizes my life—and ever since has had it locked away.

**ATALANTA:** Congratulations. You can never die.

**MELEAGER:** I know that I *will* have to die—someday—and so does my mother. And it has driven her insane. She never leaves her room. She watches the chest with the log inside day and night. My father has considered her dead to him.

**ATALANTA:** Was she killed in front of your very eyes? I don't see how this is pertaining.

**MELEAGER:** Ever since I can remember, my mother has had a guard about me—someone to watch my every step. Over the years, this constant fear has destroyed her mind. Her love has turned to hate. She hates anything that could take me away from her. She has forbidden me to marry—threatening to destroy the log herself if I should do such a thing. And so I am cursed to be alone the rest of my life.

**ATALANTA:** *(quietly)* I am sorry, but to me that would be a great thing—no one to ever tell you what to do.

**MELEAGER:** Have you never desired a companion? Someone to share your life with?

**ATALANTA:** No—never. I was raised wild, and I think I shall always be wild.

**MELEAGER:** I hope not. But come, Atalanta. If nothing else, let us be friends.

**NARRATOR:** He held out his hand. She glanced at it hesitantly but then took it in her own.

**ATALANTA:** Agreed. Now, sleep, princeling. I have a feeling that you and I are going to be going on a long journey tomorrow.

**NARRATOR:** She was right. The next day, the chief pledged the help of the hunters to Prince Meleager of Calydon, and they made ready to depart.

**MELEAGER:** Atalanta, have you ever been out of Arcady?

**ATALANTA:** No, this has always been my home. What is Calydon like?

**MELEAGER:** A lot like this country—wild and free.

**ATALANTA:** Then I shall like it. How big is this boar, did you say?

**MELEAGER:** Men say that it is ten to twelve feet tall.

**ATALANTA:** Men? Men always exaggerate.

**NARRATOR:** The two companions rode at the front of the procession—laughing and jibing. The chief rode with a satisfied look on his face.

**CHIEF:** Perhaps our little wild girl will find love after all.

**NARRATOR:** At the back of the procession, two old men rode with downcast looks upon their faces. They were the uncles of Meleager, the brothers of the queen.

**UNCLE ONE:** We do not need this rabble to kill the boar!

**UNCLE TWO:** Especially that female whelp. Look at her—flirting with the prince. Does she think that she will *ever* become a princess?

**UNCLE ONE:** Not if I have anything to say about it.

**NARRATOR:** They rode for many days until they finally came to the wilds of Calydon. They pitched their tents and made camp in the forest and prepared their weapons and their beasts for the hunt the following day.

**ATALANTA:** (*proudly*) I say that I shall be the first to slay the boar.

**MELEAGER:** Really? I think *I* shall get there first.

**ATALANTA:** (*playfully*) You? Ha! You are a woman! That beast is from Artemis. It will see your shaking hand and your pale face and know that it has nothing to fear.

**NARRATOR:** And so the two stayed up late into the night of the eve of the great hunt. In spite of Atalanta's efforts, they had become fast friends.

The morning broke light and crisp, and an early horn sounded that the hunt had begun. Meleager rode his magnificent steed into the forest, while Atalanta ran lightly at his side.

**CHIEF:** Hunters, stay close! Keep your spears in front of you! The boar will charge without warning.

**NARRATOR:** They went deeper and deeper into the wilderness. The prince's uncles and their men were obviously poorly trained for woodland travel and soon began to swear at the thick foliage.

**ATALANTA:** We have lost all element of surprise by your thoughtless crashing through the underbrush! This is pointless!

**MELEAGER:** Quiet, uncles. We must not give our prey an advantage—

**NARRATOR:** His words were cut off by an otherworldly roar. The giant form of a black beast burst forth from the trees and tore through the men to the company's left. Bodies flew through the air as the bloody tusks flung them like rag dolls.

**ATALANTA:** (*yelling*) Get away from him! He is mine!

**MELEAGER:** Atalanta, be careful!

NARRATOR: Atalanta and Meleager charged toward the boar, which was now trampling its victims into the ground. Its bloody snout lifted from the earth, and its red eyes stared at them menacingly.    Its unearthly voice boomed out.

BOAR: *(scary voice)* Do you know who sent me, mortals?

ATALANTA:   Artemis has sent you, and I will send you back to her, pig.

BOAR: I shall like to see you try.

MELEAGER:   What are you saying to it?

NARRATOR:   The roaring beast charged forward. Atalanta stood her ground. With it only paces from her, she leapt into the air and buried her spear into the back of its neck. It squealed a squeal of the souls tormented in Hades and stumbled to the ground. Meleager was there in a flash and drove his sword deep into its throat.

BOAR: *(rasping)* Artemis will be revenged.

NARRATOR:   The red light of its eyes flickered and faded. Meleager and Atalanta smiled at each other in triumph. The rest of the party was quickly making its way over to the scene of the battle.

UNCLE ONE: Victory! The beast is dead, I see. To whom shall we give the body?

UNCLE TWO: He who dealt the killing stroke shall have it.

MELEAGER: It was Atalanta. She was the one who killed the boar.

ATALANTA:   No, I must confess it. I only injured it. It was the prince who killed it.

UNCLE TWO:   As a prince should. What an embarrassment if he should be shown up by a ratty girl.

MELEAGER: *(angrily)* Silence! I won't have you speak to her that way. *She* shall have the body. I could not have killed the boar without her.

UNCLE ONE: *(angrily)* Preposterous! Giving the body to a *girl*—a worthless nomad! Never!

MELEAGER:   *(even angrier)* I have said my piece.

UNCLE TWO:   *We* do not care about what you have to say. In fact, nephew, I believe it is time you ran home to your mother. We have business to settle here.

UNCLE ONE: Yes! Men, kill this scum! They have fulfilled their usefulness!

NARRATOR:   The hunters stirred at once, but the Calydonian soldiers moved in closely around them—weapons at the ready.

MELEAGER: *(shocked)* What are you doing?

UNCLE ONE:   We can't have the kingdom knowing that we enlisted the help of filthy *nomads* to kill this beast. Surely you understand, nephew. Our honor is at stake! Kill them at once! The girl as well!

MELEAGER:   Noooo!

NARRATOR:   Meleager drew his sword and jumped toward his grimacing uncles. Atalanta and the hunters, too, jerked into the fray. The battle went quickly. The trained Calydonian soldiers were no match for the honed senses of the hunters. The Calydonians began to retreat back to the city. Atalanta saw the bent form of Meleager and came to his side. He was kneeling by two covered bodies.

**MELEAGER:** *(quietly)* I killed them. They tried to kill you.

**ATALANTA:** They were evil men.

**MELEAGER:** But they were my mother's brothers. Men run back now to tell her the news. I have betrayed my family—for a woman.

**ATALANTA:** You have done the right thing! What is there to worry?

**MELEAGER:** I have killed the beloved ones of my mother. Her retribution shall be swift.

**NARRATOR:** He was right. The survivors from the skirmish soon reached the city walls wailing. When the queen heard the news, she tore her cloak and then furiously dug a hidden bundle from a dusty trunk. She raged as she threw it upon the roaring fire. Quickly the thin wrapping burned away, and a simple aged log was revealed beneath. She laughed the laugh of the mad. *(crazed laughter)*

Back in the wilderness, Meleager fell to the ground in pain.

**ATALANTA:** Meleager!

**MELEAGER:** *(weakly)* Artemis has had her revenge. The prophecy of the Fates has come true. I can feel it!

**ATALANTA:** *(frantically)* No! I can save you! I'm strong! I can save you!

**NARRATOR:** Atalanta cradled the body of her friend in her arms, and it began to glow. Meleager cried out in pain.

**MELEAGER:** *(weakly)* Atalanta—I love you—I loved you the moment I first saw you.

**ATALANTA:** I know, my friend. I know.

**NARRATOR:** She held him tightly—as tight as she could—but her strength could not help him. She felt his weight disappear from her arms, and the body of the prince crumbled into ash. Then, for the first time in her life, she wept.

The legends of Atalanta did not end here. She went on to many mighty deeds. But from this time on, she was a changed person. She did not swagger as she did before. She did not boast as loudly. She was never again afraid to take the help of a friend. In a world where women could not, she became one who *could* and *did* go down in history as the greatest female hero of all time.

## DISCUSSION QUESTIONS

1. What are some of the reasons that Atalanta is *not* a typical Greek hero?
2. Do you think Atalanta is a good role model for women? Explain.
3. If you could change one thing about the ending to Atalanta's story, what would it be? Explain.
4. Do you think Atalanta is too prideful?
5. What is significant about Meleager being the one who actually killed the boar?

# OEDIPUS THE CURSED KING
## TEACHER GUIDE

## BACKGROUND

Oedipus is one of Greek mythology's most notorious characters. Sigmund Freud named the Oedipus complex, a theory that all young boys feel attraction for their mothers and hatred for their fathers, after this character who inadvertently murders his father and marries his mother.

Oedipus's story has horrified and intrigued audiences for over 2,000 years. The most famous (and arguably most powerful) tragedy produced by ancient Greece is *Oedipus Rex* (or Oedipus the King) by the playwright Sophocles. Greek spectators went to the theater for the same reasons we now go to the cinema: to be entertained. But they also went to experience what Aristotle called *catharsis* or the purging of negative emotions. By experiencing the tragic fates of fictional characters, the audience members relieve themselves of their own sadness, frustration, and anger. The same theory applies to those who subject themselves to sad movies because they enjoy "a good cry."

Needless to say, Oedipus's story offers plenty of tragedy. Possibly the most tragic element of the story is that Oedipus is basically a good guy. Compared to other characters from mythology, he's a boy scout. It's not his fault that he didn't know the true identity of his parents. He was born doomed. His only crime was trying to escape his fate. This may seem like a poor reason for Oedipus to experience so much tragedy, but the Greeks equated fate with the gods. When Oedipus tries to change his fate, he's actually trying to prove the gods wrong.

Today many students read this play in high school. Those who don't often read *Antigone* instead, a drama also by Sophocles that deals with the aftermath of Oedipus's reign. Both plays deal with similar themes: What happens when one ignores the gods? How quickly can one rise to power? How quickly can one fall from grace? Thanks to these still-relevant themes *Oedipus Rex* and *Antigone* will be read for many years to come.

## SUMMARY

Shortly after giving birth to a new baby boy, Jocasta, queen of Thebes, is delivered a terrible prophecy by Tiresias, a blind prophet. Tiresias tells Jocasta and her husband, Laius the king, that the child they now hold in their arms will one day murder his father and marry his mother. Laius decides that the child cannot be allowed to live. He sends it into the wilderness with the royal shepherd with instructions to expose the child to the elements.

The kindly shepherd ignores this command and gives the child to a stranger he meets in the wilderness. This stranger is actually a servant of King Polybus of Corinth, and he delivers the baby to his sovereign, who is mourning the death of his own young son. The Corinthian king decides to adopt the baby as his son and heir, naming him Oedipus, which means "swollen foot."

Oedipus grows up believing his true parents are the king and queen of Corinth. When he turns eighteen, Oedipus journeys to Delphi to hear his fortune told by the oracle. She tells him the same prophecy that Tiresias uttered years before. Horrified, Oedipus decides that he cannot return to Corinth and decides to journey toward Thebes instead.

On the road to Thebes, Oedipus is attacked by an old traveler. Merely protecting himself, Oedipus inadvertently kills the old man. Oedipus flees the scene of the crime, continuing on toward Thebes. Next he encounters the sphinx, a beast with the head of a woman, the body of a lion, the wings of an eagle, and the tail of a snake. This beast has been killing anyone who travels the road after they fail to solve her riddle: What walks on four legs in the morning, two at noon, and three in the evening? Oedipus answers her riddle correctly: The answer is man. The sphinx kills herself in anger.

When Oedipus arrives at Thebes, the people there make him their king for slaying the sphinx and marry him to the queen, Jocasta. It is not until years later, when a famine strikes Thebes, that the truth of Oedipus's situation becomes clear. The oracle demands that Oedipus find the murderer of Laius. Oedipus calls upon Tiresias to give him advice on locating the former king's murderer. The blind prophet's answer stuns everyone: Oedipus has accidentally murdered his father and married his mother. Jocasta hangs herself in grief, and Oedipus gouges out his eyes. Creon, Jocasta's brother, assumes control of Thebes and banishes Oedipus to the wilderness, where he wanders until his death.

## ESSENTIAL QUESTIONS

- Can a person avoid his or her fate?
- Why do horrible things sometimes happen to people who deserve better?

## CONNECTIONS

*Minority Report* (2002) In this science fiction film criminals are arrested *before* they commit crimes thanks to oracle-like mutants. But the question remains—are these predictions always right, or can the future be changed?

*Sophocles's* Antigone In this "follow-up" play to *Oedipus Rex*, Antigone, the daughter

of Oedipus, must take a stand against her uncle Creon when he refuses to give her brother a proper burial.

## ANTICIPATORY QUESTIONS

- What is a *sphinx*?
- What walks on four legs in the morning, two at noon, and three in the evening?
- What is *fate*?
- It's said that men often marry women who are *like* their mothers. Do you think this is true?
- What is an Oedipus complex?

## TEACHABLE TERMS

- **Dramatic Irony**   During the course of the story, the reader knows the true identity of Oedipus's parents while Oedipus does not. This is dramatic irony.
- **Antagonist**   Having students determine exactly who or what is Oedipus's antagonist helps them develop an understanding of this term. (*Fate* or *the gods* is the most common answer.)
- **Irony**   The idea of a blind prophet is ironic. Even though Tiresias can see the future, he cannot see the world around him.
- **Author's purpose**   The ancient Greek playwright Sophocles is the main source for this myth. What is he trying to say about those who try to change their fate?

## RECALL QUESTIONS

1. What is the prophecy concerning Oedipus?
2. What does the name *Oedipus* mean?
3. What is the riddle of the sphinx?
4. Why do the people of Thebes make Oedipus their king?
5. What does Oedipus do once he sees Jocasta has hanged herself?

# OEDIPUS THE CURSED KING

## CAST

| | |
|---|---|
| **OEDIPUS** | *Young Prince* |
| **JOCASTA** | *Queen of Thebes* |
| **TIRESIAS** | *Blind Prophet* |
| **LAIUS /OLD MAN** | *King of Thebes* |
| **POLYBUS** | *King of Corinth* |
| **SERVANT** | *Servant to Polybus* |
| **SHEPHERD** | *Servant to Laius* |
| **SPHINX** | *Strange Creature* |
| **GUARD** | *Watchman of Thebes* |
| **CREON** | *Brother to Jocasta* |
| **MAIDSERVANT** | *Servant to Jocasta* |
| **ORACLE** | *Oracle of Delphi* |

**NARRATOR:** In the midst of a howling storm, Jocasta the queen of Thebes was giving birth. Grouped about her in a sweaty bundle, her maidservants attended her, dabbing her fiery face, and ushered her wailing son into the world.

**MAIDSERVANT:** *(frightened)* She is weak! She may not even live to see the dawn. This child is cursed to be born on such a night.

**NARRATOR:** The maidservant gazed sadly at her mistress. Jocasta was nearly a child herself, barely sixteen—the king, a man of thirty. King Laius came bursting into the stifling room. He had been eagerly awaiting the birth of his heir. The maidservant displayed his child to him, and he took him into his arms.

**LAIUS:** *(anxiously)* A boy?

**MAIDSERVANT:** Yes, your majesty.

**LAIUS:** *(overjoyed)* Praises to Zeus! Oh, my beloved wife, you have done your husband well!

**NARRATOR:** He put a hand to her sweat-streaked face.

**JOCASTA:** *(weakly)* Laius. Laius.

**MAIDSERVANT:** *(grimly)* The queen is not well. She has lost much blood. She may not survive the night.

**LAIUS:** *(softly)* You cannot die, Jocasta. You've just brought our happiness into the world. You must live to see this blessing of ours grow into a—*(startling boom of thunder)*

**NARRATOR:** Laius stopped in mid-speech. A flash of lightning had silhouetted a dark form standing near the doorway—a new arrival to the birthing chamber.

**JOCASTA:** *(frightened)* Laius!

**LAIUS:** *(angrily)* Who's there? How dare you enter our royal quarters! Explain yourself at once!

**NARRATOR:** The wiry frame of a man stood forward. In a smooth motion he threw his muddy traveling cloak back from his shoulders. Darkness shrouded him once again.

**LAIUS:** *(enraged)* Speak, spy! What is your purpose here? Speak! Or we will burn the words out of you. What have you seen?

**NARRATOR:** Yet another flash from the skies lit the face of the stranger. Two bulging eyes overflowed their sockets—a milky glaze across the pale irises.

**TIRESIAS:** *(coyly)* See? I see nothing in this world, my king. But in the next, I see much.

**NARRATOR:** The king and his young wife stared in horror. The child let out a shriek. *(wail of a child)*

**TIRESIAS:** Silence that child. I am sent from my master with a message for you.

**LAIUS:** You will make no orders here. What master would you have higher than me? I am the king, and there can be no higher.

**TIRESIAS:** Not so. I serve Lord Apollo, your majesty.

**NARRATOR:** These words caught Laius by the throat. Olympus had sent this man with the news of Apollo, god of prophecy, upon his lips.

**LAIUS:** *(nervously)* Forgive me. Your master is surely higher than I. What news do you have for me? Will my wife die from this birth?

**TIRESIAS:** Do not forget your place in the world, king. The gods see and direct all. *(pause)* Your wife *will* die because of the birth of your son—but not for many years hence.

**JOCASTA:** *(terrified)* Laius, what does he mean?

**TIRESIAS:** *(angrily)* Were you not warned about this child? Were you not told what an abomination he would be to your country?

**LAIUS:** *(hesitantly)* Warned? Well, yes. But that was years ago. I am a king! I must have a son! Who will rule after me?

**TIRESIAS:** The jackals and the dark creatures of night will rule after you, Laius king. The oracle spoke then, and the oracle speaks now. If Laius shall have a son, that son will slay him.

**JOCASTA:** No!

**TIRESIAS:** But I have said only half, my lady. If Jocasta shall bear a son from Laius, that son will come to share her bed in unholy love.

**NARRATOR:** The queen cried out and fell back upon her bed in a swoon.

**LAIUS:** *(yelling)* Silence! Do not speak those words! I forbid it!

**TIRESIAS:** I speak as I am commanded. These words have been spoken before, but you chose not to listen. They fly from my lips once again—one final warning against this child.

**LAIUS:** *(forcefully)* Leave immediately, or I will have you gutted—your head stuck on a pole.

**TIRESIAS:** I am quite safe from your threats. Lord Apollo keeps me close to his side. You have heard his words. Heed them.

**NARRATOR:** A thunderclap—one much bigger than the others—shook the walls of the chamber. When the flashing subsided, the blind man was gone—vanished without a trace. The serving women rushed to the queen, while the king stared at the wriggling child in his arms.

**JOCASTA:** *(reviving)* What can we do? What can we do? Our baby!

**NARRATOR:** Laius rounded angrily upon the servants.

**LAIUS:** *(determined)* Leave us at once! Forget what you have seen and heard here this night, or I shall flog you within an inch of your lives.

**NARRATOR:** The serving women fled terrified. They had witnessed the cruelty of Laius before. As the final maidservant darted past, the king caught her by the arm and pulled her close.

**LAIUS:** Fetch the royal shepherd. Tell him it is time to prove his loyalty to his king.

**MAIDSERVANT:** *(stammering)* Yes—yes—my lord.

**NARRATOR:** Freed from his grip, the woman dashed from the room. Laius turned and lowered his newborn son into his wife's pleading hands. Frantically, Jocasta searched the face of her husband.

**JOCASTA:** *(frantically)* Is it true? What can we do?

**LAIUS:** *(angrily)* Quiet, woman! I'm trying to think!

**JOCASTA:** *(whimper)*

**NARRATOR:** Gritting his teeth, Laius clenched his hair within two fists. He turned quickly and ripped a dagger from his belt.

**LAIUS:** Now do exactly as I command. Hold up the child!

**JOCASTA:** *(crying out)* Laius! No!

**LAIUS:** Do as I say!

**NARRATOR:** The frightened girl raised her child up into the air. The king moved closer—dagger in hand.

**LAIUS:** Child born on this hateful night, you are no longer the heir of Thebes. I curse you as the gods have cursed you. You are no son of mine.

**NARRATOR:** Spitting upon the infant, he seized its two tiny, kicking feet and pushed the point of the dagger through each. Blood gushed forth, and the child wailed. *(wailing child)*

**LAIUS:** He will show these scars forever. They will show that he was born a commoner, an illegitimate—no son of the king. The king shall have no son.

**NARRATOR:** In the darkness the royal shepherd entered, panting and frightened.

**SHEPHERD:** *(out of breath)* You sent for me, your majesty?

**NARRATOR:** The king turned—the wailing, blood-stained child in his arms.

**LAIUS:** Take this boy into the wilderness and leave him on the mountain of Kithairon to die.

**NARRATOR:** Horrified, the servant looked up to his master.

**SHEPHERD:** But—but, your majesty. Who is this child?

**LAIUS:** You need know nothing more. Do as I say—or you will find your neck stretched by the executioner's rope.

**NARRATOR:** The shepherd took the infant into his arms and backed slowly from the chamber. The queen began to weep again, and the king held his head to hers.

**LAIUS:** *(whispering)* Shhhhhhh. Forget that child. Pretend he died in the womb. Forget him. His memory will fade soon enough.

**NARRATOR:** And so in the midst of a tempest as the earth had never seen, the baby was carried into the night by loyal hands. The kind shepherd had known as soon as he had taken the bundle into his arms that he would not be able to leave it to die. As he pushed through the battering rain into the wilderness, he formulated a plan.

The night sky lit up like noon for a moment. The jagged peak of Kithairon towered above.

**SHEPHERD:** *(to the baby)* Tonight, the gods are angered. But you do not fear them, little one. The heavens have crashed, but you haven't made a sound.

**NARRATOR:** The rough man stopped and looked down into the bundle he shielded from the rain.

**SHEPHERD:** If you do not fear the gods, why should I fear a king? We'll find you a home and tell your wicked parents that you have died. It will be our little secret.

**NARRATOR:** Soon the storm subsided, and the thin glow of dawn broke the horizon. On one of the many mountain paths, the shepherd happened upon a traveler.

**SHEPHERD:** Which way are you headed, brother?

**SERVANT:** I return to Corinth. I serve the king there.

**SHEPHERD:** Take this child for me. Thebes is no place for him. Find him a good home. Living with me in the wilderness is no fate for such a child.

**NARRATOR:** The traveling servant saw the shepherd's urgency, and he agreed to take the child.

**SHEPHERD:** I cannot thank you enough. *(to the child)* Goodbye, little one. I wish you all the happiness in the world.

**NARRATOR:** The Corinthian servant bore the child back to his homeland. Upon his return, he was greeted with horrific news. A sudden plague had taken the life of the newborn prince. The king of Corinth, the servant's master, sat brooding and mourning the loss of his son.

**SERVANT:** *(meekly)* Sire, I know your loss is great, but I believe the gods have given you a second chance. A stranger in the wilderness gave me this child, an orphan, and told me to find it a good home. Will you take it as your own and forget your grief?

**NARRATOR:** King Polybus marveled at such a coincidence and at once declared the intervention of Olympus. He accepted the baby as his own son and named him prince of the realm.

**POLYBUS:** But his feet have been wounded! What trials this child has already suffered! We shall call him Oedipus for his swollen feet. Relax, little Oedipus, your troubles are over.

**NARRATOR:** Many years passed. The boy Oedipus experienced the happiest of days that any child could. He was kept completely ignorant of the royal adoption, which had so changed his fate. The child with the swollen feet soon grew into a young man, and when he reached eighteen years of age, he prepared for the ancient ritual of manhood.

**OEDIPUS:** *(confidently)* Father, I am ready.

**POLYBUS:** To do what, my son?

**OEDIPUS:** To go to the temple at Delphi, of course. To visit the oracle.

**POLYBUS:** It's a long road. Are you sure you're up to it? You can always go next year, you know.

**OEDIPUS:** I'm ready to hear my fate and become a man.

**POLYBUS:** Your mother and I will miss you terribly. I remember my own journey to the oracle, you know. Be careful, and hurry home.

**OEDIPUS:** I will.

**NARRATOR:** The journey from Corinth to Delphi proved uneventful. Excitement fueled each and every one of Oedipus's steps. When he at last climbed the crooked mountain that housed the oracle's cave, his heart beat in furious anticipation.

**OEDIPUS:** *(cautiously)* Hello? Is anyone in there?

**NARRATOR:** Inside the cave turned into a cavern, and Oedipus cautiously made his way into its mouth. The air soon became cool, and hissing mist rose from the cracked floor.

**ORACLE:** *(booming voice)* Enter, young man.

**NARRATOR:** A woman was seated on a tall, metal stool ahead in the darkness.

**OEDIPUS:** *(nervously)* It is I, Oedipus.

**ORACLE:** *(quiet laugh)* Swollen foot. I know your name—and its meaning.

**OEDIPUS:** I am the prince of Corinth. I've come to hear my fortune.

**ORACLE:** *(slyly)* Fortune would be an odd word for a future such as yours.

**OEDIPUS:** *(scared)* What do you mean?

**ORACLE:** *(grimly)* All ahead is darkness— darkness of mind—darkness of thought.

**OEDIPUS:** For me? Are you serious? This is Oedipus.

**ORACLE:** *(dry laugh)* Everyone always expects happiness. Not everyone can be happy. I don't deal in lies—only truth. Now listen closely. Once it is said, I will speak no more. *(pause)* Oedipus, you are destined by high Olympus to commit two horrible sins.

You shall murder your father—and marry your mother.

NARRATOR: The heart of the young man went cold.

OEDIPUS: *(weakly)* No. No. There must be some mistake. *(pleading)* It's—it's only a prophecy. It can be changed—right? Oh please tell me it can be.

NARRATOR: But the oracle only closed her eyes and bowed her head. She had spoken.

For hours the boy lay upon the mountain, stunned, listening to the wind rip through the crags. When he did finally rise, he did so completely against his will.

OEDIPUS: *(decidedly)* If this truly is my fate, I will undo it.

NARRATOR: With weary, halting steps, he descended the mountain. At its base, two paths stretched out before him. One led to a home that he could no longer return to. The other—into the wild, the unknown.

OEDIPUS: Goodbye, Father. Goodbye, Mother. You won't understand, but at least you will be saved from your wretched son.

NARRATOR: Oedipus struck out, down the unknown path, fleeing fate with the words of the oracle burning in his mind.

Slow steps broke into a run, and at last he fought back tears. He ran and ran until his sides ached as if they would split open. Then he lay down in the dirt and remained still. The summer sun beat down upon him, and the bright, white light consumed his mind until he knew nothing else.

OLD MAN: *(yelling)* Halt! What is going on here? Stop! Stop!

NARRATOR: Oedipus opened his weary eyes. Through the swirling dust, he saw an old man snarling down at him from on horseback. The boy sat up.

OLD MAN: *(angrily)* Get out of the road, you miserable peasant!

NARRATOR: Oedipus rose as the old man glared at him fiercely. Behind him there followed a group of servants.

OLD MAN: *(sarcastically)* Sorry to interrupt your nap. It's hard enough to get our caravan down this road without riff-raff lying across it.

NARRATOR: Heat rushed to Oedipus's face.

OEDIPUS: *(dangerously)* Watch it, old man. You're dealing with someone who is cursed.

NARRATOR: The old man roared with laughter.

OLD MAN: *(loud laugh)* We are certainly frightened. We should have ridden over you when we had the chance. *(forcefully)* Now, trash, move! Or we will move you ourselves.

NARRATOR: Immediately, anger thrilled through every vein of the boy's body.

OEDIPUS: *(roaring)* I will not!

OLD MAN: *(coldly)* Very well.

NARRATOR: The man pulled a knotted whip from his satchel, raised it up into the air, and brought it swiftly down toward Oedipus's face. *(cry of pain, whip-crack)*

The boy ran forward, avoiding the blow. Seeing nothing beyond his own rage, he barreled into the side of the old man's horse. *(neigh of a horse)*

**OLD MAN:** (crying out) Ah!

**NARRATOR:** The force of the blow knocked the old man from his mount. Flailing his arms madly, he fell—pitching to the side—landing hard upon his neck.

**OEDIPUS:** (yelling in a frenzy) Ha! Who controls the road now, you old buzzard?

**NARRATOR:** Oedipus seized the whip from the man's limp hand and turned upon the servants.

**OEDIPUS:** (yelling) Who's next?

**NARRATOR:** Terrified, the remaining travelers fled.

**OEDIPUS:** (yelling) That's right! Run, you cowards! Run from the cursed one!

**NARRATOR:** Oedipus seethed with satisfaction as he saw the last of them disappear down the road.

**OEDIPUS:** Your friends have abandoned you, old man.

**NARRATOR:** The boy turned back to the fallen form. It remained motionless—its head turned at an odd angle. The rider-less horse nuzzled its master.

**OEDIPUS:** (breathlessly) I killed him. I killed him.

**NARRATOR:** He stared at the whip in his hand and then threw it to the ground.

**OEDIPUS:** She was right. If I'm capable of this, I *am* a monster.

**NARRATOR:** A sudden fear burned inside of him—fear of himself, fear of the deed done by his own hand. He did all he knew how to do: He fled.

He traveled for days, haunted by his dreams and hunted by phantoms. He took no notice of where his feet led him. Landscapes rose and fell. So it was no surprise that he did not happen to see that the roadside fields soon became barren or that he met no more travelers. Even the shining whiteness of the bones that littered the roadway escaped his notice.

It took the towering form of the sphinx to stir his attention.

**SPHINX:** (otherworldly) Halt, mortal.

**NARRATOR:** Oedipus looked up from his daze, but his eyes remained bleary. The most bizarre creature he had ever seen was seated beside the road. The head of a woman was gazing imperiously down at him. That is where the creature's womanhood ended. The furry body was that of a lion with the wings of an eagle and terminated in the tail of a snake. The sphinx was resting upon her bed of bones—licking her paw and flicking her scaly tail cat-like back and forth.

**SPHINX:** You're awfully calm for being in the presence of a monster.

**OEDIPUS:** (daze-like) I could say the same for you.

**SPHINX:** I have killed a hundred men. Their bones litter the roadways. Do you not fear me?

**OEDIPUS:** (numbly) I fear only myself.

**NARRATOR:** A smile of intrigue passed over the sphinx's womanly face.

**SPHINX:** Perhaps you wish to die. Is that why you've sought me out?

**OEDIPUS:** Kill me if you must. Rid the world of the cancer you see before you.

**SPHINX:** Don't be too hasty, mortal man. I don't kill for the sake of killing. I'm actually a very refined creature. I believe in giving everyone a sporting chance.

**OEDIPUS:** *(sarcastic)* How noble. A civilized monster.

**SPHINX:** I will give you the same chance I have given everyone else who happened to pass this way—the chance to solve my riddle.

**OEDIPUS:** Riddles are for children. What if I refuse to play?

**NARRATOR:** The sphinx smiled at him.

**SPHINX:** *(beastlike)* Then I shall eat you—slowly.

**OEDIPUS:** I'll play your little game. At least if I lose, my misery will come to an end.

**SPHINX:** *(happily)* That's the spirit. I'm also very fair. If on the off-chance you actually win, I will voluntarily forfeit my own life. Here is my riddle.

**NARRATOR:** The sphinx cleared her throat and spoke in a resonating voice.

**SPHINX:** What creature walks on four legs in the morning, two legs at noon, and three legs in the evening?

**NARRATOR:** The wind lazily whipped up the dirt around them.

**OEDIPUS:** How much time do I have to answer the question?

**SPHINX:** As long as my patience holds out.

**NARRATOR:** Though he did not will it, Oedipus's mind began to move and click.

**OEDIPUS:** *(absentmindedly)* Perhaps she does not mean only one day. There is a morning and an evening to life.

**SPHINX:** *(growing impatient)* Your time is running out.

**OEDIPUS:** Life changes many creatures. Many creatures walk on two legs, and many creatures walk on four legs. But three legs—there is the riddle.

**SPHINX:** Enough of your babbling! Do you know the answer or not?

**OEDIPUS:** Of course, that's it!

**SPHINX:** *(angrily)* My patience is growing thin!

**OEDIPUS:** Man. The answer is man.

**SPHINX:** *(angrily)* What?

**OEDIPUS:** We crawl in the morning of our lives, we walk on two legs in our prime, and when we are old, we walk with a cane.

**NARRATOR:** Oedipus smiled in spite of himself. A bizarre light had come into the Sphinx's eyes, and she shrieked. *(nightmare shriek)* With huge swoops of her wings and a gust that pushed Oedipus to the ground, she took to the air, howling and wailing. She didn't fly far, but climbed high and then fell, fell down into the nearby sea—extinguishing her own life.

**OEDIPUS:** *(understated)* Huh. I guess she was a civilized monster after all.

NARRATOR: A sudden corner was turned in Oedipus's mind. He felt his spirits revive. He still held the power to put the past behind him. As he continued on the path, he noticed for the first time that nothing was growing for miles around. The sphinx had brought a curse upon the land. At last a set of shining city walls gleamed in the distance. They shone out like hope—a new start.

When Oedipus neared the massive gates, he found them bolted against him.

GUARD: (shouting) Who's there?

OEDIPUS: (shouting) A traveler!

GUARD: There have been no travelers on this road for months! The sphinx has killed them all.

OEDIPUS: Let me in! I have killed the sphinx.

NARRATOR: The guard looked down at the boy in shock. He turned to his fellow guards and conversed in hushed tones. (sounds of whispering in hushed tones)

GUARD: (hesitantly) Very well. Come inside. We shall take you to Creon the regent. He will decide what to do with you.

NARRATOR: The gigantic doors opened. Oedipus was taken roughly by either arm and escorted into the city.

OEDIPUS: Everyone seems a bit on edge here. What city is this?

GUARD: You are in Thebes, stranger. You have come at our darkest hour.

NARRATOR: Soon Oedipus found himself in the royal hearing hall. The Creon they had spoken of was a thin, serious man wrapped in a black robe. He looked at Oedipus distrustfully.

CREON: (suspiciously) Are you a spy? Tell only the truth.

OEDIPUS: No, sir. As I told the guards, I am a traveler.

CREON: If you are a traveler, where did you come from?

OEDIPUS: I came here from Delphi.

CREON: (snorting) Impossible! There is a monster that kills any who travel on that road! And bandits, too. Our king was murdered by a band of them just days ago. He had avoided the sphinx as he traveled to speak to the Oracle of Delphi. So how did you survive?

NARRATOR: Oedipus told Creon about his entire journey.

CREON: So you claim to have killed the sphinx by guessing its riddle? (laugh) Ridiculous.

NARRATOR: So Oedipus spent many days in the Theban jail. Finally, word came to Creon that no trace of the Sphinx could be found. The news spread through the city that the mysterious stranger had indeed slain the monster. It was Creon himself who came to free Oedipus from his cell.

CREON: I have to apologize for doubting you, young man.

OEDIPUS: I understand your doubt. I can hardly believe it myself.

CREON: The people are overjoyed. They sing your praises. I have also been charged to tell you that they wish to make you their king.

**OEDIPUS:** *(shocked)* Me? Why?

**CREON:** You have saved us. I am the people's humble servant. If they wish you to rule them, I will not stand in their way.

**NARRATOR:** Oedipus could barely believe it. Was this truly his good fortune? Had he escaped his destiny at last?

**OEDIPUS:** *(happily)* I accept.

**CREON:** There is one thing you should know. In order to legitimize your claim to the throne, we ask that you marry our queen. Her time of mourning for her husband has ended, and she is still young enough in years.

**OEDIPUS:** May I meet her first?

**CREON:** Certainly.

**NARRATOR:** The queen pleased Oedipus. He was surprised at her beauty. True, she was some years older, but she wore them well. There was still life and love within her.

Oedipus became the king of Thebes, and it seemed that he had in fact escaped the foul prophecy of his past. With Jocasta, his new wife, he was exceedingly happy. And once again the years passed by like a breeze. Together they raised a royal family, two boys and two girls, each with the vibrant glow of life in their eyes. Oedipus all but forgot his past, and the darkness that had threatened to consume him. Thebes loved their king, and it seemed that a happy ending would be had after all.

Then came the drought. The skies refused to give up their rain, crops failed, and the people began to starve. Only the gods could be the source of such a misfortune.

**OEDIPUS:** Send a man to Delphi at once. Ask the oracle what must be done to remedy this problem.

**NARRATOR:** It was strange, but Oedipus barely remembered the prophecy the oracle had spoken to him so long ago. All he knew was that the prophecy had been spoken in error. He had proved it false.

A messenger was dispatched and returned in haste with the oracle's words: The murderer of the old king must be found and brought to justice. Then, and only then, the skies would give forth rain once again.

**JOCASTA:** *(joyfully)* Thank the gods! They are crying out for justice at last!

**OEDIPUS:** I was told of Laius's death when I came here. I'll send out the soldiers to search the highways. Any bandits there must be put to death. Then we will have rain.

**NARRATOR:** This news relieved Oedipus. It seemed an easy solution. He called for Creon.

**OEDIPUS:** Creon, brother-in-law. Do the men who traveled with Laius when he was murdered still live?

**CREON:** I am sure they do, my lord. If you remember, it happened shortly before you arrived here in Thebes.

**OEDIPUS:** Do you remember their names? May we question them?

**CREON:** They were servants and slaves. They barely understood what they saw happening.

**OEDIPUS:** *(angrily)* There must be some way of solving this riddle! The gods would not leave us without a solution.

**CREON:**   There is blind man who wanders near Thebes, who is said to have the sight of the gods.

**JOCASTA:**   *(excitedly)* Tiresias! Of course. He will tell us what we need to know.

**OEDIPUS:**   Summon him. Let us put an end to this mess.

**NARRATOR:**   Word was sent out through Thebes: Tiresias must be brought before the king. The old blind man came soon enough, led there by a young boy. He stood proudly before the throne.

**TIRESIAS:**   *(old voice)* What does King Oedipus wish to know of the gods?

**OEDIPUS:**   Tiresias, Delphi has sent us a message. We must find the man who murdered Laius the former king. Only then will our land be healed.

**TIRESIAS:**   This land will never be healed while you sit upon the throne, my lord.

**OEDIPUS:**   *(in shock)* What did he say?

**JOCASTA:**   *(angrily)* How dare you speak to the king in such a way!

**NARRATOR:**   The old man began to laugh a cruel laugh.

**TIRESIAS:**   *(mockingly)* You fools. Do you not see?

**CREON:**   *(angrily)* Do you mock your king?

**TIRESIAS:**   I mock those who deserve it. Come, boy. We must leave.

**NARRATOR:**   The old man turned to go.

**JOCASTA:**   *(loudly)* Stop! Tell us what we want to know!

**TIRESIAS:**   What can the past hold but sadness? Why dig up things long buried? Let your kingdom die and then perhaps you will live.

**OEDIPUS:**   *(coldly)* Tell us, or I will have you put to death.

**TIRESIAS:**   *(slowly)* I do not fear you, but do you not fear my words?

**OEDIPUS:**   Nothing you say can shake us.

**TIRESIAS:**   Very well. I know the man whom you seek, king. He is here in this very room.

*(loud gasping)*

**OEDIPUS:**   *(yelling)* Where, Tiresias? Where?

**TIRESIAS:**   The man you seek is yourself. You yourself killed the king—or do you not remember?

**NARRATOR:**   They all froze, and Jocasta was the first to break the silence.

**JOCASTA:**   *(laugh)* I see his game now! He's making a joke.

**CREON:**   *(angrily)* Lies! Oedipus never met Laius! Who has bribed you to say such treachery?

**TIRESIAS:**   *(sadly)* I expected as much. Fools refuse to see the truth.

**OEDIPUS:**   *(slowly)* I can assure you, noble seer, I have never killed anyone.

**NARRATOR:**   Tiresias smiled.

**TIRESIAS:** You tried to run—and now you try to lie. But nothing can save you. Do you forget so soon? There was an old traveler, who attempted to break you with his whip.

**NARRATOR:** The stomach of Oedipus sank into his feet.

**OEDIPUS:** *(stunned)* But that man was no king. He was a dusty traveler on the road to Delphi.

**TIRESIAS:** Would a king wear his crown on such a journey?

**CREON:** *(figuring it out)* No. He would dress as a commoner. He was going to see the oracle.

**OEDIPUS:** *(numbly)* But I didn't know.

**TIRESIAS:** You still fail to see the whole picture, my lord.

**JOCASTA:** *(angrily)* What do you mean? What other treason would you dare utter here, you madman?

**TIRESIAS:** My lady, you of all people should have seen the similarities. You should have looked at Oedipus and seen him for what he truly is—your and Laius's son.

**NARRATOR:** The queen laughed a strange laugh—half snort, half shriek.

**JOCASTA:** *(ranting)* Impossible! Our child was cast into the wilderness. Laius pierced his feet to mark him for death.

**NARRATOR:** Tiresias nodded grimly.

**TIRESIAS:** I remember the night very well, my lady. Perhaps we should ask the king. sir, what marks do you bear upon your feet?

**OEDIPUS:** *(numbly)* Two scars. *(realizing)* But my father was the king of Corinth.

**TIRESIAS:** The shepherd who was sent with you into the wilderness took pity on you. If only he had killed you as he had planned. His mercy has cursed you.

**CREON:** *(angrily)* You lie!

**TIRESIAS:** I expected such disbelief. I have sent for the shepherd. He dwells near the mountain still. He will be here soon enough to verify my story.

**OEDIPUS:** But I was no shepherd's son! I was raised as a prince! How do you explain that?

**TIRESIAS:** That kind shepherd gave you to a passing traveler to take into Corinth. That man presented you to his lord, the king of Corinth, who adopted you as his son.

**NARRATOR:** Jocasta stared at Oedipus in wordless horror.

**OEDIPUS:** *(in disbelief)* How could I have known? How could I have known?

**JOCASTA:** *(softly)* Then it was true. Our child did murder his father—and—and—married—

**NARRATOR:** She looked to Oedipus with white, trembling lips.

**JOCASTA:** *(whispering)* Forgive me. *(yelling)* What have I done?

**NARRATOR:** Crying to the heavens and tearing her gown, Jocasta rushed from the room.

**OEDIPUS:** *(crying out)* Jocasta, no!

**TIRESIAS:** *(loudly)* You can fight it no more. You have fought it since you were born. Accept it! Accept your curse!

**OEDIPUS:** *(screaming)* No! No!

**NARRATOR:** Oedipus dashed after his fleeing wife, grasping blindly at her flowing robes. She rushed into her chambers, and the door slammed in his face.

**OEDIPUS:** *(yelling)* Jocasta!

**NARRATOR:** He began to throw himself against the door attacking it with all his might.

**OEDIPUS:** *(wailing)* Open the door! Open the door!

**NARRATOR:** When at last the door splintered and he broke through, he immediately hid his eyes in horror. Dangling from the ceiling was the body of his queen—her eyes pale and looking heavenward.

**OEDIPUS:** *(weakly)* No—no—no. Why have you done this to me?

**NARRATOR:** He stumbled forward and fell to the floor beneath her suspended feet. His hand grasped something cold. It was a brooch pin, fallen from her neck.

**OEDIPUS:** *(angrily, insane)* Why? Why should a man live in such a world? Why should I see such a monstrosity? My wife and mother dead before my very eyes? And all because of me. I have been blind—blind! Now, I will be blind forever.

**NARRATOR:** Gripping the point of the pin, he drove it sharply into each of his eyes. Blood poured down his cheeks, and sobs racked his body. Creon appeared in the doorway and gasped at the horror before him.

**CREON:** *(calling out)* Tiresias! Tiresias! Come and tell me what I should do! The queen is dead, and the king has gone mad.

**NARRATOR:** The blind man was already there, placing a calm hand on Creon's shoulders.

**TIRESIAS:** Pick him up. Wash him. And send him away. Thebes is yours again. Let it be healed.

**NARRATOR:** Creon turned to the prophet in confusion.

**CREON:** This man is my brother-in-law. Surely I owe him more than that.

**TIRESIAS:** You have asked, and I have told you. Listen to the will of the gods.

**CREON:** But his children…

**TIRESIAS:** His daughters will go to him and care for him when they are older and ready to accept their parents' sin. Until then, he will roam—blind and forgotten.

**CREON:** I don't know.

**TIRESIAS:** He did not listen to the gods. Will you ignore their commands as well?

**NARRATOR:** Creon paused.

**CREON:** Very well. I will send him into the wilderness.

**TIRESIAS:** It is what must be done.

**NARRATOR:** The servants were sent for, and they came timidly into the horror of that place. They took down the body of the queen and bandaged the wounds of the king.

**CREON:** *(sadly)* I mourn for such a wretched man.

**TIRESIAS:**   *(quietly)* Do not mourn too loudly, King Creon. Sadness will be no stranger to your own home. Farewell—until our next meeting.

**NARRATOR:**   And so the stooped and bandaged form of Oedipus was led away and left again to the will of the wild. He walked blindly now with broken steps, running his fingers over parched lips, trying to remember his former life. He would wander alone for many years, cursed and spurned by the gods—until they finally took pity and allowed him to pass beneath the earth, where his wearied soul at last could find rest.

## DISCUSSION QUESTIONS

1. Could Oedipus have escaped his fate?
2. What is Oedipus's flaw that brings about his destruction?
3. Do you feel sorry for Oedipus? Explain.
4. What do Tiresias's parting words foreshadow for Creon?

# NARCISSUS AND ECHO
## TEACHER GUIDE

## BACKGROUND

Narcissism is a common term in our culture. Those who suffer from it have an unhealthy obsession with themselves. *Echo* is common term as well, the official name for the reverberation of sound waves. Both of these words stem from mythology. The myth of Narcissus and Echo is mainly about misguided love. Echo the nymph loves Narcissus shallowly while Narcissus loves only himself. It's a quick tale, one that might seem flippant when compared to hero tales or epics like the *Iliad*. It doesn't possess enough drama to be heartbreaking; after all, its players are a bit ridiculous. It's better when it's played for laughs as it is here. But this myth does show connections the Greeks made between nature and myth. This story explains the birth of the Narcissus flower, why its petals droop down toward the water, and why we can hear our voice echoed back to us under the right conditions. Myths were, in their most primitive form, a way of explaining away the mysteries of the world. In modern times science has taken over the job of explaining nature, leaving myths free to be simply entertaining stories.

## SUMMARY

Echo is one of the silliest nymphs who ever lived and cannot control her tongue. One day one of her sister-nymphs asks her to keep a look-out. The nymph is having a tryst with Zeus and wants Echo to watch for Zeus's jealous wife, the goddess Hera. Echo stupidly agrees, unaware of what is going on. Hera soon appears in search of her husband and tries to question Echo about his whereabouts. In her usual way Echo rambles on, unintentionally stalling the goddess. Hera realizes that by talking to the silly nymph, she has made Zeus aware of her presence and given him enough time to escape. Since she cannot punish Zeus's nymph lover, she decides to punish Echo for her part in the affair. She declares that Echo will never again speak with her own words; she will only be able to repeat the last words spoken to her. With this curse cast, Hera disappears.

The story then turns to Narcissus, who is the most beautiful boy ever born. Hordes of girls follow him wherever he goes, begging for one look, word, or touch. But Narcissus will have nothing to do with them. Echo, now rendered nearly silent, encounters the boy and falls in love with him as well. She searches for a way to express her feelings to him. At last, using his own words, she catches his attention and conveys her intentions. Narcissus only sneers at her offer, and Echo wilts. After the boy is gone, Echo prays to the goddess Nemesis for revenge.

Narcissus sits down by a clear pool and suddenly catches sight of the only creature whose looks rival his own. He falls instantly in love and begs the creature to be his. Unfortunately, he realizes his love is trapped by some spell within the pool of water. Rather than losing his new-found love, Narcissus sits by the pool day and night, whispering sweet nothings, until at last he dies of starvation—never guessing he has fallen in love with his own reflection. The gods make the Narcissus flower to grow where he died—a flower whose petals droop down at the water's edge.

Echo alone witnesses Narcissus's death, but it does not bring her the happiness she seeks. She goes into the mountains and slowly fades away until only her voice remains.

Some say you can still hear her today, stealing our words and using them as her own.

## ESSENTIAL QUESTIONS

- What is the difference between narcissism and healthy self-esteem?
- What is the connection between nature and myth?
- How important is physical beauty?
- How important is the ability to express yourself?

## CONNECTIONS

*The Picture of Dorian Gray*, a novel by Victorian writer Oscar Wilde, tells of the story of an exceptionally good-looking young man, Dorian Gray, who secures a deal with a higher (or maybe we should say, *lower*) power so that he will never age and lose his beauty. Even though his physical beauty never deteriorates, Dorian Gray's soul becomes corrupted by a series of evil deeds fueled by his selfish vanity. Like Narcissus Dorian Gray feels only for himself and is obsessed with physical beauty.

## ANTICIPATORY QUESTIONS

- What is narcissism?
- Do you know where the echo got its name?
- Do you know a myth or tall tale that explains something in nature?
- Is it rude to dominate a conversation?

## TEACHABLE TERMS

- **Euphemism**   The phrase Hera uses on pg. 63 "frolicking in the fencerows" is a euphemism for what she would probably rather say.
- **Tone**   While the myth of Narcissus and Echo is often told seriously, this version creates a different, humorous tone. Asking the question *Was this story told seriously?* will help you analyze its tone.
- **Flat and round characters**   Narcissus is a flat character because he does not change during the course of the story. On the other hand, Echo is a round character because she (at least partially) realizes the error of her ways.
- **Personification**   The goddess Nemesis, mentioned on pg. 66, is the personification of retribution or divine justice.
- **Descriptive language**   The paragraph describing Echo's transformation on pg. 67 is an effective example of descriptive language.

## RECALL QUESTIONS

1. Which goddess punishes Echo?
2. What is her punishment?
3. Who is Narcissus's one true love?
4. What does Narcissus's part of the story explain about nature?
5. What does Echo's part of the story explain about nature?

# NARCISSUS AND ECHO

## CAST

| | |
|---|---|
| **GIRL ONE** | *One of Narcissus's Admirers* |
| **GIRL TWO** | *One of Narcissus's Admirers* |
| **GIRL THREE** | *One of Narcissus's Admirers* |
| **NARCISSUS** | *Handsomest Youth* |
| **ECHO** | *Chatty Nymph* |
| **NYMPH** | *Woodland Nymph* |
| **HERA** | *Queen of the Gods* |

**NARRATOR:** Narcissus was the most beautiful boy who ever lived. It was said that his mother was a woodland nymph and his father a river god, yet Narcissus was born mortal. His only immortal quality was his god-like good looks. Wherever he went, girls flocked to him in droves. Though they cried, begged, and pleaded to be his, the boy would have none of them.

**GIRL ONE:** *(excitedly)* Narcissus! Over here! Here!

**GIRL THREE:** Out of my way! He's mine! He's mine!

**GIRL TWO:** *(scream)* I touched his hand! I really touched his hand!

**NARCISSUS:** *(sigh)* Calm yourselves! What are you? Women or beasts! Give Narcissus some peace and quiet!

**GIRL THREE:** *(crazy)* Please! Make me your wife!

**NARCISSUS:** *(haughtily)* Ha! That's a laugh. Just take a look at yourselves! Obviously none of you are worthy of Narcissus. When I meet one whose beauty equals my own, then—and only then—will I love.

**NARRATOR:** At this the girls wilted.

**NARCISSUS:** But with such impossible standards, why get my hopes up?

**NARRATOR:** In the region where Narcissus dwelt there also lived a band of woodland nymphs. One in particular, a dimwitted and chatty nymph named Echo, happened to hear of Narcissus's legendary beauty one day.

**ECHO:** *(rapidly)* Narcissus is his name. They say he's a complete dreamboat—what does that mean anyway? Dreamboat? Anyway they say he's to die for. In fact, several girls already have—died that is. They committed suicide just to get his attention. Can you imagine? Committing suicide just to get someone's attention? Sounds pretty pathetic to me. I've never liked anyone that much—although I did have a thing for Apollo a while back. But who am I kidding? I'm a nymph! I have a thing for everyone!

**NARRATOR:**   The other nymph, whose ear Echo was bending, found a spot to interject.

**NYMPH:**   *(interrupting)* Fascinating! By the way, Echo, will you do me a favor?

**ECHO:**   A favor? Oh, that sounds serious. Just last week Artemis herself asked me to do her a favor. We were having the most lovely chat, but she suddenly got a leg cramp, so she asked me to go fetch her brother, Apollo— y'know, the god of medicine. When I came back, she must have gotten better, because she was gone—but you know—

**NYMPH:**   *(interrupting)* Great. I'm kind of in a hurry. I'm supposed to be meeting a—um, friend—here in a minute.

**ECHO:**   Well, that's so sweet. That reminds me of a friend I used to have. She was my best friend growing up—did I ever tell you about her? She was a water nymph, so she was bit wet behind the ears, if you know what I mean—

**NYMPH:**   *(angrily)* Stop! *(nicely)* I mean, I haven't finished yet, dear. My friend's wife doesn't know we're meeting, so if she happens this way, maybe you could distract her?

**ECHO:**   Sure, that would be great—I mean, are you two planning some kind of surprise party for his wife or something? I love surprises. There was this one time when I found all of my friends hiding from me, and when I asked why, they said they were throwing me a surprise party—but the strange part was it wasn't even my birthday or anything—

**NYMPH:**   That's nice. Well, my friend is waiting. Just remember: If his wife shows up, distract her.

**ECHO:**   Distract her? Well, I can tell you one thing, I'm probably not very good at distracting people. What am I supposed to say? I'm not very good at coming up with stuff right off the top of my head—

**NYMPH:**   *(gritting her teeth)* You're doing pretty well right now! Just talk to her, Echo! Keep her entertained! Welcome her to our woods!

**ECHO:**   Oh well, I can sure handle that all right—I mean, if our woods had an official greeter, I think it would be me. Most people say that I have an infectious personality—or do they say *infected*? I can't remember. My memory's just not what it used to be. I was telling—

**NYMPH:**   Gotta run! Bye! *(under her breath)* Idiot!

**NARRATOR:**   Echo's sister nymph disappeared into the underbrush.

**ECHO:**   *(quietly)* Uh. Well, okay. Seems like everyone's in a hurry. No time to talk. Hurry. Hurry. Hurry.

**NARRATOR:**   Echo smiled to herself and sat down upon by the edge of a small, clear stream. She leaned over the rippling water and admired her reflection.

**ECHO:**   At least I always have you to listen. Talking to yourself is better than not talking at all.

**NARRATOR:**   Her mind soon returned to her mission.

**ECHO:**   *(to herself)* I wonder who her mysterious married friend is? Surely it's not this Narcissus everyone's been talking about. No, no, it couldn't be him. He's not married. Plus he's sworn to only love the one whose beauty equals his own. Tee hee. I wonder...

**NARRATOR:** She returned to her reflection. After staring into her own eyes for a time, she broke the surface with a slap of her hand.

**ECHO:** Nah. Probably not. But a nymph can dream, can't she?

**NARRATOR:** Little did Echo know that the nymph's visitor was Zeus himself, on yet another one of his extra-marital escapades. And the wife that the nymph had mentioned was none other than his vindictive queen, Hera.

Echo had just fallen silent—for once—when she noticed the leaves of the trees vibrating about her.

**ECHO:** I wonder what that is. You know, it could be an earthquake. The last time Poseidon caused one of those, I remember a whole—

**NARRATOR:** The leaves shook themselves free from the trees and were caught up in a ferocious whirlwind. In the midst of this, there appeared a feminine form.

**HERA:** *(booming)* Where is he?

**NARRATOR:** The form of Hera solidified, and before Echo could react, the angered queen of Olympus was stalking toward her.

**HERA:** You there! Nymph! Answer when you're spoken to!

**ECHO:** Oh, you were talking to me! I'm sorry. I really didn't know for a second—in fact I was kind of taken aback by that dramatic entrance of yours. Do you do that all the time or only when you're going to surprise parties?

**HERA:** *(sharply)* Cut the chit-chat! Obviously you're not *she*, but I bet you know where *she* is!

**ECHO:** So you're looking for a she now? That's funny, when you first showed up, I thought you said he. I've always had a hearing impediment though, so it's no wonder. By the way, I'm Echo, and it's very nice to know that I'm not *she*—whoever that is—because you seem very intense about finding this mystery woman and this *he* you keep talking about. Say, you're one of the goddesses, aren't you? Don't tell me! I'm good with faces. Aphrodite! You're Aphrodite, aren't you?

**NARRATOR:** Hera's anger exploded in a burst of rage.

**HERA:** *(roaring)* Silence! I would do the world a favor and cut out your prattling tongue, but as you might have noticed, I'm kind of in a hurry!

**NARRATOR:** Echo closed her mouth sheepishly.

**HERA:** I am looking for Zeus. Perhaps you've heard of him? He is my husband. Now I know he's around here somewhere, frolicking in the fencerows with one of you little hare-brained hussies.

**ECHO:** Oooh—I must say I have seen your husband. Let me congratulate you for marrying so well. I have my own eye on a high-born lad as well. So that must mean that you are Hera, Queen of Heaven. Oh my! I forgot to curtsey. You must think I am the rudest nymph who ever lived—

**NARRATOR:** Hera's eyes filled with flames of hatred.

**ECHO:**  I thought I saw Zeus once—only from a distance—but then my friend told me that it was only a cloud—but you know I could have sworn it was him. He's the one with the big beard, right? Sometimes I get you all confused. If you've seen one god, you've seen them all, that's what I say—

**HERA:**  *(violent scream)*

**NARRATOR:**  The barren trees burst into flames. Hera grabbed the frightened nymph by the wrist.

**HERA:**  Either you tell me where they are, or you're going to be a worthless pile of ashes.

**ECHO:**  My—my—my—I am so sorry—I apologize my queen—they're here—or somewhere close by—I—I—just get so nervous—and I can't stop talking.

**NARRATOR:**  There was a flash of light away through the trees, and Hera's gaze jerked toward it. Something bright shot heavenward, leaving behind a cloud-like trail.

**HERA:**  There he goes! There he goes! I knew it! He will pay for this! He will rue the day that he ever—

**ECHO:**  Well, that's great, your majesty. You know I'm so happy that I could help. I always say it's better to help people than—

**HERA:**  *(crazy)* Help? I was going to catch him red-handed. I wanted him to watch while I ground his little playmate into fertilizer, but you—you kept me from it—with that blasted tongue of yours!

**ECHO:**  You know, I can tell you're upset with me, but I think it's always best to get a good night's sleep before you make any hasty decisions—I mean, you definitely don't want

to do anything you regret—like this one time my uncle—

**HERA:**  You don't learn do you? Fine! So one floozy has flown the coop, but you'll make a fine replacement.

**NARRATOR:**  The nymph began to back away.

**HERA:**  Since you are so fond of the sound of your own voice, you—Echo—are forever cursed. You always wanted the last word, didn't you? Well, now you'll have it! *(evil laugh)*

**NARRATOR:**  Hera snapped her fingers, wiped her hands clean, and gazed coolly at the nymph.

**HERA:**  No need to thank me for sparing your life. And for future reference, stay away from my husband.

**NARRATOR:**  Then Hera was gone. Echo couldn't believe it. She was sure that Hera would kill her, but here she was alive. She *was* cursed—whatever that meant.

There was a rustling in the brush, and Echo's sister nymph appeared looking quite frightened.

**NYMPH:**  Thanks for stalling her, Echo. We heard her yelling. What did she do to you?

**ECHO:**  To *you*. To *you*.

**NARRATOR:**  In surprise Echo brought her fingers to her lips. They had acted without her control. She had meant to say so much more.

**NYMPH:**  What? I don't understand. I heard her yell something about being cursed.

**ECHO:** *(sadly)* Cursed. Cursed.

**NARRATOR:** Huge tears formed in Echo's eyes. Then her sister nymph perceived what had happened.

**NYMPH:** Oh, Echo. I'm so sorry for you.

**ECHO:** For you. For you.

**NARRATOR:** Echo ran from the grove.

**NYMPH:** Where are you going?

**NARRATOR:** As she ran, she covered her mouth. She did not wish to answer, but her lips moved of their own will.

**ECHO:** *(crying)* Going. Going.

**NARRATOR:** Her voice was lost forever. From that time on, Echo lived apart from the other nymphs. She couldn't stand the sight of them. They were so frivolous and carefree. She had been that way once. Now she only wanted to be alone in her misery.

Yet one day as she sat within the damp cave she now called her home, she heard a voice not far off, the voice of a young man.

**NARCISSUS:** Let's see those hags find Narcissus out here. It's almost a crime for such good looks to be out here in the middle of the wilderness where no one can see their glory. An absolute waste. But look! Even nature is not more beautiful than Narcissus.

**ECHO:** *(to herself)* Narcissus! Narcissus!

**NARRATOR:** She crept to the mouth of her cave to get a glimpse of the legendary boy. Once she beheld his golden face, her cold heart was revived. He was everything the legends said: a mortal beauty with no rival.

**NARCISSUS:** Look on me, nature. See that the gods have created something truly perfect in Narcissus—something that is completely worthy of a world's share of love.

**ECHO:** *(dreamily)* Love! Love!

**NARRATOR:** Narcissus was marching away proudly, addressing the forest around him. Echo fell silently into step behind him. A new hope had entered her heart. How many had failed to entice this boy? Maybe she was the one who would at last be his match. She would have no words to profess her love. But, she told herself, true love needs no words. *(snap of a twig)* The boy turned at the sound.

**NARCISSUS:** *(loudly)* Who dares interrupt the walk of Narcissus? If you've come for a glimpse of my beauty, take it and be on with your miserable little life. *I said*, who's here?

**NARRATOR:** Echo stepped around the bend in the path and beamed proudly.

**ECHO:** *(loudly)* Here! Here!

**NARRATOR:** The boy stared at her in annoyance.

**NARCISSUS:** All right. You've had your look. Now be on your way.

**NARRATOR:** Echo's smile wilted.

**NARCISSUS:** *(hatefully)* Well, what do you want? A souvenir? A lock of the hair of Narcissus? I don't think so. The only hand that will ever touch my hair will be the hand of my wife.

**NARRATOR:** Echo folded her arms across her chest.

**ECHO:** Wife. Wife.

**NARRATOR:** Slowly the mouth of Narcissus curled into a smirk.

**NARCISSUS:** *(laughing)* I would rather die than give a homely creature like you power over me.

**ECHO:** *(weakly)* Power over me. Power over me.

**NARCISSUS:** Oh please. Don't sulk. You look bad enough as it is.

**NARRATOR:** The golden boy turned on his heel and shuddered.

**NARCISSUS:** Yikes.

**NARRATOR:** As Echo watched him disappear into the trees, something crumbled inside of her. And even though her lips could not speak it, she formed a prayer in her mind. She prayed that some god, above or below, would make Narcissus come to know the same heartbreak she had felt.

It was Nemesis, the goddess of retribution, who heard her prayer.

Narcissus continued through the forest and came at last to a secluded pool. Its waters were so clear and its surface so completely undisturbed that nothing obscured its mirror-like surface.

**NARCISSUS:** Even Narcissus—a god among men—grows thirsty and must drink.

**NARRATOR:** The boy bent to the waters, but stopped short. There, just below the surface, was the most glorious creature he had ever seen. There was an odd feeling in his chest—an unfamiliar tingling—accompanied by a lightness of the mind.

**NARCISSUS:** *(breathlessly)* Who or what are you? You who have at last made Narcissus feel love!

**NARRATOR:** He examined the flawless face intently. There they were—the very features he had imagined—the shining eyes, the pink lips, even the lustrous hair of his dreams.

**NARCISSUS:** Only I—among all living things—can rival your beauty, sweet one. Speak! What is the name that the gods have given to such splendor!

**NARRATOR:** His love did not answer—only stared back at him expectantly.

**NARCISSUS:** *(excitedly)* Don't be coy! Surely you are some goddess or some nymph! Speak! You have nothing to fear!

**NARRATOR:** No reply.

**NARCISSUS:** Please! You must tell me your name! I will die if I do not hear it!

**NARRATOR:** Nothing.

**NARCISSUS:** What prevents you from speaking? Are you under some spell? Are you trapped in this magical pool? Come! Let your love, Narcissus, free you from this prison!

**NARRATOR:** He reached into the pool, searching for the form to match the face, but this disturbed the surface of the water.

**NARCISSUS:** *(panicking)* No! Don't go! I will die if you leave me! *(calming)* There! There! You are returning. You looked scared before. You did not want to leave me either, did you?

**NARRATOR:** The boy re-seated himself by the side of the pool.

# ORPHEUS AND EURYDICE
## TEACHER GUIDE

### BACKGROUND

Even the ancient Greeks knew that music was a powerful force; the story of Orpheus, the mythical musician, shows us this. Of course, music is just one facet of the myth: Love is another. Orpheus so loves his wife that he is willing to venture into the Underworld to retrieve her soul. Yet it is not love alone that allows Orpheus to descend into Hades and return alive. Many have loved just as deeply, but only Orpheus possesses the ability to *artistically express* that love and loss in such a way that re-creates these emotions in the hearts of monsters, gods, and other creatures that have never before felt such things. It is only because of this ability to stir empathy in others that he is able to succeed in his quest. For this reason the Orpheus myth is an enduring metaphor of the way music can affect the soul.

This script tells only a portion of Orpheus's myth. After Orpheus's rescue of Eurydice from the Underworld fails, the musician roams for many years lamenting her loss and swearing never to love again. (It is during this time that he appears in the myth of Jason and the Argonauts.) While wandering in Thrace, Orpheus comes upon a maenad ritual. (Maenads were the crazed female followers of the wine god Dionysus who reveled in sexual debauchery and bloody sacrifices.) These women approach Orpheus lustily, but when he will not submit to their sexual advances, they rip him limb from limb. They throw Orpheus's severed head and his lyre into the nearby river. The lyre continues to play and the head continues to sing as they float downstream. The people who find Orpheus's head keep it and establish it as an oracle, for it begins to sing of the future.

### SUMMARY

Orpheus is the son of Apollo, the god of music, and lives atop Mount Parnassus with his mother Calliope, one of the nine eternal muses who inspire art in mortals. When Orpheus is just a toddler, Apollo presents his son with his first lyre (harp). Orpheus is a musical prodigy, and as he grows up, he supplies the muses with continuous dancing music. Melpomene, the muse of tragedy, eventually tires of Orpheus's upbeat tempo and suggests that the mortal boy go to earth and live among his own kind. His mother doesn't like this idea, but Orpheus is fascinated with the idea of earthly love and decides to go down into the world to look for true love. As he descends the mountain, Orpheus plays a beautiful song on his lyre, which causes rocks, trees, and even a river to move out of his way and let him pass.

At last in the world of mortals, Orpheus meets a young shepherd girl named Eurydice and falls instantly in love; the two are soon married. The god Hymen appears during their wedding feast and presents the newlyweds with a bad omen: Hymen's torch, instead of burning cleanly, smokes. (Hymen was the god of wedding feasts who blessed or cursed marriages.)

Not long after their wedding, Eurydice is chased by a satyr (goat-man) in the field where she watches her sheep. While she runs, she steps on a poisonous snake lying in the grass and is bitten. (In alternate versions of the myth, Eurydice is either dancing with her bridesmaids or being chased by a fellow shepherd when she is bitten by the snake.) Orpheus arrives in time to witness his wife die.

Orpheus's heart breaks, and he roams the countryside lamenting Eurydice's death. Those who once welcomed his music shut their doors against his dirges of gloom and doom. At last his sad songs reach Olympus, and the gods dispatch Hermes to give Orpheus hope. If Orpheus is brave enough to descend into the Underworld, his music might have enough power to move the heart of Hades and win back his lost love. Orpheus follows a path down into Hades. At the sound of his music, the three-headed hell-hound Cerberus moves aside for him, and Charon the Boatman of the Underworld ferries him across the Styx without a coin. Orpheus's music even charms Hades, who agrees that the boy can lead the soul of Eurydice back to earth provided that he never looks at her as she follows behind him. If he does, Eurydice must return to the Underworld. Orpheus begins his ascent yet doubts that the spirit of his love is really behind him. Before they are completely out of the Underworld, Orpheus turns to look at Eurydice, and her spirit fades back into the darkness.

## ESSENTIAL QUESTIONS

- What exactly is music and why is it so powerful?
- Can love overcome death?

## CONNECTIONS

*Black Orpheus (1957)* This award-winning film directed by Marcel Camus modernizes the myth of Orpheus and Eurydice by setting it in 20th century Brazil. Orfeo (Orpheus) is a musically-talented streetcar conductor who falls for Eurydice during Carnival, the Brazilian equivalent of Mardi Gras. When Eurydice dies unexpectedly, Orfeo consults a voodoo priestess to find out how to bring her back from the dead.

## ANTICIPATORY QUESTIONS

- Who is Orpheus?
- How did the Greeks view the afterlife?
- Is music powerful?
- How does musical talent change a person's life?
- How has music impacted *your* life?
- Can love triumph over death? Explain.

## TEACHABLE TERMS

- **Simile** On pg. 73 Orpheus muses on the nature of love by making two similes: Is love like lightning or slow like the growth of a tree? The students can discuss these similes, deciding which better describes love, or they can create their own descriptive simile.
- **Personification** Several inanimate objects—a rock, a tree, and a river—are personified in the first part of this story. Also the muses are personifications of the various types of art.
- **Idiom** On pg. 75 Eurydice tries to tell Orpheus why she is dying. She says "snake in the grass," which he takes as the idiom for a two-faced scoundrel.
- **Tone** Although this script relates tragic events, it uses a lighthearted tone. One good example of this: Orpheus and Eurydice's comical exchange as she lies dying on pg. 75.

## RECALL QUESTIONS

1. Who are the muses?
2. How does Eurydice die?
3. What are two obstacles Orpheus faces in the Underworld?
4. Hades tells Orpheus not to do what?
5. What happens at the very end of the story?

# ORPHEUS AND EURYDICE

## CAST

| | |
|---|---|
| APOLLO | *God of Light and Music* |
| ORPHEUS | *Talented Musician* |
| CALLIOPE | *Orpheus's Muse Mother* |
| MELPOMENE | *Muse of Tragedy* |
| CLIO | *Muse of History* |
| URANIA | *Muse of Astronomy* |
| THALIA | *Muse of Comedy* |
| ERATO | *Muse of Love Poetry* |
| ROCK | *A Rock* |
| RIVER | *A River* |
| TREE | *A Tree* |
| EURYDICE | *Beautiful Maiden* |
| SATYR | *Amorous Goatman* |
| HERMES | *Messenger God* |
| HADES | *Lord of the Underworld* |

**NARRATOR:** It was no wonder that the boy Orpheus could sing as well as he could. After all, his father was Apollo, the god of poetry and music, and his mother was one of the nine eternal muses. With genes like that Orpheus was destined for greatness. His mother and her sister-muses raised him on the heights of Mount Parnassus, which wasn't quite as ritzy as Mount Olympus, but it worked well enough for a group of un-married free-spirits on a budget. Every day the muses danced and danced and danced— that's how they inspired mortal art, by dancing—until Helios's last rays passed from the sky. Some might (and did) call this lifestyle boring, but it was what amused the muses.

When Orpheus was nearly three years old, the god Apollo appeared on Mt. Par-nassus, and after winking at a few of the dancing muses, presented his young son with a shining lyre.

**APOLLO:** Son.

**ORPHEUS:** Yes, Father.

**APOLLO:** This is the lyre. It holds more power than any shield or sword and can pierce man's heart just as deeply. Use it well.

**NARRATOR:** The tiny boy took the lyre and plucked its six strings with his chubby fingers. New musics—notes never before heard on the earth—sprang forth.

**APOLLO:** That's my boy! Why he's a musical genius already.

**CALLIOPE:** Sisters, our dancing is paying off! My son will be the greatest musician who ever lived!

*(murmuring of the muses)*

**NARRATOR:** Orpheus took to the lyre like other boys took to running or wrestling. His songs were the most beautiful ever heard, and as the muses danced and danced, he played and played—his notes keeping the exuberant beat. Fifteen years passed in this manner. It was then that his aunt Melpomene, the muse of tragedy who had become somewhat tired of always jigging and frolicking, piped up.

**MELPOMENE:** *(annoyed)* Calliope, dear, would it be possible to get *your son* to slow his tempo? My feet have been numb for the last six months. I don't want to wear them out. We *are* dancing for eternity here.

**CALLIOPE:** Orpheus, dear, you know we never tire of your wonderful music, but why don't you play something slower? Something somber? All of your songs happily bounce and leap, but your tempo is exhausting.

**ORPHEUS:** But, Mother, I have never felt sadness. How can I play an emotion I've never felt? I've lived here with you and my eight dancing aunts my whole life. What do I have to be sad about?

**MELPOMENE:** *(shocked)* What? There is tragedy everywhere! War, famine, death! Homicide, suicide, fratricide, matricide, insecticide! Haven't you heard? The world is full of misery!

**CALLIOPE:** *(shocked)* Melpomene! Please!

**ORPHEUS:** What are these things? I've never heard of them?

**MELPOMENE:** Oh brother. That's it. Enough is enough. Calliope, it's about time you sent that boy down into the world—the real world. He's not a god! He's a mortal!

**CALLIOPE:** Melpomene!

**MELPOMENE:** Well, he should know. The boy's nearly eighteen years old. You can't keep him up here in la-la land forever—fattening him up on nectar and ambrosia! He needs to go down and see what the real world is like.

**ORPHEUS:** What could there possibly be down there that I'm missing out on?

**NARRATOR:** The other muses, whose feet had also blistered because of Orpheus's happy harping, chimed in.

**CLIO:** History, my boy! On earth you could study the great deeds of men!

**URANIA:** Astronomy! On earth you can look up to the night sky and study the stars!

**THALIA:** *(laughing)* Comedy! In Athens they make the funniest plays!

**ERATO:** Love!

**ORPHEUS:** But I have love here. I have the love of my mother.

**MELPOMENE:** May the Fates save the boy! We're talking about *romantic* love. That's more than love for your mother.

**CLIO:** Unless your name's Oedipus.

*(all the muses laugh)*

**MELPOMENE:** Go to earth and find a girl. Maybe she'll break your heart, and then your music will know true depth.

**NARRATOR:** Calliope was furious at her sister for giving such advice, but the mention of love had stirred Orpheus's heart. If he were truly a mortal, his place was on the earth. And, besides, this eternal dancing did tend to get a bit old.

**ORPHEUS:** I will go!

**CLIO:** Bravo! Now we will have a nephew who will make history!

**URANIA:** A nephew whose image Zeus can hang in the stars!

**THALIA:** A nephew to laugh at!

**ALL:** Thalia!

**MELPOMENE:** *(to herself)* Or maybe a nephew worthy of tragedy.

**NARRATOR:** And so Orpheus left the mountain top. The muses each unclasped one hand to wave goodbye but continued their considerably slower dancing. As he lost sight of them, Orpheus noticed tears on his mother's cheeks.

While Orpheus made his way down the mountainside, he sang an I-don't-know-where-I'm-going-but-I-can't-wait-to-get-there ditty. It was an upbeat song, of course, about his quest for love. There was no path to speak of on the slopes of Mt. Parnassus, but as Orpheus sang and walked in step, the rocks politely rolled to the side and made way before him.

**ROCK:** Best of luck to you, Mr. Orpheus. When you find love, don't take it for *granite.*

**NARRATOR:** Soon Orpheus saw a turgid mountain stream gushing down the slopes, blocking his way. He continued to sing, and it was no surprise to him that the stream stopped flowing for him, and he walked across its dry bed.

**RIVER:** Best of luck to you, Mr. Orpheus. Don't let the world *drown* your enthusiasm.

**NARRATOR:** And further down, where the forest began, tangled trees had grown up through the rock, making it impossible to pass. Orpheus kept walking and kept singing. The trees heard his song, unwrapped themselves from one another, untangled their thickets, and let the boy through.

**TREE:** Bravo, Mr. Orpheus! If anyone or anything gets in your way, we'll tear them *limb* from *limb!*

**NARRATOR:** By the time he reached the bottom of the mountain, Orpheus had already learned a valuable lesson about the world: Rocks, streams, and trees make really bad jokes. More disturbing than the puns was the fact that he had no idea where to go next. He had set out on a quest to find love, yet no one had explained to him where love lives or how love works.

**ORPHEUS:** Does this love thing just strike—like lightning? Or is it slow and stealthy like the growth of a tree?

**NARRATOR:** Orpheus did not have to walk far until he saw someone sitting on a large rock in the midst of a field. It was a girl. She had raven black hair pinned behind her ears and was watching a few tufts of sheep nibble on the field-grass.

**ORPHEUS:** Hello, I am Orpheus.

**NARRATOR:** The girl turned to him in surprise.

**ORPHEUS:** I've come to earth to find love. My songs can move stone, divert streams, and bend mighty trees.

**EURYDICE:** Sounds dangerous.

**ORPHEUS:** Would you like to hear one of my songs?

**EURYDICE:** Sure. Why not? I've just been sitting here watching sheep all day.

**NARRATOR:** Orpheus began to play a perhaps-I-have-found-the-love-of-my-life tune, and something inside the girl's mind shifted. Up until then she had seen only a boy—one who seemed a little off in the head. Now she was looking upon someone she loved.

**EURYDICE:** (*lovey-dovey*) Beautiful boy, thou hast charmed my heart!

**ORPHEUS:** Is that a good thing?

**NARRATOR:** The girl jumped from the rock into the surprised arms of Orpheus and planted on his lips a first kiss magnitude ten.

**ORPHEUS:** (*breathlessly*) I have found love after all!

**NARRATOR:** The current of their love threatened to sweep the two young people away, so marriage followed quickly. Eurydice—that was the girl's name—made all the arrangements, and Orpheus sang an I'm-getting-married-and-I'm-happy-about-it jingle. During the marriage ceremony, the god Hymen appeared among the shadows, holding aloft a burning torch.

**EURYDICE:** Orpheus, look. This is a good sign. There is the god Hymen—come to bless our marriage. My sister will be so jealous. He never showed up at her wedding, and, turns out, her husband already had a wife in another village.

**NARRATOR:** But instead of burning cleanly, the god's torch started to smoke. It smoked so much that it stung the eyes of the guests and caused the bride to cough.

**EURYDICE:** (*coughing*) Maybe I spoke too soon.

**NARRATOR:** Yet after the god had disappeared and Orpheus had struck up his lyre with a nevermind-bad-omens song of celebration, the lighthearted spirit of the wedding returned.

Each day of their married life, Eurydice went to the meadow where they had first met to watch her sheep. Orpheus went with her and sang a sheep-watching song. At the sound of his lyre, the sheep would clump up or scatter just as he desired.

In the fall a nearby village requested that Orpheus come and sing for them. They'd been hit by a plague, and their hearts needed revival. Orpheus agreed to go and sing them a cheer-up-and-heal-up melody, so Eurydice went to the meadow alone during his absence.

**EURYDICE:** Watching these sheep is so much harder without my wonderful husband. Thanks to his lyre music all I had to do was leave them alone, and they'd come home, wagging their tails behind them.

**NARRATOR:** Eurydice realized that she was talking to herself and dissolved into a reverie, which further dissolved into a noonday nap. This is why she did not notice the mischievous goat-man who tender-hoofed his way up to her rock.

**SATYR:** A beautiful nymph—asleep on a rock! Easy pickings!

**NARRATOR:** It should be a testament to Eurydice's beauty that the goat-man mistook her for a nymph because it is the sole job of goat-men to pursue nymphs day and night.

This is one reason why they're frowned upon in polite society. (The other is that they don't wear pants.)

When Eurydice awoke with the shadow of a wormy goat-man hovering over her, she let out a shriek.

**EURYDICE:** *(scream)* Get away from me, you horrible goat-man!

**SATYR:** Actually we prefer the term *satyr*.

**NARRATOR:** Not in the mood to debate terminology, the maiden jumped from the rock and tore through the tall meadow grass.

**EURYDICE:** Help! Help!

**NARRATOR:** This is exactly what the goat-man had hoped she would do. Goat-men love a chase. Although the girl ran with all her speed, he clipped and clopped along at her heels.

**SATYR:** *(amorously)* My sweet, my sweet! Let us end this ridiculous charade! You know you want the goat-man.

**EURYDICE:** Dream on, weirdo!

**NARRATOR:** Unfortunately, in their chase, the maiden stepped upon a very poisonous snake slinking in the proverbial grass. (Everyone has been told that snakes are more afraid of you than they are of them, and this is supposed to be comforting. Yet, in most cases, humans don't have fangs and bite when frightened—while snakes do.) This snake sunk its fangs into Eurydice's tender ankle.

**EURYDICE:** *(cry of pain)*

**NARRATOR:** The snake, which was about to have cardiac arrest over its terror of humans, slithered away, and Eurydice fell into the grass. The poison worked quickly.

**SATYR:** Whoa! I've never seen an ankle swell up that quickly! Is that oozing pus? *(nervously)* Uh…well…I better be going now.

**EURYDICE:** Get back here and help me! This is all your fault, you stupid goat-man!

**SATYR:** *(distantly)* Satyr. Goodbye.

**NARRATOR:** When Orpheus returned to the meadow from his journey, he did not see Eurydice where she normally perched on her rock. He searched the meadow until he saw the sheep gathered in a clump around her fallen body. The girl's lips were blue, and her ankle was grossly swollen. He held her tenderly in his arms.

**ORPHEUS:** What has happened?

**EURYDICE:** *(weakly)* Goat-man!

**ORPHEUS:** What?

**EURYDICE:** *(weakly)* Snake in the grass!

**ORPHEUS:** *(between tears)* Please! Don't call me names, my love, or I will die!

**EURYDICE:** Oh nevermind.

**NARRATOR:** With that Eurydice's irritated soul sank down into the Underworld.

It is said that Orpheus cried enough tears to make their own salty river. He had found love only to lose it. His songs, which had up till then brought mirth, were now haunting dirges for Eurydice. He wandered the countryside—his body thin and his eyes sunken from fasting—playing his languid laments.

Though their tone had changed, his tunes

still held power. To those villages who wanted rain, his music brought drought. To those whose homes were nearly flooded by spring rains, dismal deluges accompanied his dreary notes. Each day he sang for the night to come quickly. He forbade the stars to shine and told the darkness to linger past the dawn.

Those who heard him approaching—men and women who had once welcomed him—closed their windows tight and snuffed their lamps, so he would pass on and take his gloom elsewhere. His lamenting at last reached the ears of Olympus and moved the hearts of the mightiest of the immortals.

One night as Orpheus staggered forward mumbling and plucking with bleeding, feeble fingers, a dark form blocked his path. The bard paused in his song.

**HERMES:** *(booming)* Mortal Orpheus! I am come from high Olympus to tell you to stop your mourning!

**ORPHEUS:** *(angrily)* Why do you gods care if I mourn? You are the ones that created my suffering! I want *all* the gods, *all* the mortals, and even the earth herself to suffer—*as I suffer!*

**HERMES:** Creepy. But, pray tell, what is the source of your suffering? Why do you sing?

**ORPHEUS:** For my lost love, Eurydice! Taken from me in the blossom of youth! *(begins to sing again)* Eurydice! Eurydice!

**HERMES:** Please! No more! Your music has had its desired effect among the immortals. It has even sobered Dionysus—and that takes some doing. So you're mourning for your love. That's tough. It really is. But there are other fish in the sea. Take my father Zeus for example. I can't tell you how many mortal women he's incinerated...or flattened...or mutilated...or turned into bears. But, you

know, he doesn't let it get him down! He gets right back out there—and usually the same day. *(pause)* Hmmmm. Okay. Maybe *he* isn't the best example.

**NARRATOR:** The musician's nostrils flared with anger.

**ORPHEUS:** I could never find another love like Eurydice! She was my sun! My goddess! My *very life!*

**HERMES:** Hmmm. I never thought of that. You could kill yourself—but that's too stagey. *(mockingly)* Look at me, I'm killing myself! It's *so* overdramatic. But listen: the gods have sent me with a suggestion for you.

**ORPHEUS:** They know of a way to get my love back?

**HERMES:** Of course, we do. As the poets say: Death is not the end, just an intermission.

**ORPHEUS:** Do you mean—?

**HERMES:** Yes, Orpheus, the gods are telling you to go to Hades! The Underworld! Take your golden lyre, go to Hades himself, and melt his heart with your music. It just might work. Your songs have all of us on Olympus absolutely depressed. I promise. Zeus hasn't had an affair in weeks, Dionysus hasn't touched a drop of wine, and Hebe can't bear to bear her cup. If we want a drink, we have to get it ourselves! It's barbaric!

**ORPHEUS:** But it's impossible. I'm not a hero like Heracles.

**HERMES:** Listen to me, my boy, *you* have the greatest weapon of all. I should know. I invented it. That lyre right there is stronger than any sword or shield. They may pierce the body, but music pierces the soul!

**ORPHEUS:** You're right! What do I have to lose?

**HERMES:** Well, your life, but—

**ORPHEUS:** I will do it! I will get back my love!

**HERMES:** That's the spirit! You'll find a foul-smelling cave to the west. Follow it down into the Underworld. Hades is filled with all types of creepies and crawlies, but your music will keep them at bay. Farewell, Orpheus!

**ORPHEUS:** Farewell.

**NARRATOR:** As the messenger god vanished, Orpheus steadied his nerves by playing an encouraging prepare-to-do-the-impossible serenade upon his lyre and struck out toward the foul-smelling cave. Within the depths he faced many frightening specters, but his melody was stronger than them all. When the musician neared, the six eyes of Cerberus moistened with tears, his three snouts sniffed, and three necks bowed submissively as the beast whimpered to the side of the path. When Orpheus came to the banks of the River Styx and beheld Charon the miserly boatman leaning heavily upon his oar, a song of sorrow was the only toll he had to pay. As Charon poled the singing boy across the river, he shook his head. Orpheus was the only passenger he had ferried without a coin. At last Orpheus came before the grim god Hades whose eyes—like those of an insect—held no feeling of any kind.

**HADES:** Since you have made it this far, you may play, mortal. But, be warned: My heart is made of stone.

**NARRATOR:** Yet as Orpheus played his love-is-love-even-in-Hades anthem, something hitherto unseen in the Underworld happened. A bit of sediment slowly collected in the corner of Hades's eye. It formed into a tear-shaped deposit on the god's grey cheek. Then the earth—above and below them—shook with a deep tremor, and a crack like pick on stone was heard. It was the sound of Hades's heart breaking.

**HADES:** Very well. Take your love. Her spirit will follow you out. But you cannot look on her face until you are both fully in the light of your father, Apollo—the earth-light—once again. If you do, she will return to me. Light to light, shade to shade.

**NARRATOR:** The god's finger flicked the newly-formed stalactite from his eye.

As he walked back to the surface, Orpheus sang a love-is-not-swallowed-up-in-death chorus. The guardians of the Underworld—as before—did not hamper his progress, but bowed in acknowledgement of his supreme gift.

Orpheus knew he could not look behind him, but as he drew nearer and nearer to the surface, he became more and more eager to know for certain that the spirit of Eurydice followed behind. When he crossed back over the Styx in Charon's ferry, he tried to gauge whether or not the craft seemed burdened with the weight of an extra body. When he passed before the glittering eyes of Cerberus, they tracked his progress but never even once glanced behind him to where his Eurydice supposedly followed. Doubt redoubled its gnawing at his heart.

**ORPHEUS:** (*to himself*) Is Hades making a fool out of me?

**NARRATOR:** The end of the tunnel appeared like a lamp in the darkness. He was nearly home free. The very moment his foot crossed the threshold of light, he whirled anxiously around. *She* was there, behind him in the tunnel—shimmering on the air like a mirage. There was a look of sadness on her face, a look of disappointment—as if he had forgotten her birthday.

**EURYDICE:** Oh, Orpheus. Too soon.

**NARRATOR:** Then he saw what she saw. Although he stood in the light of the world, she still stood in the darkness of the Underworld.

**EURYDICE:** Farewell, my love.

**NARRATOR:** Orpheus lunged out toward her, but his arms embraced only air. The spirit of the girl bowed its head and faded out to the music of Orpheus's staccato sobs.

## DISCUSSION QUESTIONS

1. How does this myth show the power of music?
2. Discuss the quote "'Tis better to have loved and lost than never to have loved at all" and how it applies to this story.
3. Is love more powerful than death? Explain.
4. If Orpheus had succeeded in bringing his wife back from the dead, would that be fair to others who had lost a loved one? Explain.

# THE GOLDEN FLEECE

## TEACHER GUIDE

## BACKGROUND

Jason's quest for the legendary Golden Fleece is exceptional among the hero tales of ancient Greece because of its all-encompassing cast of characters. Not just *one* hero journeys for the fabled prize, but almost every other Greek hero is along for the ride as well. Hercules, Atalanta, and Orpheus (characters who have their own tales elsewhere) pop up in Jason's story to give him a hand. According to some versions of the myth, even the hero Theseus (a.k.a. the Minotaur-slayer) and Atalanta's friend Meleager were along for the ride. Another helper acquired along the way is the Colchian witch Medea, who becomes Jason's lover. Her spells aid the heroes time and time again.

In a story with so many heroes, teamwork becomes an important factor. It is not just one character who is responsible for the quest's success; instead each hero contributes his or her unique talents toward the overall success of the group. Even though Jason is the leader (and the hero who receives top billing), the truth is he could never succeed without the help of his companions. For this reason the voyage of the Argonauts has always been a testament to the power of teamwork.

## SUMMARY

Beginning with the backstory of the Golden Fleece, the story tells of two children, Phrixus and Helle, who are the children of a powerful king. After their father puts away their mother in favor of a younger wife, Phrixus and Helle begin to fear for their lives. Their new stepmother is ruthless and forms a plot to have them publicly executed. The stepmother parches the kingdom's seed reserve, intentionally ruining the harvest for the following year. She then bribes a messenger sent to the Oracle of Delphi to blame this misfortune on the "cursed" children of the king. The spineless king sees little choice other than to publicly execute his own children. The gods, who are angered by the queen's trick, send a flying, golden ram to rescue the children. Phrixus and Helle escape their execution on the back of the magical beast, but Helle does not hold onto the ram's fleece tightly enough and falls into the sea. The ram bears Phrixus to the faraway land of Colchis, where the boy ritualistically sacrifices his rescuer. Bearing the golden fleece of the ram, Phrixus goes before the king Æetes and presents him with the magical item in return for safe passage through his lands. After this Phrixus fades into legend.

The story shifts to the mountain dwelling of Chiron the centaur, a famous trainer of heroes. Here an exiled prince named Jason has lived for many years—ever since Pelias, his much-older cousin, violently seized the throne that rightfully belonged to him. When Chiron sends Jason to gather water, Jason helps an old woman, who is actually Hera in disguise, across a river. When Jason returns, Chiron tells him that the time has come for him to travel to his father's former kingdom, face his cousin, and regain his throne. As Jason journeys toward the kingdom, he breaks one of his sandals and enters the ruling city wearing only one shoe. Unbeknownst to Jason, King Pelias has been warned by an oracle that a man wearing only one shoe will overthrow his kingdom.

When Jason confronts his cousin and reveals his identity, the cowardly king is terrified and devises a way to get rid of Jason once and for all. He proposes that Jason prove his right to rule the land by retrieving the

Golden Fleece from the faraway land of Colchis. (Pelias and Jason are both related to the legendary Phrixus.) Pelias's crooked nobles agree to this, and Jason impetuously accepts the quest. Once out of the presence of the king, Jason realizes that he has been given an impossible task. At Jason's lowest point, the goddess Hera decides that she will be his benefactress since she has seen his goodness. Using her messenger, the rainbow goddess, Iris, Hera spreads word of Jason's heroic undertaking throughout Greece. Through Iris, Jason learns that the shipwright Argos has agreed to make him a peerless ship that he will use to sail to Colchis. In addition, Atalanta, a female Greek hero, Orpheus, a magical musician, and Heracles, the most famous hero of all, arrive to aid Jason on his voyage. Jason realizes that some god or goddess must be blessing his endeavor.

Before he sets out on his quest, Jason sees the form of his old master, Chiron the centaur, in the stars of the sky. Chiron tells Jason that he has died, but he will watch over Jason as he sails on his quest. Here is where the first part of the story ends.

## ESSENTIAL QUESTIONS

- What does it take to be a good leader?
- Why are mythical and real-life quests important? What lessons can they teach?

## CONNECTIONS

*Jason and the Argonauts* (1963) This cult classic film re-tells the voyage of Jason and is famous for its monsters created by stop-motion effects master Ray Harryhausen.

## ANTICIPATORY QUESTIONS

- Heroes often journey to find magical items. What are some of these items?
- Who are some of the most famous Greek heroes?
- What is the Golden Fleece?
- What are some of the common elements in the hero stories you have read so far?

## TEACHABLE TERMS

- **Exposition** The background story of the Golden Fleece is a form of exposition, for it gives readers information that they will need to know in order to understand the rest of the story.
- **Slang** Phrixus uses the term *c'mon* on pg. 83. This is an example of slang.
- **Understatement** Most of Orpheus's dialogue in this story is understatement since he dryly underplays his reactions to the events around him. Another example is the Ram's line "I hate it when that happens" on pg. 83 directly after Helle falls to her death.
- **Verbal irony** On pg. 87 when Jason mutters that a "limping teenager" will really strike fear into King Pelias, he is using sarcasm, a form of verbal irony.

## RECALL QUESTIONS

1. Who raised Jason after he was exiled from his father's kingdom?
2. Why is Jason arrested when he journeys to Pelias's kingdom?
3. What challenge does Pelias say Jason must complete in order to prove he is king-material?
4. Which god or goddess decides to come to Jason's aid?
5. Who are two of Jason's famous helpers?

# THE GOLDEN FLEECE

## JASON AND THE ARGONAUTS: PART I

### CAST

| | |
|---|---|
| **JASON** | *Young Hero* |
| **PELIAS** | *His Evil Cousin* |
| **OLD WOMAN/HERA** | *Queen of the Gods* |
| **ZEUS** | *Lord of the Gods* |
| **ORPHEUS** | *Depressed Musician* |
| **HERACLES** | *Famous Strongman* |
| **ATALANTA** | *Famous Female Hero* |
| **CHIRON** | *Centaur, Hero Trainer* |
| **PHRIXUS** | *Young Prince* |
| **HELLE** | *Sister of Phrixus* |
| **KING** | *Father of Phrixus* |
| **INO** | *Stepmother of Phrixus* |
| **IRIS** | *Rainbow Goddess* |
| **RAM** | *Ram Sent by Hermes* |
| **GUARD** | *Guard of the City* |
| **MAN** | *Man from the Crowd* |

**NARRATOR:** In the far-off land of Colchis upon the limb of an aged tree, there hung a golden fleece. The quest for this fleece is one of the greatest stories ever told. In ancient times many brave adventurers set out to claim this prize—and few returned.

The story of the Golden Fleece began with a king who grew tired of his queen. Although she was the mother of his two children, she had become too overweight and frumpy for his vain tastes, so he sent her away to live in a far part of his kingdom. (*sounds of weeping*)

**HELLE:** (*weepy*) I miss Mother.

**PHRIXUS:** (*weepy*) Why did she have to go, Father?

**KING:** She and I had...differences. I had outgrown her, and she had outgrown the palace. Ha! But I have found you a new mother—a better mother—one that will be a queen more befitting of me. I present to you my bride-to-be—Ino.

**NARRATOR:** The king introduced the children to a sly-looking woman, who was as thin as a reed.

**INO:** (*warmly*) Oh, what darling children!

**KING:** See, my little willow-wand, I knew you would love them! Well, I've got a kingdom to run. I'll leave you three alone to get acquainted.

**NARRATOR:** The children looked at their stepmother dubiously. As soon as the king's footsteps had faded down the hallway, the queen's forced smile sank down into a scowl.

**INO:** Listen up, you little twerps—I am going to run the show around here.

**PHRIXUS:** You may be the new queen, but you will never replace our mother! She is twice the woman you are.

**INO:** *(laugh)* Ha! At least! Someone should have told her to lay off the pork chops.

**PHRIXUS:** You may have beguiled my father with your beauty, but we see your ugly heart.

**INO:** You two little runts make me sick!

**HELLE:** Maybe you should try eating something.

**INO:** Grrrr. Soon your father and I will have new children, and they will sit on his throne—not you brats.

**PHRIXUS:** Over our dead bodies.

**INO:** Exactly.

**NARRATOR:** The new queen had already fabricated a plan to end the children's lives. She sent her servants to parch the kingdom's supply of seed. When the seed was planted and failed to sprout, the king sent a messenger to the Oracle of Delphi, asking why this curse had descended upon the kingdom. But Ino intercepted the messenger and bribed him to give the king a false message—it was the king's own children whose actions had cursed the harvest. Now they must die as a sacrifice to the vengeful gods.

**KING:** What? There must be some mistake!

**INO:** Oh, the little darlings! Boo-hoo! *(pause)* But the oracle has spoken! Call the royal executioner! No reason to prolong the inevitable!

**KING:** My dear, I—

**INO:** Look! I can give you more children—better children. Finish this! Now!

**NARRATOR:** So the weak-willed king signed the death warrant on his two young children. On a gray morning soon afterward, he led his unwitting son and daughter toward their own execution.

**PHRIXUS:** Father, where are we going?

**KING:** *(heavily)* We are going to stand before the people, my son.

**NARRATOR:** Phrixus could tell that something wasn't right. The king's eyes seemed glazed, and he could hear an angry crowd shouting in the distance. *(distant crowd muttering)*

**PHRIXUS:** *(whispering)* Helle, what do you think that noise is?

**HELLE:** Maybe it is a surprise party! My birthday is coming up soon!

**PHRIXUS:** Something's wrong. I can feel it.

**NARRATOR:** Fortunately for Phrixus, the gods decided to intervene and save them from this horrible fate. They were angered by Queen Ino trying to shed innocent blood in their name. So they sent him a rescue.

**RAM:** Pssstt. Kid, over here!

**PHRIXUS:** What?

**NARRATOR:** Phrixus turned. A golden snout was sticking around the corner of a nearby building.

**RAM:** Shhhhh! Come over here!

**HELLE:** Who are you talking to?

NARRATOR: It was a ram—a golden ram—its fleece shining like the sun. It waved a furious hoof at Phrixus.

RAM: Get over here, you idiot! Quickly! Or you'll be caught!

NARRATOR: Phrixus grabbed his sister's arm and pulled her toward the animal's hiding place.

RAM: Quickly, Phrixus. You and your sister must climb on my back. I am sent from Hermes. I will carry you to safety.

PHRIXUS: Quickly! C'mon!

HELLE: What are you doing?

PHRIXUS: Climb on! Didn't you hear the ram? It's our way to escape.

HELLE: No—I—

NARRATOR: Pulling his sister along, Phrixus jumped onto the back of the golden ram and dug his heels into its sides.

RAM: Okay, that's enough! Kicking is *not* necessary!

NARRATOR: The animal leapt in the air and soared heavenward. (*whooshing of a flying ram*)

PHRIXUS: We're flying, Helle! We're flying!

HELLE: (*screaming*) Ahhhhhhh!

PHRIXUS: Hold on!

NARRATOR: The flying ram had already cleared the palace walls. Far below them, the children saw their father turn and feebly wave his arms at their escape.

HELLE: Poor Father! He will miss us!

RAM: Yeah right. He was planning to kill you as a sacrifice to the gods. Now, hold on tight. I've got a schedule to keep.

NARRATOR: On they flew. Soon they were out over the sea—the waves crashing beneath them.

RAM: This sea is called the Unfriendly Sea. Guess why! Just don't look down.

NARRATOR: The children held on tighter.

HELLE: (*scared*) Phrixus, I'm slipping.

PHRIXUS: Ram, can you fly slower? My sister is losing her grip.

RAM: If I go slower, the creatures that we fly swiftly over will catch us—and then, we will all die.

PHRIXUS: Helle! Hold on!

HELLE: I'm slipping! I can't—

NARRATOR: Suddenly, Helle lost her grip, and she fell from the back of the ram. Phrixus watched her disappear down into the black waves below.

HELLE: Ahhhhh… (*fades away*)

PHRIXUS: Nooooooo!

RAM: I hate it when that happens.

NARRATOR: Helle met her death amid the tumultuous waves. Through blinding tears, Phrixus held on until the golden ram set him down on the shore of a strange land.

**RAM:** Here we are—Colchis, the land beyond the Unfriendly Sea. Now, go seek out the king of this land.

**PHRIXUS:** But my sister...

**RAM:** Yeah, sorry about that. My maximum occupancy is one.

**PHRIXUS:** You could have told me that before we escaped!

**RAM:** You live, you learn...unless you die. If it makes you feel better, I'm a goner, too. You will find a knife behind that rock. To show your thankfulness to the gods, you must sacrifice me.

**PHRIXUS:** But you just saved my life!

**RAM:** Hey, you've got the easy part. I have to die here. It must be done.

**PHRIXUS:** Okay...if you insist.

**RAM:** Make it quick. *(sigh)* What a world!

**NARRATOR:** Phrixus sacrificed the ram as the gods wished. Then he cut the shining fleece from the ram—a symbol of its undying beauty. He continued on to the palace of Æetes, the King of Colchis, who received him well and offered him a home there. In return, Phrixus gave the Colchian king the Golden Fleece. Then Phrixus and the fleece faded into legend.

**CHIRON:** And that is the origin of the Golden Fleece. It still remains in Colchis, but many Greeks dream of returning it to our land someday. The image of the golden ram that rescued Phrixus also appears in the stars of the sky. *(pause)* Jason?

**NARRATOR:** On a high mountain in the hill country of Greece, the centaur Chiron had just finished lecturing his young pupil, Jason, who was slumped on a nearby rock.

**CHIRON:** *(sternly)* Jason, have you been listening? *(loudly)* Jason!

**JASON:** *(waking up)* Huh, what?

**NARRATOR:** The boy sat up suddenly.

**CHIRON:** *(sigh)* You *must* pay attention to your lessons. How do you ever expect to become a hero?

**JASON:** Hmph. What do boring tales have to do with being a hero?

**CHIRON:** Everything. If you do not know the past, you are doomed to repeat it.

**JASON:** But I want to fight!

**CHIRON:** That will come soon enough. Patience is a virtue many centaurs do not have. So it is with humans, too. But I have learned it and so shall you.

**JASON:** *(angrily)* I am a prince to a kingdom that has been stolen away from me. I need to do *something* to get it back!

**CHIRON:** *(sigh)* And how exactly are you going to do that?

**JASON:** Listen! I have it all planned out. I will go and challenge my cousin Pelias, tell him that he is a villain and a coward, and then run him through with a sword! *(pause)* That is, if I even had a sword.

**CHIRON:** Think, young one. What would happen then? Many men would strike you down before you had time to savor your revenge. Your cousin is the king after all.

**JASON:** On a throne that's supposed to be mine!

**CHIRON:** What good is a throne if you're not smart enough to use it? Instead of desiring to be powerful, perhaps you should learn to be wise.

**JASON:** *(childlike)* Learning is boring.

**CHIRON:** But it is only learning that will make you great. Knowledge is the only treasure that no one can take away from you. Now it is time for mathematics. Get out your abacus.

**NARRATOR:** Jason was a young prince, who had been raised in a mountainside cave by the wise centaur, Chiron. His father had been king of the Greek city-state of Iolcus until Jason's cousin, Pelias, had violently seized the throne. With his father missing and presumed dead, his mother had fled the land, leaving baby Jason in the care of Chiron.

Jason was half-heartedly calculating on his abacus.

**JASON:** Soooo…when are you going to teach me how to use a sword?

**NARRATOR:** Chiron, swishing flies with his long tail, continued reading his scroll and did not look up.

**CHIRON:** There is not much to it. There is a blunt end and a sharp end. Hold it by the blunt end. Swing the sharp end toward your enemy. Stop swinging when either he or you is dead.

**JASON:** That's it? You taught me the name of every star in the heavens, but you can't teach me more than that about being a warrior?

**CHIRON:** If you want to be a great warrior, you will need steady hands and balance.

**JASON:** Steady hands! Balance! I can do it!

**CHIRON:** Then go gather two jars of water from the river and return without spilling a drop. Then perhaps we can talk…

**JASON:** About being a great warrior?

**CHIRON:** About fixing some supper.

**NARRATOR:** Chiron had taught Jason everything he knew: the learning of the ancients, the layout of the stars, the stories of the old heroes, learning that filled Jason's head to the point of bursting, yet he had never taught him how to swing a sword or to shield himself from a heavy blow.

Jason lugged a pair of large jars down to the river, grumbling to himself as he went.

**JASON:** Some hero I'll be. Hopefully, I can *think* my enemies to death. *(sarcastically)* It's Jason, the mighty warrior! And look out! He's got a protractor!

**NARRATOR:** At the river's edge Jason threw the heavy jars down angrily upon the ground. *(clattering sound)*

**OLD WOMAN:** *(elderly voice)* Young man.

**NARRATOR:** Jason turned. An old woman, heavily wrapped in a traveling cloak, tottered at the edge of the river.

**OLD WOMAN:** I must get to the other side of this river. Will you help me?

**JASON:** *(to himself)* Great. My first mighty quest.

**NARRATOR:** Jason was in such a foul mood that he wanted to refuse, but Chiron had taught him always to be polite and helpful to those in need.

**JASON:** Sure, ma'am.

**OLD WOMAN:** Oh, thank you!

**NARRATOR:** Jason took the old woman into his arms and waded across the swift-flowing river.

**OLD WOMAN:** My, my. What a strong young man, you are! I have a granddaughter that I must tell about you.

**NARRATOR:** Jason deposited the old woman safely upon the far shore.

**OLD WOMAN:** Thank you, sonny. I would have never made it by myself.

**NARRATOR:** Then she locked her deep-seeing eyes onto his.

**OLD WOMAN:** Your master is right. Wisdom is the true mark of a great warrior.

**JASON:** Wait. How did—?

**NARRATOR:** Then suddenly the old woman was no longer there. Jason shook his head in disbelief.

**JASON:** Huh. What? She can't cross a river, but she can sure make herself scarce quickly!

**NARRATOR:** Jason filled his jars and, grunting under the weight, returned to the mountainside cave where his master was waiting.

**JASON:** Here is the water—and I didn't spill a drop.

**CHIRON:** You are ready.

**JASON:** Seriously? The water jug thing was the true test?

**CHIRON:** No. The gods have spoken. It is time for you to set out.

**JASON:** But my training—

**CHIRON:** I will teach you all you need to know about warfare before you go, but it will not take long. The mind is the weapon of greatness. I have spent all these years sharpening yours as much as I could. At times, I fear it is still quite blunt. Let us begin.

**NARRATOR:** Chiron, the teacher who would train many of the great Greek heroes, taught Jason all that he knew of the art of war. When he was finished, the centaur beamed at the boy proudly.

**CHIRON:** Now, I am ready to give you a gift—one I have been preparing for you.

**JASON:** *(excitedly)* What is it? My own weapon? At last!

**CHIRON:** No, but rather a garment to turn away the rain as you travel.

**NARRATOR:** Chiron held up a cloak made from the skin of a leopard.

**JASON:** *(not impressed)* A leopard skin?

**CHIRON:** Do not look down upon it. The mighty leopard gave you his hide. It is a wondrous gift. Wear it well. I had hoped to give you something more...

JASON: *(hopefully)* A sword?

CHIRON: A haircut.

NARRATOR: Chiron motioned to Jason's long hair, which cascaded down to his shoulders.

CHIRON: Not everyone appreciates a mane like we do. But you must be off. Follow the road. You have learned the way. Claim your birthright, but along the way, do not forget wisdom, for only it can save you.

NARRATOR: Jason placed the leopard skin over his shoulders and prepared to depart. Yet before he did, he embraced the centaur warmly.

JASON: Thank you—for everything.

CHIRON: Until our next meeting...farewell.

NARRATOR: So Jason left the only home he had ever known. The road moved quickly. He was soon out of the mountains and approaching Iolcus, his father's once kingdom. As he walked, he pondered.

JASON: I've always dreamed of challenging my cousin. But how will I do it? *(pause)* I will use my mind. That's it! I have been trained by Chiron the Wise. Ha! This may not be so hard after all!

NARRATOR: At this moment, the strap on his left sandal gave way, and in his shock, he tripped and fell face first to the ground.

JASON: *(angrily)* Great. My sandal is broken. This is just what I need. I guess I'll have to limp into the palace with one sandal. That'll strike fear into my enemy—a limping teenager.

NARRATOR: But little did Jason know, what he wore was *exactly* the thing to strike fear into his cousin. After seizing the throne, Pelias had been confronted by an oracle, who told him that while his fortune was great, he should fear one who came wearing only one shoe. Fearing these words, the king had set the palace guards to watch for a man who wore only one shoe. If a man fit this description, they were to bring him immediately before the throne—for a speedy execution.

GUARD: Stop, boy!

JASON: Me?

GUARD: Why do you only wear one shoe?

JASON: *(jokingly)* I'm starting a new trend.

GUARD: Come with me.

NARRATOR: The guard grabbed Jason and dragged him toward the palace.

JASON: *(frightened)* I was only joking!

NARRATOR: Thrown roughly to the ground, Jason was shocked when he looked up to behold the king—the repugnant swine he had come to face. He was even a bit more swine-like than Jason had imagined with his dangling jowls and rotund body to match.

PELIAS: *(to guard)* Bring me a sword. Let's execute this wretch at once!

JASON: Wait! You can't do this!

PELIAS: Why not? I *am* the king. You will tell me your name...then I will kill you.

JASON: Why? Because I'm wearing one shoe? Is the law of this land that no one can wear only one sandal? That's the stupidest thing I've ever heard!

**PELIAS:** This is my kingdom. I make the laws. Everyone wears two sandals at all times. The most loyal wear three. Anyone foolish enough to wear only one is put to death. Now, give me your name, or I will cut it out of you.

**NARRATOR:** The fat king advanced with his sword—his eyes glittering with hate. It was then that Jason remembered the lore that Chiron had taught him.

**JASON:** Halt! You cannot kill me! I am your relative, Jason. My father is the rightful king of this realm. If you murder me, the Furies will haunt your mind day and night for such a crime!

**PELIAS:** *(gasping)* Jason?

**NARRATOR:** Pelias's face twisted into a look of extreme anger and then melted away to a look of supreme happiness.

**PELIAS:** *(sugary tone)* Jason, my boy. Guards, put this sword away please. There will be no need for that today. *(happy laugh)* So, tell me, my cousin, where did your father manage to hide you away all these years?

**JASON:** I was raised in the countryside by Chiron the centaur.

**PELIAS:** Chiron, you say? I'm sure he taught you some of his *horse* sense. I've heard he's a bit of a *nag*. But you're home now! Thank goodness! We've been worried sick!

**JASON:** I see through your sweetness. I've come to claim the throne that is rightly mine—a throne that I see you have been keeping warm in my absence with your enormous rear.

*(murmuring and giggling from the crowd)*

**PELIAS:** *(gritting teeth)* But, young prince, I have only been keeping it for you. I will gladly step aside and let the true heir take his place.

**JASON:** Thank you.

**NARRATOR:** Could it really be this easy? Chiron had been right. He hadn't needed weapons at all.

**PELIAS:** But first, let us call in all the nobles. *(to guards)* Guards, send for the nobles. They are gathered in the main hall. Tell them that my cousin has returned.

**JASON:** I expect you to stay true to your word.

**PELIAS:** Of course, of course. True as day.

*(murmuring from the nobles)*

**PELIAS:** Ah, here we are. Great men of this realm, look who has returned—the son of the former king!

*(murmurs from the crowd)*

**JASON:** *(loudly)* I have come to claim my father's throne.

**PELIAS:** And so he has. But, dear nobles, I must pose you a question—how do we know that this boy is who he says he is? Just who is this long-haired, leopard-skin-wearing freak? Jason—if that is your name—how can you prove that you are your father's son?

**JASON:** I—I—

**PELIAS:** *(slyly)* That's what I thought. Now, I am a fair man. I suggest a task for this boy. Jason, I assume you know the tale of Phrixus and his magnificent Golden Fleece?

**JASON:** Uh…of course, I do. But what does it have to do with me?

**PELIAS:** I'm so glad you asked. Phrixus is one of our relatives, you know. His fleece is a symbol of our family's greatness. If you are truly part of our family, it would not be above you to retrieve this artifact for our beloved kingdom. It should be returned to Greek soil, where it rightfully belongs!

*(murmurs of approval; "Yes" from the nobles)*

**JASON:** *(confidently)* Sure. No problem. Sounds like a cinch.

**PELIAS:** Oh, what a brave boy! You must be the old king's son! Who else would volunteer to sail across the Black Sea to the barbarian land of Colchis?

**JASON:** Ummm…what?

**PELIAS:** Colchis is at the very ends of the earth. Didn't you know that?

**JASON:** Erm.

**PELIAS:** Someone should have paid closer attention to his geography. So, it's a very simple test—if you are truly the king's son, bring back the Golden Fleece and receive your kingdom…or die trying. *(chuckle)*

**NARRATOR:** Jason's face stayed emotionless, but inside, his stomach was churning. He had been tricked. Now he had no choice.

**JASON:** *(numbly)* I have sworn to bring back the Golden Fleece, and that is what I will do.

**PELIAS:** Wonderful. Spoken like a true relative of mine.

**JASON:** *(hatefully)* You didn't let me finish. I will bring the fleece…and with it your destruction.

**PELIAS:** *(laughing)* Ooooh. I'm shaking.

**NARRATOR:** As he stalked out from the palace, Jason felt heat boiling behind his eyes.

**JASON:** This is impossible! There's no way I could possibly survive a trip to Colchis. It's leagues away across the sea. I have no ship, no crew, no hope!

**NARRATOR:** After wandering the lonely streets, Jason found the city docks and stared despondently out over the sea he had pledged to cross. It was here—his will lost—that he caught the eye of Hera as she gazed down from high Olympus.

**HERA:** This boy, Jason—what do you know of him, husband?

**ZEUS:** *(distractedly)* Hmmm—nothing, dear—nothing.

**HERA:** *(annoyed)* Oh, I forgot. The only mortals you pay attention are young females.

**ZEUS:** That boy could pass for one easily enough. A weak-looking lad.

**HERA:** But his heart is good. He carried me across a river when I was in a disguise. I appeared as an old crone.

**ZEUS:** I thought you said you were in a disguise. *(chuckling)*

**HERA:** *(angrily)* Insult him and me all you want! His destiny is to become a hero, and I will help him do so!

**ZEUS:** Dear, we should not interfere with the destinies of mortals.

**HERA:** Really? And how many of your sons have you sent on to be mighty heroes?

**ZEUS:** Hera....

**HERA:** Do you deny Jason help because he, out of all the others, is not the putrid offspring of your insatiable loins?

**ZEUS:** You have said your piece!

**HERA:** Have I? I am not a thing to be ordered about. *(softly)* I will help this boy because no one else will. He is no son of Zeus, yet I will see to it that he goes on the greatest quest man has ever known!

**NARRATOR:** So Hera sent her messenger, Iris the rainbow goddess, throughout Greece, spreading the word of the great quest. Many heroes heard of this mighty undertaking and started to make their way to Iolcus. Such a magnificent prize attracted the greatest and most powerful champions in all of ancient Greece. Meanwhile, Jason wandered the city aimlessly—unaware of the work Hera had begun.

**JASON:** How am I ever going to do this? Chiron said to use my mind. I have to think!

**IRIS:** Sir. You are Jason, correct?

**NARRATOR:** Jason looked up to see a young girl with a plain face standing before him. It was odd, but for a second, he thought he saw her eyes gleam with a purple light.

**IRIS:** I have a message from Argos the shipwright. Your ship will be sea-worthy in a few months. He has received your order.

**JASON:** My order? What do you mean?

**IRIS:** *(pointing)* He lives just over there. You may ask him yourself.

**NARRATOR:** He looked where she pointed, toward a distant part of the shorefront.

**JASON:** But I didn't order any—

**NARRATOR:** Jason turned back to argue, but the girl was gone. A giant rainbow had spread across the bay. Iris had done her duty.

**JASON:** The gods must have arranged this. I will need men to sail the ship! And supplies! I need to get busy!

**NARRATOR:** Over the following months Jason asked all the men of Iolcus—who was brave enough to go with him? He found working a trade and making a harvest easily outranked a dangerous mission to the far ends of the earth. He had hit another wall—until one day.

**ATALANTA:** Excuse me, *man*.

**JASON:** Look, miss, I'm really busy. I'm trying to—

**ATALANTA:** Get brave people to go on your voyage. I know. I've come to tell you that I'll come with you.

**JASON:** Well, that's very nice, *sweetie*, but we won't be needing any women on this voyage. We can do our own cooking and cleaning.

**NARRATOR:** Jason suddenly felt his arm being painfully pinned behind him.

**JASON:** *(in pain)* Ah! On second thought—welcome aboard.

**ATALANTA:** I am Atalanta. You will soon find that I am as strong as any man, though somewhat smarter.

**JASON:** Nice. *(pause)* Wait! I have heard tales of you! You are a mighty warrior—for a female. And who is that with you?

**NARRATOR:** A sad-looking boy slumped behind her—golden-haired with fair skin, a lyre thrown over his shoulder. He seemed to be moaning softly to himself.

**ATALANTA:** This is Orpheus. We traveled the road together. He's a bit mopey, but you'll find that his music is as good a weapon as any. And that's not necessarily a compliment.

**JASON:** I've heard tales of him as well. I welcome you both. *(under his breath)* Great. A girl and a harp player. What a fearsome group.

**NARRATOR:** Suddenly, angry shouts came from across the marketplace. A crowd was gathering around some sort of scene.

**MAN:** Put it down, you brute, put it down!

**ATALANTA:** What is that noise?

**JASON:** I don't know.

**ORPHEUS:** *(sadly, monotone)* Some man is holding an ox cart in the air.

**JASON:** What?

**NARRATOR:** They ran to see what all the commotion was about. A large man, like Orpheus had said, was holding an ox cart over his head—the ox still dangling from it.

An old cart-driver was screaming irately at the strongman.

**MAN:** My cart! My cart! Thief!

**HERACLES:** Quiet, puny man. Do you not know who I am? You almost ran me over with this tiny cart!

**MAN:** Put it down! Put it down!

**HERACLES:** *(annoyed)* Here, I'll put it down.

**NARRATOR:** The large man dropped the ox cart onto the old man. *(crash and groaning of an old man)*

**HERACLES:** Some people have no manners.

**JASON:** *(to Atalanta)* Who is that man?

**ATALANTA:** Isn't it obvious? It's Heracles.

**JASON:** What's he doing here?

**ORPHEUS:** *(dryly)* He's come to join you.

**JASON:** Me? Why me?

**ORPHEUS:** *(even drier)* Maybe he's like me. Nothing better to do.

**ATALANTA:** Heracles! Over here! HERE! *(under her breath)* Big dumb brute.

**HERACLES:** Hello, small peoples. I am Heracles. Can you tell me where to find Jason?

**NARRATOR:** With the giant man so close, Jason suddenly found that he had lost the ability to speak. Chiron had told him many stories of what this renowned strongman had done.

**JASON:** Erm. I am Jason.

**HERACLES:** You're smaller than I thought. Such a great quest for a small man? Can you not talk, little one?

**JASON:** Errrr…

**HERACLES:** Ha! I kid you!

**NARRATOR:** Heracles slapped Jason on the back—knocking him to the ground.

**JASON:** Oof!

**HERACLES:** Sorry. I have come to join you. With the mighty Heracles on your journey, you shall not fail.

**ATALANTA:** Riiiight…

**ORPHEUS:** *(sighing loudly)* I'm tired. Life used to be so good.

**HERACLES:** What's his problem?

**ATALANTA:** His one true love died.

**HERACLES:** *(sadly)* I know how he feels.

**ORPHEUS:** *(somewhat hopefully)* Did you lose your love to Hades as well?

**HERACLES:** Err—sort of.

**ATALANTA:** Did your closest friend disintegrate before your very eyes?

**HERACLES:** No…I sort of murdered my wife and kids. *(quickly)* But it wasn't my fault…exactly.

**ATALANTA:** Well, I'll be keeping my distance now.

**NARRATOR:** Jason couldn't believe it. In front of him stood two of the greatest heroes Greece had ever known—and Orpheus—all of them offering to accompany him on his journey.

**ATALANTA:** Well, let's not stand around here in the middle of the street all day. We will have to elect a captain—hopefully, someone competent.

**HERACLES:** Our captain shall be Jason! This is his quest after all.

**ATALANTA:** Well…

**HERACLES:** *(yelling)* And if anyone challenges that, I will crush them with my massive arms! So when do we leave, captain? We are a hearty crew, thirsting for adventures!

**JASON:** Oh! You're talking to me! Uh…tomorrow. I just received word that our ship is ready.

**HERACLES:** What is our ship's name?

**JASON:** The Argo.

**ORPHEUS:** *(emotionally drained)* Catchy.

**NARRATOR:** And so this band of heroes retired for the evening, preparing themselves for their voyage the next day.

But Hera's power had not yet been fully revealed. There were more—other heroes—late arrivals yet to come. Peleus, the father of Achilles, came first, tall and regal. Then came the twins Castor and Polydeuces, the impulsive and eager brothers of Helen of Sparta. And with them came many brave men—all vowing to follow young Jason to the ends of the earth. Hera had done well.

At the harbor with his new vessel rocking

silently in the bay, Jason stared up at the stars—the same stars Chiron had trained him to memorize.

**JASON:** Chiron, I see that you gave me knowledge for a reason. I just wish you were here to help me use it.

**NARRATOR:** As he spoke these words, he noticed a cluster of stars that he had never seen before.

**JASON:** That's odd. Chiron taught me every star in the heavens.

**NARRATOR:** These stars began to shimmer and dance. To his astonishment, they shifted and formed a shape. In that shape, Jason saw his old teacher.

**JASON:** It can't be! *(shouting)* Chiron!

**CHIRON:** There is no need to shout. I can hear you.

**JASON:** Master, I don't understand. What's happened to you?

**CHIRON:** After you departed, I knew that you would need help, so I went in search of Heracles. I ran into him at my cousin's wedding. He's a sucker for centaur weddings apparently. Things went sour. Too much wine was drunk. Long story short—Heracles got into a big, drunken brawl, and I caught a stray poisoned arrow in the hoof.

**JASON:** *(sadly)* I—I didn't know.

**CHIRON:** It's not the worst way to die. The good news is that Zeus has placed me in the stars so that I might watch over you.

**JASON:** *(excited)* That's great! I think I'm going to need all the help I can get.

**CHIRON:** You have mighty helpers—helpers of legend. I have trained many heroes, Jason, but you, my son, will travel the farthest and see the most. You will face many challenges. But you are favored by the gods—no small feat. Use what I taught you of the stars to guide your ship. You will sail far across the Black Sea—to the ends of the earth. Do not forget your old teacher, Jason. I hope that I have taught you well. Now is the test. Farewell.

**JASON:** Farewell.

**NARRATOR:** The stars faded from Jason's eyes. The dawn was breaking. This was to be the greatest day of his life, the day that he began the most legendary quest ever undertaken by any man of any time—the quest for the Golden Fleece.

## DISCUSSION QUESTIONS

1. Why is it important to know the back-story of the Golden Fleece?
2. Is Chiron right—is the mind the greatest weapon?
3. What lesson does Jason learn about his education with Chiron? Explain.
4. What is heroic about Jason?
5. So far how does the story of Jason repeat earlier hero motifs? Explain.
6. The quest for the Golden Fleece is a multi-hero story. What do you think the addition of heroes like Heracles, Orpheus, and Atalanta contributes to this story?
7. So far has Jason been wise—or just lucky? Explain.

# ABOARD THE ARGO

## TEACHER GUIDE

### BACKGROUND

The Argonauts do not have a multimillion dollar movie franchise like the *Avengers* do, but they might deserve one. After all, the Argonauts were the original super-group—a collection of previously-established heroes who join forces to complete a common goal. It's an idea that sells, and this story tells us that it has been selling for almost 3,000 years.

Even though the ancient Greek heroes do not have secret identities or the ability to shoot laser beams out of their eyes, they are still the ancient equivalent of modern superheroes. The sons of Boreas the North Wind, who were present on Jason's voyage in the original myth, *were* able to fly—which is getting closer. Plus, Heracles did have some amazing super-strength, not to mention some Incredible Hulk-like rages.

Even powerful heroes realize the importance of teamwork. By the time the Argo sailed, the Greek heroes had already achieved some amazing individual feats: Atalanta had hunted the Calydonian Boar, Orpheus had descended into the Underworld, and Heracles had completed twelve impossible labors. Yet when they signed up to accompany Jason on his mission to Colchis, they put their egos to the side and accepted the role of a team member—which was probably not easy for such widely renowned heroes. They all accepted the leadership of Jason, an inexperienced young man, for one simple reason: It was his quest, not theirs.

Even a legendary team like the Argonauts would be worthless without a good leader. Over the course of the story, Jason proves himself to be as much a hero as the rest of his companions by his resolve and determination to reach his goal. There is a saying that a good leader must be a good follower, too. Jason is never afraid to give someone else the lead when he knows that their talent is what the group needs to succeed. For all of these reasons the journey of the Argonauts is the ultimate tale of teamwork.

### SUMMARY

Several episodic adventures make up the second half of Jason's story. First, the crew encounters the island of the Lemnian women, a fierce tribe of women warriors who have no men among them. They take Jason and his male crew as their husbands, but Atalanta begins to wonder what has happened to the men of the tribe. She learns that the Lemnian women murdered their men and suspects they will soon do the same to the Argonauts. She persuades Jason and his men to leave the island.

As the Argo passes through the strait that leads to the Black Sea, six-armed giants begin to hurl boulders from the mainland. Heracles uses his massive strength to deflect these projectiles and save the ship.

Next, while stopping on an island to refresh their supplies, a young crew member is pulled into a spring by a group of amorous nymphs. This boy is Hylas, Heracles's armor-bearer. No one knows where Hylas has gone to, so Heracles leaves the Argonauts and their quest to search for him.

On yet another island Jason and his crew encounter Phineus the prophet, a man with a unique punishment. The gods have forced him to sit forever at a table covered in food, yet before he can ever eat of the feast, creatures called Harpies (half-bird, half-woman) come and befoul it. The Argonauts observe this happening and fight the Harpies off. The rainbow goddess, Iris, appears and stops the Argonauts from slaying the Harpies. Because of their bravery, she says Phineus will no longer be punished. He rewards the Argonauts by telling them how to sail successfully past a pair of clashing rocks that rise up out of the sea and destroy ships.

Using Phineus's advice, the Argonauts sail between the rocks and arrive at an island that is home to birds that can fire their wings like arrows. The Argonauts are helpless against the assault of these birds until they ask Orpheus to sing to them. Hearing Orpheus's song, the birds despair and drown themselves in the sea. Then the Argonauts sail on to Colchis—the land of the Golden Fleece.

## ESSENTIAL QUESTIONS

- Why is teamwork important?
- How do you become a good leader?

## CONNECTIONS

*Argonautica* This Greek epic poem, written in the third century B.C., is the definitive version of the quest of Jason and the Argonauts. Its author, Apollonius of Rhodes, was reportedly the head of the great library of Alexandria. He incorporated a large amount of research into his storytelling and mainly mimicked the epic style of the poet Homer.

## ANTICIPATORY QUESTIONS

- What do you think will happen in the second half of Jason's story?
- What skills do the Argonauts have that will come in handy on their adventure?
- What good do you think the Golden Fleece will accomplish in Jason's life?
- What sights do you think Jason and his crew will see on their voyage?

## TEACHABLE TERMS

- **Character Development** Examine how Jason's character has developed over the course of the story. Has he become more mature? Has he grown into his position as a leader?
- **Onomatopoeia** (*Shoom!*) on pg. 104 and (*Zing! Zing! Zing*) on pg. 106 are examples of onomatopoeia.
- **Comedy Relief** Orpheus is an example of a character that provides comedy relief in the story. His comments often add a humorous touch to serious events.
- **Episodic Narrative** This myth is an example of an episodic narrative as it is told through a series of small episodes or adventures.

## RECALL QUESTIONS

1. Who or what try to destroy the Argo as it sails through a narrow strait?
2. What happens to Hylas, the armor-bearer of Heracles?
3. What type of creature punishes Phineus the prophet?
4. Why do the Argonauts release a dove from their ship?
5. How do the Argonauts defeat the birds of Ares?

# ABOARD THE ARGO

## JASON AND THE ARGONAUTS: PART II

### CAST

| | |
|---|---|
| **JASON** | *Leader of the Argonauts* |
| **HERACLES** | *Mighty Hero* |
| **HYLAS** | *Heracles's Armor-bearer* |
| **ATALANTA** | *Mighty Female Hero* |
| **ORPHEUS** | *Depressed Musician* |
| **HYPSIPYLE** | *Warrior Woman* |
| **WOMAN** | *Warrior Woman* |
| **PHINEUS** | *Tormented Prophet* |
| **IRIS** | *Messenger of the Gods* |
| **NYMPH ONE** | *Water Spirit* |
| **NYMPH TWO** | *Water Spirit* |
| **SOLDIER** | *Soldier from Colchis* |
| **ÆETES** | *Ancient King of Colchis* |
| **MEDEA** | *Witch Daughter of Æetes* |

**NARRATOR:** In the faraway land of Colchis, the home of the legendary Golden Fleece, the princess Medea awoke to a vision. She at once went to tell this vision to her father, the king.

**MEDEA:** Father, I have had another vision.

**ÆETES:** *(hoarsely)* Speak, girl.

**MEDEA:** I saw the young Greek. He and his crew have set sail. They are being aided by Hera, queen of the gods. They come for the Golden Fleece.

**ÆETES:** *(calmly)* Good, daughter, good.

**MEDEA:** *(angrily)* Father! We cannot let them have the fleece. They are filth! They do not deserve to set foot in our land.

**ÆETES:** Patience, Medea. It is with patience that the spider, Arachne, spins her web—not haste—and so she catches her prey. We must do the same.

**MEDEA:** *(irritated)* Your will be done, Father. Good night.

**NARRATOR:** What the princess of Colchis had seen in her dream was true. Jason and his Argonauts had finally embarked. The crew hoisted the sail, and the Argo pulled out to sea.

**HERACLES:** A fine day for sailing, little Jason. *(claps his hand on Jason's shoulder)*

**JASON:** Oof! Yes, a perfect day.

**ATALANTA:** So, do we have any idea what stands between us and Colchis?

**JASON:** Miles and miles of sea.

**HERACLES:** Monsters to be sure.

**ORPHEUS:** *(hopefully)* Death, I hope.

**JASON:** It will be no easy feat—that's for sure. We'll have to stay on our guard.

**NARRATOR:** They sailed for many weeks, and Jason used his knowledge of the stars to pilot the ship. Day after day, Orpheus sang of his lost love, Eurydice, and moved even the manliest of men to tears.

**ORPHEUS:** *(depressed)* And that is how I lost my love.

**HERACLES:** *(sobbing)* It's sooo sad!

**ATALANTA:** Oh, please. He sings that song about ten times a day. Maybe he should row a bit instead!

**ORPHEUS:** *(moaning)* How can I row when my heart is broken?

**ATALANTA:** I'll break more than your heart if you don't start pulling your weight!

**HERACLES:** Ha-ha! She is a fiery lass.

**ATALANTA:** And just what exactly is that supposed to mean, you muscle-headed moron?

**HERACLES:** Hey, girly! Who you calling a…a…whatever you said?

**NARRATOR:** Jason stepped in the midst of the arguing heroes.

**JASON:** Now, let's all be calm. If we cannot work together, this voyage is doomed. Thank you for the inspiration of your music, Orpheus.

**ATALANTA:** *(grumbling)* All it inspired me to do is jump overboard!

**JASON:** Speaking of that, we need to stop and go ashore for supplies—food and fresh water.

**ORPHEUS:** There's a rather dangerous-looking island to the east.

**JASON:** That is where we will have to go ashore. Who's coming with me?

**HERACLES:** I will go! Hylas, fetch my armor!

**HYLAS:** *(eagerly)* Yes, sir.

**HERACLES:** Hylas and I have been together on many voyages. He is an orphaned lad. I have taken him under my wing. I think of him as a son.

**ORPHEUS:** That could be dangerous.

**HYLAS:** Here you are.

**HERACLES:** Thank you, boy. I'm ready to go ashore.

**NARRATOR:** And so the Argo pulled in close to the strange isle. Jason and Heracles stepped off the boat. The island was thick with vegetation. Tangled vines and large-leaved plants prevented easy travel. But they pressed onward. After an hour of struggling through the underbrush, Jason and Heracles emerged into a clearing. There in its midst, a ring of quaint huts emitted wispy columns of smoke.

**HERACLES:** I smell danger here, Jason. We should not stay here a moment longer than necessary!

**NARRATOR:** At that moment, a figure stepped forth from the furthest hut. It was a tall, dark, beautiful woman. She was soon followed by many more of her kind—tall, beautiful women.

**HERACLES:** On second thought, perhaps we should stay here.

**NARRATOR:** Heracles pulled forth his hunting horn and sounded a great note upon it—a signal for the rest of the men to come ashore. *(hunting horn)* The rest of the men and Atalanta soon appeared from the underbrush.

This island was Lemnos, and these were the famous Lemnian warrior women. The woman they had first seen was their leader, Hypsipyle.

**JASON:** Where are your men?

**HYPSIPYLE:** We have no men.

**HERACLES:** I like those odds.

**ATALANTA:** Oh, please.

**NARRATOR:** Days later, supplies and quest forgotten, the Argonauts still camped on the island. In every corner of the Lemnian village, Jason's men reclined—some being fanned, others being fed grapes, others drinking from goblets held by the Lemnian women.

**ATALANTA:** Where is Jason? I have to speak to him!

**ORPHEUS:** He is in the hut of the queen. *(sigh)* I hate love.

**NARRATOR:** Atalanta found Jason reclining upon some cushions as Hypsipyle, the queen herself, fed him grapes with her bronzed hands.

**ATALANTA:** Jason, can I speak to you for a moment?

**JASON:** I'm kind of busy. What is it?

**ATALANTA:** I know you all are living out some desert island fantasy here, but don't you find it slightly odd that there just happens to be *no* men on this island?

**JASON:** Nooo—not really.

**ATALANTA:** Think, you stupid man! There had to be men here at some point. These girls didn't just fall out of the sky.

**JASON:** What's your point?

**ATALANTA:** Something's strange. I'm going to get to the bottom of this.

**NARRATOR:** And she did. Atalanta found a moment to take the Lemnian queen aside.

**ATALANTA:** Okay, level with me, sister. Why exactly are there no men on this island?

**HYPSIPYLE:** Because they outlived their usefulness—and we destroyed them.

**ATALANTA:** Hmmm. Impressive. Psychotic—but impressive.

**HYPSIPYLE:** We women of Lemnos forgot the love-goddess Aphrodite in our sacrifices. In revenge that goddess cursed us with a terrible plague.

**ATALANTA:** Leprosy?

**HYPSIPYLE:** Rancid body odor. Our husbands were repulsed by us and sought out companionship with women from other lands. That was their last mistake.

**ATALANTA:** So you wiped out all the men for their unfaithfulness?

**HYPSIPYLE:** Every father, husband, and boy. All except for my father—the former king. I secretly spared his life and put him out to sea in a wooden chest.

**ATALANTA:** Isn't it kind of hard to keep your race alive without any men?

**HYPSIPYLE:** Travelers happen by here, and we take them as husbands.

**ATALANTA:** And then dispose of them, I guess?

**HYPSIPYLE:** We have found disposable husbands are the best.

**ATALANTA:** Then my crewmates and I must be gone from here immediately!

**NARRATOR:** The Lemnian queen stepped forward menacingly.

**HYPSIPYLE:** I don't think so. We outnumber you ten to one, and we are mighty warriors.

**ATALANTA:** Are you threatening me? Because you're not very good at it. Listen to a real pro. You will let our crew depart, or I will tell the rest of your female-power warriors that you spared your own father when they had to put theirs to death. I don't think they will take too kindly to that, do you?

**HYPSIPYLE:** Grrrr. Just try and get your man friends to leave. No man will leave this island willingly. Our allure is too great.

**ATALANTA:** You don't know these men like I do.

**NARRATOR:** Atalanta went at once to find Jason and tell him all that she had learned.

**ATALANTA:** (*whispering*) Jason, we have to get out of here! These women are dangerous!

**JASON:** Ha! Dangerous?

**ATALANTA:** Although they *definitely* aren't acting like it right now, they detest men. In fact, they murdered all the men that once lived here.

**JASON:** But they're so friendly!

**ATALANTA:** They just use men to repopulate their race! Once the honeymoon's over, they'll murder you, too!

**JASON:** Hmmm. But maybe not.

**ATALANTA:** (*cry of disgust*) You men are all alike!

**NARRATOR:** After much persuasion, Atalanta finally convinced Jason that they must leave. Quickly, they set about finding every man and relaying the news. The men were not happy. Here on Lemnos they had found the women of their dreams. Yet they admitted that they had taken a vow to follow Jason to the ends of the earth, so they grudgingly agreed to depart.

**WOMAN:** Should we stop them, my queen?

**HYPSIPYLE:** No, let them go.

**NARRATOR:** It was with sad faces that the crew snuck back to the Argo—leaving their Lemnian loves behind. They hoisted the sail and set the Argo back out to sea, continuing on toward Colchis. Many of them wept as they watched the island of Lemnos fade into the distance.

**ATALANTA:** No need to thank me for saving you.

**JASON:** (*glumly*) Don't worry.

**ATALANTA:**  Those women were going to murder you, you know.

**JASON:**  Yeah, but what a way to go.

**NARRATOR:**  To encourage the heartsick men, Orpheus sang a song about the loss of love, but this only made them feel worse.

Soon the Argo neared the narrow strait that led to the Black Sea called the Hellespont—named for Helle, the sister of Phrixus who had drowned there long ago.

**HERACLES:**  Ah! What beautiful mountains!

**JASON:**  We must be careful. They call the Black Sea the Unfriendly Sea for a reason. Chiron told me that dangerous giants live in the mountains nearby. They are monsters who have six arms each and wear leather loincloths.

**ATALANTA:**  Uhh…is the leather loincloth thing an important detail?

**NARRATOR:**  As the Argo passed through the strait, a sudden splash near the ship almost caused it to capsize. *(gigantic splash)*

**JASON:**  Look! There! Monsters!

**NARRATOR:**  Jason was right. On the shore to either side were giants with six arms each. Muscle upon muscle padded their enormous bodies. With their massive hands, they pried loose more chunks of the mountains to hurl at the ship.

**ATALANTA:**  Unfriendly Sea, huh? That must be the welcoming party.

**JASON:**  We will be pulverized! We will all die!

**ORPHEUS:**  Finally!

**HERACLES:**  No! Not while Heracles is aboard! Row swiftly, and Heracles will protect you!

**JASON:**  Man your oars!

**ATALANTA:**  *(grumbling)* I hate that phrase!

**JASON:**  Just row!

**NARRATOR:**  Roaring with anger, the giants sent more boulders sailing into the air, and the sky above the Argonauts grew dark with falling projectiles. *(whistling of falling boulders)* While every other Argonaut grabbed up an oar, even Orpheus, Heracles stood in the midst of the ship, cracking his knuckles as the boulders descended upon them.

**ATALANTA:**  There are too many of them! We will be crushed!

**NARRATOR:**  But Atalanta underestimated Heracles.

**HERACLES:**  *(war cry)* Arhhhh!

**NARRATOR:**  With superhuman speed and strength, the fists of the strongman flew into action. Fragments of boulder filled the air as Heracles deflected or crushed each and every one of the deadly missiles. *(Bam! Bam! Bam!)*

**HYLAS:**  Behind you, Heracles!

**NARRATOR:**  Heracles deflected the final boulder as the Argo pulled through the strait into the open sea. Seeing their prey eluding them, the six-armed giants roared in anger. *(distant roaring of giants)*

**ATALANTA:**  *(taunting)* Ah, don't get your loincloths in a bunch!

**HERACLES:** Now you see the strength of Heracles!

**JASON:** Heracles, you have saved us!

**HERACLES:** *(breathing heavily)* I know. Now I have only one request. Care if we pull over for a drink of water? Heracles thirsts!

**NARRATOR:** As soon as they were a safe distance from the mountains of the giants, they pulled the Argo into shore.

**HERACLES:** Hylas, boy! Let's fetch some water! I am parched!

**HYLAS:** I can handle it, Heracles! You stay here at the ship and rest.

**HERACLES:** Ah! There's a good lad!

**NARRATOR:** Hoisting a jar upon his shoulder, Hylas, Heracles's armor-bearer traveled inland to find a source of fresh water. At last he discovered a crystal clear pool in the midst of the forest.

**HYLAS:** Ah, here is a spring!

**NYMPH ONE:** *(seductively)* My, my! What a handsome young man!

**HYLAS:** *(nervously)* Who's there?

**NARRATOR:** Two slinky, feminine forms rose from the depths of the pool. They were the nymphs who lived in the spring.

**NYMPH TWO:** Hello, handsome.

**NYMPH ONE:** Perhaps you should stay here with us, pretty one.

**HYLAS:** N-n-nooo…I must be getting back to Heracles.

**NYMPH TWO:** Come swim with us. Tee hee!

**HYLAS:** No! Let me go!

**NYMPH ONE:** I have his hand!

**NYMPH TWO:** Come into the pool with us, beauty.

**HYLAS:** I—no—

**NYMPH ONE:** *(angrier)* Stay with us.

**NYMPH TWO:** Forever.

**NARRATOR:** Before he could react, the two nymphs pulled the poor young boy into the pool. Below the surface, they caressed his body as he struggled for breath. Soon, amid their adoration, he stopped thrashing, and life left him. The nymphs cooed bubbles of pleasure. And there, in the bottom of their enchanted pool, they kept the body of Hylas as their eternal treasure—his beauty forever still.

**HERACLES:** Hylas! Hylas!

**NARRATOR:** Back at the ship, the Argonauts waited for Hylas's return with anxious faces.

**ATALANTA:** He's been gone too long! Something must have happened to him!

**NARRATOR:** Then Heracles himself went to look for the boy. The strongman found Hylas's water jug where he had dropped it by the spring. The Argonauts split up and combed the countryside, but no sign of Hylas was found.

**HERACLES:** *(emotionally)* He has disappeared! Why did I let him go alone?

**JASON:** I'm afraid we must sail on.

**HERACLES:** I refuse!

**JASON:** But that means you have to stay behind!

**HERACLES:** So be it.

**ORPHEUS:** Oh well.

**HERACLES:** I am sorry that I could not have been of more help, but the lad is like my son. I must find him.

**JASON:** You've got to do what you think is best. Farewell, Heracles. Thank you for your help.

**HERACLES:** Farewell, brave companions.

**NARRATOR:** With that, Heracles turned and started walking. His shadow was soon lost amongst the trees. He would wander for many years, searching for Hylas, shouting his name at every step, scouring the earth, but the young boy was never seen again.

The Argo sailed on. The crew kept watch on the sea for signs of danger, but no danger came. Supplies once again ran low, but they feared what disasters lay in wait upon land.

**JASON:** We must go ashore. We will take only a few men—as many as can be spared. The fewer lives risked, the better.

**ATALANTA:** I'm coming, too.

**JASON:** Of course, I count you among the men.

**ATALANTA:** (satisfied) Good.

**ORPHEUS:** I will go, too.

**JASON:** Really? It will be dangerous. Hylas went ashore, and he was never seen again.

**ORPHEUS:** Exactly. Here's hoping.

**NARRATOR:** So Atalanta, Jason, and Orpheus went ashore.

**ORPHEUS:** There are Harpies nearby.

**ATALANTA:** Shhhhhh! How could you know that?

**ORPHEUS:** Just a sixth sense. Whenever something bad is about to happen, I always feel it.

**ATALANTA:** What about something good?

**ORPHEUS:** (surprised) Something good? I don't think that's ever happened.

**NARRATOR:** Above the tree-line rose a plateau. In the middle of this high spot, there was set a long table and seated at it the figure of a solitary, old man.

**ATALANTA:** Someone is there! We must be close to some civilization.

**NARRATOR:** They climbed the steep embankment that led up to where the man sat. The table before him was piled with food—exotic dishes, suckled meats, fine pies, anything the body could wish for. Yet the man looked feeble and emaciated. He was hunched forward and did not look up when the group approached.

**JASON:** Old man, can you tell us where we might find food and water?

**NARRATOR:** The old man looked up, his eyes unglazed, and he jumped.

**PHINEUS:** Ghosts! Or are you real?

**JASON:** We are real. We don't want to hurt you. We just need information.

**PHINEUS:** *(crazy)* Visions of the future? Ghosts from the past? What is the present? Who knows? Who knows?

**ATALANTA:** I think he's gone senile.

**ORPHEUS:** Lucky.

**JASON:** We only need to know where to find—

**NARRATOR:** But Jason was cut off. The old man began to scream, falling from his chair, shrieking to the skies.

*(screeching of the Harpies)*

**PHINEUS:** *(screaming)* The Hounds of Zeus!

**NARRATOR:** Swooping low, three winged creatures darted from the sky. Atalanta pulled Jason to the ground. The beasts shrieked as they came—Harpies, head of a woman, body of a bird. A stench came with them, a stench that made it painful to breathe.

**ATALANTA:** We're trapped!

**NARRATOR:** But the Harpies did not move to attack the travelers or the old man. They simply stopped their dives and flapped their foul wings above the food on the table. As the three watched, the green of the Harpy stench caused the food to wilt—puckering with foulness. The Harpies let out staccato cries, almost laughter, as they watched with their black, bird-like eyes.

*(Harpy screech)*

**ORPHEUS:** What are they doing to the food?

**NARRATOR:** The old man had crawled close to them.

**PHINEUS:** They are my curse, my curse. I am a prophet, and I have offended Zeus with my prophecies. I am doomed to stay on this island—starving—for eternity.

**JASON:** *(whispering)* Why do you not eat?

**PHINEUS:** The Harpies! They come and ruin my food before I can even think of touching it. That is my punishment. Tomorrow, the food will be restored, and a new day of torture will begin! Food, oh how precious it is! Do you perhaps have some on you?

**JASON:** No, we were hoping you had some.

**ATALANTA:** *(angry)* Gods or no gods, no creature should suffer such a fate!

**NARRATOR:** Atalanta rose up, bow in her hand, and released a shaft. *(Shoom!)* A nearby Harpy shrieked, an arrow in its shoulder, and turned its cruel talons toward her. *(Harpy screech)*

Atalanta already had another arrow nocked into her bow. But the Harpies had stopped moving. They hovered in midair, perfectly still. To her surprise, Atalanta found that she, too, was unable to move.

**ATALANTA:** *(through clenched teeth)* What's happening?

**NARRATOR:** The air started to flash, color coming from everywhere—blue, red, green, yellow, orange. The outline of a woman materialized in the midst of the light—a regal woman with purple eyes.

IRIS:  I am Iris, the messenger of Hera. *I have stopped you.*

ATALANTA:  Why?

IRIS:  No man—or woman—may kill the Harpies. They are the Hounds of Zeus.

ATALANTA:  Watch me.

IRIS:  Girl, you would do well to learn some respect for those above you. There is no need for any more fighting here. Phineus has suffered long enough. Olympus has declared his punishment ended. The Harpies will no longer plague him.

NARRATOR:  Atalanta found she could move again as the Harpies began to wing themselves away.

PHINEUS:  Thank you, oh thank you, beautiful messenger of the gods.

IRIS:  I have not saved you. The bravery of these Argonauts has. Give them your thanks.

PHINEUS:  *(turning to Jason)* I am a great seer. Tell me where you are going! I know the way from here to any country.

JASON:  We seek Colchis and the Golden Fleece.

PHINEUS:  The fleece! A mighty quest! But know this—between this shore and that, there are two great rocks that rise out of the sea. A terrible danger lurks between them. Once something has passed between these rocks, they rise up to smash it to smithereens. They are a curse from the heavens.

ATALANTA:  I have heard of these rocks.

PHINEUS:  If you sail between them, they shall crush your craft.

JASON:  Is there a way around them?

PHINEUS:  No, not to Colchis. But do this— capture a bird on these shores. Let the bird fly between the rocks. They will crush it. Then when they are lowering from their attack, quickly sail through.

JASON:  Will that actually work?

ORPHEUS:  Probably not.

PHINEUS:  After you pass through the clashing rocks, you must visit the dark island you see next. There dwell the birds of Ares. They can fire their feathers like arrows, their beaks are as sharp as bronze…and their dung is poison.

ORPHEUS:  Sounds like fun.

ATALANTA:  More birds? Didn't we just fight the Harpies?

JASON:  Yes, but the Harpies had the heads of women, so they were twice as deadly.

ATALANTA:  Watch it!

PHINEUS:  On that island you will find the key to entering the land of Colchis. Many thanks to you, Jason, for saving me, an old man.

IRIS:  The voyage must be continued. Hera has smiled upon you. Sail well, young Jason.

NARRATOR:  Iris raised her hand, and the world about them filled with radiant light. They blinked. They were back on their ship— provisions piled all around them.

**ORPHEUS:** That was easy.

**NARRATOR:** And so they set sail once again. When they neared the two gigantic, clashing rocks that Phineus had spoken of, they released a dove. It met its death between the crags. *(cry of a bird)*

**JASON:** Now is our chance! The rocks are lowering! Row! Row!

*(whooshing of water and wind)*

**NARRATOR:** As the rocks lowered into the water, the Argo sailed between them.

**JASON:** *(happily)* We made it!

**ORPHEUS:** Ahem. I hate to rain on your parade, but there's a dark, menacing island ahead—the home of the birds with killer poop.

**ATALANTA:** That is the island Phineus spoke of. I will have my bow ready for these foul fowls!

**NARRATOR:** All of the Argonauts disembarked on the island, watching the skies warily for a sign of attack. Suddenly the sun above them grew dim.

**ATALANTA:** Is it growing dark so soon?

**JASON:** No! Look!

**NARRATOR:** A flock of beastly birds had risen from the trees ahead. *(shrieking of birds)* Their metallic feathers clicked and clacked as they came. Then the razor-sharp raptors aimed their feathers toward the Argonauts and released them like deadly shafts. *(Zing! Zing! Zing!)*

**JASON:** Get down!

**NARRATOR:** Dodging the feathers of the birds as they sank into the trunks of the trees behind her, Atalanta released a volley of her own arrows. *(twang, twang, twang)* But they merely rebounded off the steely hide of the birds.

**ATALANTA:** Argh! These birds had all the power of their father, Ares! They were built for war.

**JASON:** Watch out!

**NARRATOR:** As the birds swarmed in the sky overhead, poisonous, purple globs of dung fell down toward them. *(Plop, plop, plop)* Some of these globs landed on the Argonauts, and they cried out in pain as the excrement seared their skin like an acid. *(cries of pain)*

**JASON:** Use your shields!

**ATALANTA:** How will we get out of here? Our weapons are useless!

**NARRATOR:** Jason glanced to his side. Orpheus was slumped on a nearby rock—sadly picking at a glob of bird-dung with a stick.

**JASON:** We have one weapon left! *(to Orpheus)* Orpheus, play us a song!

**ORPHEUS:** Eh. I don't feel like it.

**NARRATOR:** Jason could hear the bird dung sizzling as it ate through the shields of his men.

**JASON:** Please, Orpheus! Don't you want to sing about Eurydice one more time? About all that heartbreak you feel?

**ORPHEUS:** No. Actually, I think that's part of my problem. I need to move past the grief.

JASON: What? Don't you feel even a little bit depressed?

ORPHEUS: Nah. This is the best day I've had in months. It's a real breakthrough.

ATALANTA: Hurry, Jason! The dung is eating through our shields!

JASON: Just sing, Orpheus! Sing!

ORPHEUS: Oh, all right. But just so you know, my heart's not going to be in it.

NARRATOR: Orpheus picked up his lyre and began to play. (*sappy lyre strumming*) At the sound of his first note, the birds stopped their attack—hovering above to listen.

ORPHEUS: (*singing*) Oh, Eurydice! Gone forever! Doom! Despair! Death! No hope. No hope. No hope. (*pause*) Hopeless.

NARRATOR: The birds listened silently to Orpheus's lament. Then, when he at last he had finished, they flew into the distance, out over the sea, and dived down into the waves.

JASON: Orpheus! You did it! You killed…literally!

NARRATOR: For the first time, Orpheus smiled.

ORPHEUS: At least I'm good for something.

(*cheers from the Argonauts*)

JASON: You bet you are! It was your music that destroyed the only iron-feathered birds in the world!

NARRATOR: Orpheus's smile sank down into a droop once again.

ORPHEUS: I knew it. Those birds were an endangered species, weren't they? And I wiped them out. (*sigh*) Life's not fair.

JASON: (*sigh*) There's no cheering some people.

NARRATOR: Jason shrugged and turned back to Atalanta.

JASON: Now that the birds are gone, Phineus said we would find the key to entering Colchis here. What do you think he meant?

ATALANTA: Perhaps it is a magical item— or a password etched on a tree.

NARRATOR: The Argonauts headed into the nearby grove, but Atalanta stopped them short. Through the trees ahead, they could see an encampment of soldiers.

ATALANTA: Look there! They must be Colchian soldiers! See how they're dressed? They must have been trapped in these woods by the birds.

NARRATOR: Atalanta raised her bow.

ATALANTA: Let's take care of them before they see us.

JASON: Wait, Atalanta.

ATALANTA: Jason, they're Colchians— enemies.

JASON: We don't know that they're enemies. Maybe they are the key that Phineus spoke of.

NARRATOR: By Jason's command, the Argonauts greeted the Colchian soldiers in friendship. When the Argonauts told them that they had slain the birds of Ares, the soldiers breathed a sigh of relief.

**SOLDIER:** Thank you! You've saved us! We thought we would never make it off this island alive. How can we ever repay you?

**JASON:** You are from Colchis, correct? Will you guide us to your land?

**SOLDIER:** I will do better than that. I will introduce you to our king there! I will tell what brave and noble men you are.

**ATALANTA:** Ahem.

**SOLDIER:** And women.

**NARRATOR:** So the Argonauts reboarded the Argo with the Colchian soldiers in tow and sailed on.

**JASON:** See, Atalanta? These new allies will be the key to us entering Colchis safely.

**ATLANTA:** Fine. You were right. Once.

**NARRATOR:** Soon land was sighted ahead—the hilly coastline of Colchis. A massive city was laid out on the slopes.

**JASON:** There it is! Colchis! We have made it!

**NARRATOR:** The Argonauts let up a cheer. *(cheering of the Argonauts)* Jason stared at the hills of Colchis thoughtfully.

**JASON:** You know, when I first began this quest, I thought there was no way I would ever succeed. But now I see the secret of my success.

**ATALANTA:** Me?

**ORPHEUS:** Sheer dumb luck?

**JASON:** My faithful and brave companions. Who knows? Maybe our worst battles are behind us. Now that we have reached this strange land, perhaps we will be able to gain the Golden Fleece peacefully.

**ORPHEUS:** Fat chance.

**NARRATOR:** On one of the high hills appeared a sprawling palace—the home of King Æetes, keeper of the Golden Fleece, and his deadly daughter, Medea the witch.

## DISCUSSION QUESTIONS

1. Why is teamwork important to the Argonauts?
2. What unique skills does each of the Argonauts bring to the team?
3. Is Jason a good leader? Explain.
4. What new challenges do you think the heroes will encounter in Colchis?

# MEDEA THE WITCH
## TEACHER GUIDE

## BACKGROUND

In spite of the Argonauts' combined heroic prowess, it is not the accompanying heroes (or even Jason for that matter) who really determine the mission's success. Medea, the Colchian witch they add to their group, is the true key to their success. She makes it possible for Jason to obtain the Golden Fleece, she murders her own brother to insure their escape, and, in an episode missing from this version of the story, she stops a giant bronze giant, Talos, from crushing their ship as they sail by his island home. All this she does out of love for Jason, who in return for her help promises to marry her. When the Argonauts return safely to Greece and the Argonauts disband, Jason seems to forget that he has forged an even smaller team—a team of two—just Medea and he. Ultimately, he betrays that team and suffers a brutal revenge.

Medea is one of only two witches mentioned in all of Greek mythology. In this version of the story, she is a one-dimensional villain. Medea was a foreigner, and the Greeks often labeled all foreigners as cruel and barbaric.

In spite of this prejudice the ancient Greek playwright Euripides chose Medea as the subject of one of his most famous tragedies, *Medea*. He found sympathy for her character, seeing her as a wronged individual rather than an evil, foreign sorceress. Although Euripides did not change the bloody details of her revenge, he presented Medea as deeply-flawed human being. It was a step toward humanizing an inhuman character.

## SUMMARY

Jason and the Argonauts arrive at Colchis. Going before Æetes and asking for the fleece only brings jeers from the old king and his witch-daughter, Medea. In order to avoid a battle, Æetes suggests a task for Jason. If he completes the task successfully, he will receive the fleece. Jason accepts.

Knowing that Æetes's task is impossible, the goddess Hera goes to the goddess Aphrodite for a favor. She asks Aphrodite to use the arrows of Eros on Medea and cause her to fall in love with Jason. Medea, suddenly struck with love for the man whom her father has condemned to death, goes to the Argonauts' camp and tells Jason how to complete her father's task.

The next day, Jason faces the task. He must yoke a pair of fire-breathing bulls to a stone plow and sow a field with the teeth of a dragon. Medea has given him the devices that he needs to pass this test though, and he succeeds. When Æetes still refuses to give the fleece to Jason, Medea comes to him in secret and leads him to where it hangs, guarded by an enormous serpent. Medea casts a spell to put the snake to sleep, and Jason steals the fleece.

In return for her help, Medea demands that Jason make her his wife. Jason agrees to this, but once he returns to Greece with his prize, he decides to marry a Greek princess instead. Medea, who has spent many years as Jason's mistress, rages at this news and murders the two young sons she has borne for him. She sews poisonous thread into a dress and sends it as a present to Jason's new bride. She then escapes in a chariot pulled by two dragons.

Jason's story ends with heartbreak. He learns that his sons and his fiancé are dead. He begs the gods to put him out of his misery.

The remains of the Argo, which hang from the ceiling of his palace, fall down upon him and end his life.

## ESSENTIAL QUESTIONS

- Should people ever take revenge?
- Should people make promises they don't intend to keep?
- What happens once a hero's quest is over?
- Does "happily ever after" occur in real life?

## CONNECT

**Euripides's** *Medea* This ancient Greek tragedy dramatizes Medea's revenge upon Jason. The play sheds a somewhat sympathetic light on Medea—allowing her to voice her frustrations against her former love before she enacts her bloody revenge.

**Medea on Trial** Perform a mock murder trial in your classroom, wherein Medea must defend her actions. Ask students to gather information for both the prosecution and defense of Medea.

**The Fate of Orpheus** After his adventures with the Argonauts, Orpheus happens upon a group of maenads, the frenzied female followers of Dionysus. Since he refuses their sexual advances, the maenads murder him— removing his head from his body. The maenads fling Orpheus's severed head into a river, where it continues to sing as it floats down all the way to the ocean. Discuss whether or not this is the type of ending Orpheus would have wanted for his life.

## ANTICIPATORY QUESTIONS

- What new dangers will Jason face in Colchis?

- How could a witch be dangerous to Jason's quest?

## TEACHABLE TERMS

- **Situational Irony** By the end of his story the Golden Fleece has brought Jason only sadness. This is the opposite of what is expected.
- **Red Herring** is a term used to describe something in a story that seems important at the outset but ends up being insignificant. The Golden Fleece, in a way, is an example of this.
- **Mood** The mood changes throughout the course of the story. It begins lightheartedly but ends in sadness and despair.
- **Plot** The plot of Jason's story extends years past his adventures and shows scenes from his later life. Contrast this with the plots of other hero stories, which end much earlier. Discuss why the author of this myth chose to show the later years of Jason's life.
- **Symbolism** The fact that Jason is crushed by the remains of his ship is symbolic of how his quest ultimately destroyed him.

## RECALL QUESTIONS

1. Which goddess does Hera ask for help?
2. What comes from the dragon's teeth that Jason sows in the ground?
3. What kind of creature guards the Golden Fleece?
4. Which three people are murdered by Medea at the end of the story?
5. How does Jason die?

# MEDEA THE WITCH

## JASON AND THE ARGONAUTS: PART III

### CAST

| | |
|---|---|
| **JASON** | *Leader of the Argonauts* |
| **ATALANTA** | *Female Hero* |
| **ORPHEUS** | *Depressed Musician* |
| **ÆETES** | *Aged King of Colchis* |
| **MEDEA** | *Witch, Princess of Colchis* |
| **HERA** | *Queen of the Gods* |
| **APHRODITE** | *Goddess of Love* |
| **PELIAS** | *King, Evil Cousin of Jason* |

**NARRATOR:** Jason and the Argonauts had finally reached their goal—the land of Colchis, where the Golden Fleece was housed. The Colchian soldiers that the Argonauts had rescued from the birds of Ares went to the palace of their king, Æetes, and told him of the deeds of the great heroes.

**ÆETES:** Bring them to the palace.

**NARRATOR:** King Æetes, aged beyond time, still remembered when young Phrixus had brought the Golden Fleece to his realm. Times had changed. He was no longer the trusting, kind man he once was. Age had soured him.

**MEDEA:** Visitors to the throne, Father—Greeks.

**ÆETES:** *(hoarsely, almost a whisper)* You must speak for me, daughter. My voice is nearly gone.

**MEDEA:** *(sarcastically)* Yes, Medea the witch. Medea the speaker for those who cannot speak.

**JASON:** Hail, King Æetes, ruler of Colchis and keeper of the Golden Fleece.

**MEDEA:** Greeks, to what do we owe this honor? His majesty, King Æetes, is not lightly troubled. If we were not civilized people, your heads would have been cut from your necks before you reached our doorstep.

**ATALANTA:** *(under her breath)* I doubt that.

**JASON:** I am Jason, and these are the Argonauts. We have come to claim the Golden Fleece.

**NARRATOR:** Medea sneered at Jason.

**MEDEA:** The fleece? *(laughs)* My father will give the fleece to no one—especially not to a filthy Greek.

**JASON:** The fleece rightfully belongs to my people. If you won't give it to us, we will have to take it.

**MEDEA:** *(sarcastically)* Yes, you are quite frightening—all five of you. I see no danger of the fleece going anywhere.

**ÆETES:** *(hoarsely)* Medea. Medea.

**NARRATOR:** The king motioned for his daughter to draw near to him.

**ÆETES:** Tell them that we will give them the fleece.

**MEDEA:** *(quietly)* What? Father, are you mad?

**ÆETES:** They must first complete a task for us—one that can never be completed. In this manner, we can kill these trespassers without spilling our own blood.

**MEDEA:** *(sarcastically)* What a wise father I have. *(loudly)* Greeks, we have decided that we shall give you the fleece—if you, Jason, pledge to complete a task of our choosing.

**ATALANTA:** It's a trap. Don't do it, Jason.

**JASON:** Of course, it's a trap. But how else will we get the fleece?

**ATALANTA:** We will fight.

**JASON:** Us against a whole army? This is my quest, and I will face their challenge—alone. *(loudly)* King Æetes, do you promise to give us the fleece?

**MEDEA:** If you complete this task successfully, it shall be yours. If you fail, your men shall return home—empty-handed.

**JASON:** I will take this challenge.

**MEDEA:** Good. We shall meet on the challenge field tomorrow. Bring nothing but

your sword. You shall face the challenge alone, bold one. If you fail, I will dance upon your corpse.

**ORPHEUS:** That's a pleasant thought.

**NARRATOR:** And so the Argonauts were dismissed. As they walked back to the ship, Atalanta stalked angrily ahead.

**ATALANTA:** Stupid, stupid, stupid! They will give you an impossible task! Then where will we be?

**JASON:** At least, only *I* will lose my life.

**ATALANTA:** Stupid! I didn't travel all this way just to watch you die.

**JASON:** Then don't watch.

**NARRATOR:** Night fell, but Jason found he could not sleep. Tomorrow he faced his destiny. He looked up into the night sky.

**JASON:** Master Chiron, are you there? I face a great challenge tomorrow. But how do I prepare for it if I don't know what it is?

**NARRATOR:** The stars overhead twinkled but did not respond.

**JASON:** Maybe that's why you spent so many years on my education—to prepare me for any challenge.

**NARRATOR:** He saw the outline of his centaur master in the stars. For a second he thought he saw the constellation bow its head.

**JASON:** *(sigh)* I just wish I had paid more attention. Think, Jason, think!

**NARRATOR:** Higher than the stars, the goddess Hera was looking down upon Jason.

**HERA:** Oh, Jason. I have seen you safely this far, but the Colchian king and his daughter plan to destroy you. I hate to admit it, but success in this matter will take more power than just mine.

**NARRATOR:** Hera walked through the silent halls of Olympus to the sitting room of her nemesis, the mighty Aphrodite.

**APHRODITE:** (*sweet voice*) Hera? To what do I owe this pleasure?

**HERA:** Oh, please. I know you like me as little as I like you. I have come to strike a deal.

**APHRODITE:** (*sarcastically*) Getting right to the point, I see. What do you want?

**HERA:** I know that your cuddly little son, Eros, has certain talents with his bow and arrow. I require his services.

**APHRODITE:** Ah, but these services do not come lightly. If you require my help, you must give me something in return.

**HERA:** (*coldly*) You may name your price.

**APHRODITE:** Gladly. Hephaestus, my ugly husband, bores me. His looks leave something to be desired. Therefore, I have turned my desires elsewhere.

**HERA:** It is not my concern that you are having an affair. If it were, I would *always* be concerned.

**APHRODITE:** Nice. The point is… Hephaestus grows suspicious. He suspects that I am involved with the God of War, your mightier son.

**HERA:** Is there anyone you *aren't* involved with?

**APHRODITE:** Cute. You are his mother. Soothe his concerns. Blind him to my actions, and I will grant you this favor.

**NARRATOR:** Hera bristled at this. After all, she was the protector of marriage. But then she thought of Jason.

**HERA:** Fine. It will be done.

**APHRODITE:** Oooh! Then the arrows of love are at your command.

**NARRATOR:** And so a bargain was struck between the goddesses.
Medea had gone to the palace rooftop to watch the Argo and its crew from afar.

**MEDEA:** These fools! They think they can waltz into our country and demand our greatest treasure! Ha! Tomorrow they will find out the hard way not to toy with Colchis!

**NARRATOR:** Invisible to Medea, Eros, the god of love, appeared behind her and fired an arrow into her heart.

**MEDEA:** (*cry of shock*) Ah!

**NARRATOR:** Medea felt herself overcome with instant passion. And the object of her affection? Jason, the leader of the Argonauts.

**MEDEA:** What is happening? How can I feel love for that man? He is my enemy!

**NARRATOR:** Then she nearly swooned when she realized what she had done earlier that day.

**MEDEA:** I have sentenced him to death!

**NARRATOR:** Meanwhile, Jason was standing near his ship, still thoughtfully searching the stars.

**MEDEA:** Pssst.

**JASON:** *(startled)* Who's there?

**NARRATOR:** A cloaked figure approached across the sands toward Jason. The hero drew his sword. *(Shing!)* The figure threw back her hood, revealing her face. It was the princess Medea.

**JASON:** *(surprised)* You! What are you doing here?

**MEDEA:** I—I've come to tell you that the task you will face tomorrow is impossible.

**JASON:** You call that news?

**MEDEA:** My father owns a pair of fire-breathing bulls, fearsome creatures that are untamable. But he will ask you to yoke them, drive them, and use them to plow the field.

**JASON:** *(sarcastically)* Sounds like a cinch.

**MEDEA:** Then he will ask you to sow the field with the teeth of a dragon. Once these teeth have been planted, they will instantly grow into an army of phantom warriors—too many to conquer. Even if you managed to harness the bulls, you could never defeat this army.

**JASON:** I don't understand. If I can't win, why are you telling me this?

**MEDEA:** But you *can* win. That is why I have come. I cannot bear to see you die.

**JASON:** *(confused)* Has something changed?

**MEDEA:** Everything. *(pause)* I am a sorceress. I can help you. Here. Take this ointment. Cover your body with it. It will protect you from the fire of the bulls.

**JASON:** Great. But what about the phantom army?

**MEDEA:** This.

**NARRATOR:** She held up a simple rock.

**JASON:** A rock?

**MEDEA:** Yes, there is a secret to defeating the men who spring from the dragon's teeth. Throw this rock into their midst, and they will turn upon one another—slaying themselves.

**JASON:** Fantastic.

**NARRATOR:** Suddenly, Jason paused. Was this another trick? He remembered how cold and cruel Medea had been in the throne room earlier that day.

**JASON:** Why are you doing this?

**MEDEA:** *(sadly)* Isn't it obvious? *(pause)* I do all this for you, but I ask one thing.

**JASON:** Name it.

**MEDEA:** You must take me back to Greece with you and make me your wife.

**NARRATOR:** Jason thought. He barely knew this girl—a girl who had recently smiled at the prospect of his death. Now, she was asking to be his bride. Could he love her?

**JASON:** My wife?

**MEDEA:** Yes. That is what I want to be more than anything in the world. Promise you will wed me, and I will help you.

**NARRATOR:** Everything about this seemed wrong to Jason, but he felt he had no choice. He could not do this task on his own.

**JASON:** I swear it.

**NARRATOR:** Medea smiled.

**MEDEA:** Until tomorrow then, handsome Jason. Fight well.

**NARRATOR:** She slipped back into the night as quickly as she had come. After she had gone, Jason sat down and pondered the magnitude of what he had promised. He looked up into the stars again, but the outline of his old master seemed fainter—more distant. Had he done the right thing?

The morning broke bright on the kingdom of Colchis. Near the challenge field the king Æetes was seated in a pavilion with his nobles. Medea was at his side, hiding the emotions she felt welling up inside of her. Jason took the field—sword and stone in hand.

**MEDEA:** (shouting) King Æetes wishes that you die well. You have been given your task. Release the bulls.

**NARRATOR:** Released from a great iron wagon, two giant bulls charged forth, their thick hide bristling with spikes, their breath flaming out before them. (whooshing of flame) From the sidelines Atalanta and Orpheus watched the creatures bear down on Jason.

**ATALANTA:** Stupid! (screaming) Do something, Jason!

**NARRATOR:** At once, the heaving bulls covered Jason with a fiery blast from their nostrils. (whooshing of flame) The crowd gasped, but when the smoke cleared, Jason was still standing. He pulled a long chain from his side and threw it about the two beasts' necks. They pulled away in surprise, but he had already hooked them to a large stone plow. As they pulled, the plow furrowed deep rows. Into these rows from a sack at his side, Jason dropped the dragon's teeth he had been given that morning.

**ATALANTA:** What is he doing?

**ORPHEUS:** (waking up) What? Who?

**NARRATOR:** As Medea had said they would, warriors began rising from the rows— metal helmets showing first, followed by fearsome torsos and brandished swords. There were hundreds of them. Jason turned to face them, rock in hand. He threw it into their midst. The phantom warriors fell upon one another, slashing and hacking until all their bodies littered the ground. Medea breathed a secret sigh of relief as Jason stood victorious.

**JASON:** (winded) Your majesty, I have completed this task. I must ask for the fleece.

**NARRATOR:** Shaking, the old king rose from his seat.

**ÆETES:** (hoarsely, but loud) You shall have no fleece!

**NARRATOR:** Jason's heart sank.

**MEDEA:** (coldly) This Greek has obviously cheated. He will receive no prize.

**NARRATOR:** Jason started to object, but Medea swiftly motioned for him to remain silent. She had anticipated this.

**ATALANTA:**    I don't believe it! Those cheaters! We won fair and square!

**JASON:**    No, Atalanta. It is fine. They can keep their fleece.

**NARRATOR:**    So, by Jason's command, the Greeks allowed the situation to pass. The king and his court returned to the palace, and the Argonauts slunk back to their ship. Medea was waiting there when they returned.

**ATALANTA:**    What does this cow want?

**JASON:**    Atalanta, silence. It was she who helped me to live today.

**ATALANTA:**    Helped you? What do you mean?

**JASON:**    I will tell you more later.

**MEDEA:**    Prepare your men to sail.

**JASON:**    But the fleece!

**MEDEA:**    Exactly. Now we must go and retrieve it.

**NARRATOR:**    As Medea watched her coldly, Atalanta pulled Jason aside.

**ATALANTA:**    Jason, should we trust this ice princess?

**JASON:**    We have no choice.

**ATALANTA:**    There is always a choice. Why is she helping us all of a sudden?

**MEDEA:**    *(to Jason)* We must hurry, my love.

**ATALANTA:**    Oh, I see. Yes, hurry along…love.

**NARRATOR:**    Medea scowled at Atalanta and then led Jason swiftly away from the port, toward a secluded grove of trees.

**MEDEA:**    The fleece is there in that grove.

**JASON:**    Is it not hidden?

**MEDEA:**    There is no need to hide it. It is guarded by a giant serpent—one who sharpens his teeth with the bones of adventurers like you. Now, quickly!

**NARRATOR:**    They entered the grove. Jason saw the serpent—its monstrous body coiled around a large, gnarled tree. Then he saw the Golden Fleece, the object of all his travels. Shining like the sun, it hung on a branch haphazardly, as if it had been forgotten there. Every ordeal he had passed to behold such a thing was suddenly worth it. This was a treasure worth dying for.

The serpent's eyes opened and shone with an eerie, yellow light. *(sound of a snake hissing)* Medea reached into a pouch slung at her side and pulled out a handful of dust.

**MEDEA:**    It's time for this serpent to slumber.

**NARRATOR:**    Medea threw the dust into the air, and it fell upon the snout of the snake. Then Medea began to sing.

**MEDEA:**    *(singing)*

**NARRATOR:**    It was the strangest song Jason had ever heard. He heard the voices of those he had once known in it—Chiron, his mother—and other voices, voices he had not yet heard but someday would—his children, his wife….The serpent's eyes grew heavy, and it rested its head upon the ground. *(sounds of a snake snoring)* Then Jason realized that Medea had stopped singing.

**MEDEA:** Now, my love, the fleece is yours to take.

**NARRATOR:** Jason gave Medea a questioning look but did not falter. He walked forth and scaled the side of the slumbering serpent. From this height, he was able to reach to the branch on which the fleece hung. Then he grasped it, the treasure of kings.

**JASON:** It is mine! Finally!

**MEDEA:** Now it is time to flee.

**NARRATOR:** The Argonauts were making the final preparations to leave when Jason and Medea returned. The hero held up the Golden Fleece, and all the men cheered. (*cheers of the men*)

**ATALANTA:** Look!

**NARRATOR:** A troop of warriors, their shields and spears flashing, appeared from the palace. (*sounds of angry soldiers*)

**MEDEA:** It is my brother! He is bringing warriors to apprehend us! My father must have discovered my treachery!

**JASON:** Onto the ship!

**NARRATOR:** As the soldiers closed the distance between them, the Argonauts piled aboard the ship. Jason turned to help Medea aboard, but she shrugged him off.

**MEDEA:** Wait here. I will stall them.

**NARRATOR:** Medea ran up the rocky beach to meet the charging troops—waving her arms.

**MEDEA:** Brother! I can explain! Stop your march! A truce!

**NARRATOR:** Atalanta hissed in Jason's ear.

**ATALANTA:** Now's our chance! Let's go!

**JASON:** No, we can't leave Medea. I made a promise to her.

**ATALANTA:** You promised to take that witch back with us? Jason, she can't be trusted.

**JASON:** She can. I gave her my word.

**NARRATOR:** Medea had now stopped the troops. A lone man came forward to meet with her—her brother, the prince. Yet when he drew near, a knife, drawn from under Medea's robe, glinted in the sun, and she drove it into his throat. (*dying sounds*) Jason stared in shock as Medea returned to the ship.

**ATALANTA:** What a lovely girlfriend you have there, Jason.

**MEDEA:** (*out of breath*) Now they are leaderless. That will keep them from pursuing us.

**JASON:** That was your brother! You just killed your own brother!

**MEDEA:** Yes. Do you doubt my love now? Shove off!

**NARRATOR:** With the corpse of Medea's brother lying fresh on the rocky beach, the Argonauts pushed away from the shores of Colchis. As Jason stood at the prow, he felt Medea's adoring eyes upon him. He shuddered.

**JASON:** What have I done?

**NARRATOR:** The trip home was filled with many perils, but the Argonauts had Medea. Time and time again, she saved them from certain death—all for the love of her Jason.

When they reached the shores of Jason's kingdom, it was time for the Argonauts to part ways after sharing the journey of a lifetime.

**JASON:** I cannot thank you all enough! Now I must go face my detestable cousin and retrieve my throne. I will never forget any of you or the aid you gave me!

*(cheers from the Argonauts)*

**NARRATOR:** One by one the companions parted ways.

**JASON:** Goodbye, Atalanta. I never could have made it without you.

**ATALANTA:** I know. You weren't too bad yourself.

**JASON:** And, Orpheus, your songs are truly the most…um…powerful tunes in the world. I hope someday you find some happiness.

**ORPHEUS:** I'm not going to hold my breath.

**NARRATOR:** Atalanta drew Jason aside.

**ATALANTA:** Jason, I know you have pledged yourself to this Medea woman, but take care. I fear for you. Perhaps we should stay until you have faced King Pelias.

**JASON:** All will be fine. I must go face Pelias myself. I have my prize. Thanks to you. Farewell.

**NARRATOR:** So hesitantly Atalanta bade Jason goodbye. She and Orpheus sauntered into the distance—and into legend. Jason never saw or heard from them again.

**MEDEA:** What is your plan now, my love?

**JASON:** I will show him the fleece—proving myself. Then he will give me back the throne that is rightfully mine.

**MEDEA:** Will he? He will not give that throne up without a fight. Let me play a trick upon him. Let me win back your throne for you.

**JASON:** But the fleece was the entire point of my quest.

**MEDEA:** He deserves such a trick for what he did to you, and he will get his due reward.

**JASON:** I will do what you think is best.

**NARRATOR:** The kingdom was unaware that Jason and his crew had returned. So Medea presented herself at Pelias's palace as a sorceress from afar. In the Argonauts' absence King Pelias had grown even older and fatter. His days were slipping by him.

**MEDEA:** Wise king, allow me to show you my magic. I have discovered the secret of eternal life.

**NARRATOR:** To demonstrate, Medea brought forth a gray ram, withered with age. She took her knife, cut the ram apart, and threw it into a bubbling cauldron. To the amazement of all the court, a newborn lamb sprang forth from the rising smoke of the spell. *(bleating of a lamb, gasping from the crowd)*

**MEDEA:** This rejuvenation can be done to you as well!

**PELIAS:** Then let it be done at once!

**NARRATOR:** Pelias had his own daughters, dressed in ceremonial black, surround him with their sharpened knives.

**MEDEA:** Cut him up and place him in the pot!

**PELIAS:** *(dying cries)*

**NARRATOR:** Medea chanted while Pelias's dying cries filled the throne room. When the grisly task was done, every eye was on the boiling pot, but no young king sprang forth.

**MEDEA:** *(spitting)* So passes an evil king. *(evil laugh)* Murdered by his own kin!

**NARRATOR:** The entire court gasped, Medea's eyes flashed, and she disappeared in a cloud of smoke. Medea returned to Jason and told him all that had transpired. Upon hearing of her foul trick, Jason felt disgusted.

**MEDEA:** The throne is yours again.

**JASON:** You have shamed me! Why did you do such an evil thing?

**MEDEA:** *(angrily)* To win back your kingdom! I have proved my love to you. Now, you must prove yours. You must marry me.

**JASON:** I have promised that I will do so, but I will not take back this kingdom. It was reclaimed through witchcraft and deceit. I want nothing to do with it.

**MEDEA:** I do not care where we live—as long as we are together.

**NARRATOR:** So the two fled the kingdom Jason had journeyed so far to reclaim and sought refuge in Corinth. There he pledged himself to Medea, but they did not marry. She bore him two sons. He had heard them laughing long ago in Medea's song. As Jason grew older, they were the one tiny bit of happiness in his life. He often thought of his old master, Chiron, and his great adventure for the Golden Fleece. The fleece hung as a relic now in his home, but it was meaningless. Where was the young man who once dreamt great dreams? How had this woman poisoned him?

Then, one day, the king of Corinth came to visit Jason. With him he brought his beautiful daughter. The king had heard of Jason's great deeds and his abandoned kingdom. He deemed him to be a worthy match for his radiant child. Jason looked into the girl's youthful eyes. In them, he saw hope. This was his love—not the black-hearted creature who shared his home. He felt young again, and rashly, he accepted the king's offer to be her husband. Up on Olympus, Hera mourned.

**HERA:** Oh, Jason, had I known what trouble I would bring you, I would have never linked you to this witch. Now, she will take her revenge and ruin the beautiful hero I have created. I will remember you, Jason, as you once were—shining and young. Great was your rise. Great will be your fall.

**NARRATOR:** When Medea heard of the engagement between Jason and the Corinthian princess, she was infuriated. The magic spell of Eros had grown thin. Love no longer held her heart. Hatred lived there.

**MEDEA:** *(crazy)* Deceiver! After all I have done for him! All that I have gone through! I have borne him sons! I shall poison his bride and ruin his happiness, for he has ruined mine! I have forsaken my father, killed my own brother, left my home—and for what? For what?

**NARRATOR:** In her madness, she took a marvelous gown and poisoned it so that any maiden who wore it would be consumed in flame. She sent it as an anonymous wedding present to the princess. She then took her two young sons into a closed room—dagger in her hand. Their innocent minds knew nothing was wrong.

**MEDEA:** I will destroy everything he has ever loved. I have given these life, and I can take it from them.

**NARRATOR:** The coldness of her heart became the coldness of her hand as she put the dagger to her own sons. Screaming in anger, their blood on her gown, she ran to the roof. There she conjured herself a chariot pulled by two dragons, and, jumping inside, she shrieked with joy, for her revenge was complete.

**MEDEA:** *(crazed laugh)*

**NARRATOR:** The chariot took to the sky, and she was taken out of Jason's life forever. The news came to Jason all at once. His bride-to-be had been consumed in flames—his children murdered. His mad-witch lover had fled to the skies. He was numb. He wanted to cry, but he could not. He stumbled into his meeting hall where the remnants of his once great ship, the Argo, hung suspended from the ceiling. All his life, all his adventures had come to this. How had he been so foolish? Through a window he could see the sky. The stars were just beginning to appear. He saw the figure of his old master forming in them.

**JASON:** *(sobbing)* Master—why? I don't want to live. Gods above, take me from this world!

**NARRATOR:** As if in answer to his prayer, he heard a dry rope crack. He closed his eyes and smiled. Hera had heard his final cry.

With a great groan, the enormous skeleton of the Argo crashed down upon him. *(crashing sounds)*

In that moment, he was free. Free from the pain of the world, free from grief. All was blackness around him. He saw a wide river and on the far side the silhouette of his old master—beckoning him home.

## DISCUSSION QUESTIONS

1. Where did Jason go wrong? Explain.
2. Is Medea a villain or a victim? Explain.
3. How would Jason's story have gone if Medea had not been his ally? Explain.
4. What role does the Golden Fleece play in the story? Was the quest in vain? Explain.
5. How is Jason's death symbolic?

# THE INVENTOR'S APPRENTICE
## TEACHER GUIDE

## BACKGROUND

Inventions have the power to change society for the better. Inventions such as the telephone, the light bulb, and the personal computer have revolutionized the world we live in; however, other inventions, like the atomic bomb, possess the ability to destroy society. Inventions are only a tool in the hand of the user and can be used for good or for evil.

Daedalus is Greek mythology's famous inventor. While Greek myths are filled with fighting men, Daedalus is famous for using his mind (rather than his sword) to make a name for himself. Daedalus's story is entwined with that of Theseus the hero. Theseus has many adventures, but his most famous is his journey to the island-kingdom of Crete to slay the Minotaur, a half-man, half-bull beast that lives in a subterranean maze called the Labyrinth. As you might expect, Theseus succeeds in slaying the Minotaur. In some versions of the story he his helped by Ariadne, the princess of Crete, who tells him the secrets of the Labyrinth. In others, it is Daedalus who helps the hero.

Daedalus is the ancient Greek version of Thomas Edison. He originally lived in Athens with a workshop on the Acropolis, and his amazing inventions both fascinated and terrified the people who lived there. Just as Edison was "the Wizard of Menlo Park," Daedalus was the "Artificer of the Acropolis." But his true fame did not begin until he journeyed to Crete and offered his services to King Minos. Pasiphaë, the wife of King Minos, was under a curse from Poseidon, who had made her lust after Minos's prize bull. She asked Daedalus to construct a way for her to mate with the bull, and Daedalus complied by making a wooden cow for the queen to hide in. From this unnatural union the Minotaur was born. Minos instructed Daedalus to build a prison for the Minotaur, an elaborate maze beneath his palace where those who challenged Minos's rule would meet a dark and grisly death. It became Daedalus's greatest achievement. We still use the word *labyrinth* today.

But this story takes place before these events. Daedalus is still living in Athens, trying to make a name for himself as an inventor. He has not yet learned the price that he will someday pay for fame.

## SUMMARY

Athens is the home of Daedalus, and he has made many wondrous inventions to delight the people there. With him lives his nephew, Perdix, whom the inventor considers to be a dull-witted boy. One day while Daedalus and Perdix are visiting the beach, Perdix finds a fish skeleton. In secret he uses the design in the fish's ribs to engineer a saw. When he presents his new invention to his uncle, Daedalus is overcome with jealousy because the boy has created an amazing invention. Perdix also shows another fabulous invention to his uncle, the compass. (In the original myth this was a drawing compass. Here it is a navigational compass.) In a moment of blind fury, Daedalus pushes the boy out of the high window of his workshop. As the boy falls to his death, he miraculously transforms into a bird. The goddess of wisdom, Athena appears to Daedalus and explains that she has saved the boy's life and chastises the inventor for using her gifts to further his own vain ambition. She tells him he will journey to Crete and there fashion his greatest creation. At the end of the story, the narrator notes that the perdix is a type of bird who never builds its nest too high and flies only when necessary because he remembers his fall from the Acropolis.

## ESSENTIAL QUESTIONS

- Is fame a worthwhile goal?
- How can jealousy be destructive?
- How can inventions change the world?

## CONNECTIONS

*Frankenstein* by Mary Shelley tells of an obsessed inventor named Frankenstein, who wishes to create life, but once his goal is achieved, he learns the downside to playing God. Likewise Daedalus is an inventor on a quest for fame, and the murder of his nephew shows him just how far his ambition has taken him.

## ANTICIPATORY QUESTIONS

- What inventions have changed the world?
- Who are some famous inventors?
- Can you tell about a time when you experienced jealousy?

## TEACHABLE TERMS

- **Inner conflict** By the end of the story, Daedalus has a serious inner conflict brewing between his adult obligations and his jealousy of his nephew's genius.
- **Deus ex machina** is characterized as an out-of-the-blue solution to an otherwise unsolvable problem. Perdix's transformation into a bird and Athena's appearance illustrate this term. It also alludes to the term's literal meaning: "god out of a machine."
- **Jargon** *Chisel* and *awl* referenced on pg. 124 are specific terms that a woodworker would use to describe certain tools, but

that might be absent from a layperson's vocabulary.
- **Aside** An example of a speech delivered by a character that cannot be heard by the other characters onstage occurs on pg. 125.

## RECALL QUESTIONS

1. What two inventions does Perdix create?
2. What inspires the creation of one of his inventions?
3. What place has Daedalus always dreamed of visiting?
4. What does Daedalus hope to accomplish with his inventions?
5. What is strange about the perdix bird?

# THE INVENTOR'S APPRENTICE

## CAST

**DAEDALUS**    *Athenian Inventor*
**PERDIX**    *His Young Nephew*
**ATHENA**    *Goddess of Wisdom*

**NARRATOR:** Daedalus the Athenian lived in a tall tower near the Acropolis. He was a great inventor, and his workshop was filled with all sorts of bizarre creations that showcased his skill. The Athenians spoke in awe of the Artificer of the Acropolis. Daedalus had created pictures that seemed to move and a device that could trap sound and later set it free again. Daedalus did not live alone. His young nephew, Perdix, lived with him as well. His sister, wishing the best for her son, had apprenticed him to Daedalus—to learn his wondrous craft.

Every so often the inventor and his nephew would take a walk to the seashore.

Perdix would examine the shells upon the beach, while Daedalus watched the horizon.

**PERDIX:** Uncle, each time we visit the sea, you stare at the horizon. What are you trying to see?

**DAEDALUS:** Do you know what lies out over the sea, Perdix?

**PERDIX:** Other lands. Barbarians.

**DAEDALUS:** No, not barbarians, boy. Out there in the sea is the island of Crete. It is ruled by King Minos, the wealthiest king in the world. He lives in a palace made of gold.

**PERDIX:** What does that have to do with us?

**DAEDALUS:** Everything. If you want to invent something truly magnificent, you must have the proper funding. The right backer.

**PERDIX:** But all your inventions—

**NARRATOR:** The inventor turned and looked scornfully at the boy.

**DAEDALUS:** They're toys. Worthless.

**PERDIX:** They make people happy.

**DAEDALUS:** Why do you think an inventor invents?

**PERDIX:** To help others. To make life easier.

**NARRATOR:** The inventor laughed grimly.

**DAEDALUS:** That's what I used to think. People are amused by our toys for a while, Perdix, but then they forget. They forget who first created that technology. Then what have you got? Nothing.

**PERDIX:** Then what *do* you want, uncle?

**DAEDALUS:** To create something that will last forever. To create something that people will remember for generations to come—something immortal.

**PERDIX:** Only the gods can do such a thing.

**DAEDALUS:** True. They were the first inventors. Just as the names of the gods are stamped on their creation, so will my name be stamped on mine. Then both creation and creator will live forever.

**NARRATOR:** Perdix noticed something white sticking up through the sand. He knelt and pulled it loose. It was the skeleton of a fish.

As they walked home, Daedalus brooded while Perdix examined the bones of the fish, turning it over and over and pulling the sharp edges back and forth across his finger. When they reached their home, the sky was almost dark.

**PERDIX:** Uncle, when will I be allowed to invent?

**DAEDALUS:** You? Not yet. You're still a boy.

**PERDIX:** But I—

**DAEDALUS:** I can't waste materials on your foolish ideas! Now, let's go to bed.

**NARRATOR:** When his uncle was fast asleep, Perdix snuck from his pallet and made his way into his uncle's workshop. He had been struck with an idea. He found a thin sheet of bronze, laid it upon the workbench, and taking his uncle's tools—hammer, chisel, and awl—prepared for his task. Before he began, he removed the fish skeleton from his pocket.

Perdix spent the night eagerly working on his first invention. Using the fish ribs as his guide, he recreated a similar shape in the metal. When he had finished, he tested his creation. As Perdix pulled the piece of bronze across the table top, its metal teeth dug into the wood—cutting deeper with each pull.

**PERDIX:** *(excitedly)* It works!

**NARRATOR:** He hid his invention and all traces of its construction and fell asleep.

**DAEDALUS:** Perdix, if you're not going to pay attention, there's no point in me demonstrating this for you.

**PERDIX:** I'm sorry, uncle. I'm so tired.

**DAEDALUS:** So you've said for the past few days. What has been keeping you from sleep?

**PERDIX:** *(timidly)* If I tell you, uncle, will you promise not to be angry with me?

**DAEDALUS:** Why would I be angry?

**NARRATOR:** The boy smiled.

**PERDIX:** Wait here a moment. I'll be right back.

**NARRATOR:** Perdix dashed to his sleeping chamber.

**DAEDALUS:** *(annoyed)* What has the boy done now?

**NARRATOR:** He returned with a shining piece of metal in his hands. Jagged teeth ran along its bottom side, and a handle was attached to one end. The boy held it forth proudly.

**PERDIX:** Here, uncle. This is *my* invention.

NARRATOR: Daedalus stared at the piece in disbelief.

DAEDALUS: What is it?

PERDIX: (excitedly) I call it a *saw*. It will be much quicker and more accurate than an axe. See the teeth? They dig into wood. I got the idea when we were on the beach. I saw a fish skeleton. But wait—that's not all.

NARRATOR: As the boy ran back to his room, Daedalus continued to stare at the saw. Its craftsmanship was absolutely perfect. The boy—the one he had always dismissed as a fool—was, in fact, a genius. Daedalus now held in his hands a perfect invention—brilliant, yet practical.

Perdix finally returned. He held a small circular object in his hand now.

PERDIX: This one took me much more time. I'm sorry I hid these things from you. I was so afraid you would be angry.

NARRATOR: Shaking, Daedalus took the circle from the boy. In its center was a needle. As he turned it his hands, the needle continued to point the same direction.

PERDIX: See? It always points north.

NARRATOR: The boy moved toward the window and looked out over the sea.

PERDIX: I know you spoke of Crete, uncle, and the riches there, but there are so many people here who can be helped. That's what I wanted to show you. Inventions should help people. Otherwise, they're worthless.

NARRATOR: Daedalus looked up suddenly, his face a mask of hatred.

DAEDALUS: (aside) What is this brat trying to do, anyway? I've given him a home and shelter, and how does he repay me? This was his plan all along, wasn't it? Steal the old man's secrets—and then surpass him!

NARRATOR: There was the boy silhouetted against the window—the boy who had effortlessly created two perfect inventions in the course of a week. Daedalus could not imagine the works such hands would be capable of—the wonders that such a mind could create.

DAEDALUS: (aside) It would be so easy, wouldn't it? One little push. Then these inventions would be mine. What am I saying? They're probably mine anyway. I've been talking in my sleep, and this little thief has been listening. Now he's trying to pass them off as his. No, you won't get away with it! I've caught you—like a bird in a net!

NARRATOR: Daedalus was moving forward before he knew it. It would take only one push. He knew the fall from the tower would kill him easily.

PERDIX: Uncle! What are you doing? Uncle!

NARRATOR: Perdix was a small boy, so it did not take much force to topple him over the sill. Daedalus leaned out of the window, his eyes greedily waiting for the boy's death. Perdix was spiraling down, down, down to the cobblestones below. As he fell, his arms flapped vainly at the air. In that instant Daedalus realized the magnitude of his actions.

DAEDALUS: (in shock) What have I done?

NARRATOR: Yet before the moment of impact, something strange happened. Perdix's white, flapping arms changed, somehow catching the breeze. The boy was no longer falling downward but *flying* upward. In fact, he was no longer a boy, but a bird. The bird winged itself away into the distance.

**DAEDALUS:** *(sadly)* Perdix! Perdix! Come back! Forgive me! *(quietly)* Forgive me!

**NARRATOR:** The inventor turned from the window and buried his face in his hands.

**ATHENA:** Daedalus.

**DAEDALUS:** *(scared)* Ah!

**NARRATOR:** A tall, elegant woman was standing in the midst of the room. A golden helmet covered her hair.

**DAEDALUS:** *(in awe)* Is it you, Lady Athena?

**NARRATOR:** Daedalus fell to his face.

**ATHENA:** I have saved your nephew from death. I have transformed him into a bird that will forever bear his name.

**DAEDALUS:** Oh thank you! Thank you for saving him. I was wicked and jealous—so jealous of the boy! I don't know what came over me.

**ATHENA:** Foolishly have you wished for fame. Wisdom should be used to better all mankind—not just yourself.

**DAEDALUS:** Yes! I have been a fool.

**ATHENA:** I have come to tell you that one day fame will come to you. You will design a structure so ingenious that it will be remembered for thousands of years.

**NARRATOR:** The inventor's face filled with happiness.

**ATHENA:** But your success comes at a price. Even now, the city-guards of Athens are heading here to arrest you. Did you think no one would see you push the boy from the window? King Aegeus will banish you from my beloved city.

**DAEDALUS:** Where—where must I go?

**ATHENA:** Across the sea—to the kingdom of Minos, the bull king. You will find in him a heart much like your own. You two deserve each other.

**DAEDALUS:** But this news seems so hollow now.

**ATHENA:** Remember, Daedalus, wisdom is only wisdom when used for good.

**DAEDALUS:** I will remember.

**NARRATOR:** And with that the goddess of wisdom left the repentant inventor. To this day, the perdix—or as he is known in other lands, the partridge—builds his nest close to the ground and only flies when it is absolutely necessary. He remembers all too well his great fall from the heights of the Acropolis.

## DISCUSSION QUESTIONS

1. Should Athena have punished Daedalus more severely than she did? Explain.
2. Once again this is a myth that explains something in nature. Compare and contrast this myth with "Narcissus and Echo."
3. Daedalus will appear in the next myth as well. What do you think will happen in that myth?
4. Is Daedalus *evil* or just *human*? Explain.

# DAEDALUS & ICARUS
## TEACHER GUIDE

## BACKGROUND

Flight was the goal of the Wright brothers at Kitty Hawk, North Carolina where they performed the first controlled and sustained heavier-than-air human flight in 1903. Up until this point, it seemed that flight would never be a viable means of transportation. Flashforward one-hundred years to where we live now: a world where hundreds of flights take off every hour. But according to mythology, the Wright brothers were not the first to soar with the precision of the birds.

As you learned in the previous myth, Daedalus was Greek mythology's most famous inventor, a man whose mind created the enigma called the Labyrinth. His second great achievement—human flight—was an invention of necessity, a last ditch effort for freedom. Daedalus and his young son Icarus were imprisoned by King Minos on the island of Crete. Minos controlled the seas, but he did not control the sky, so Daedalus and Icarus took to the sky.

This myth is one of the most famous in mythology. It is a cautionary tale for children who should listen to the advice of their elders. It is also a warning against *hubris*, or uncontrollable arrogance. Daedalus and Icarus should not have attempted to soar in the heavens. Only gods are allowed to do that. It also becomes more interesting when read in conjunction with the previous myth. In that story Daedalus tried to take the life of a young boy, who was instead transformed into a bird. In this myth Daedalus has his own son, Icarus. In order to live a free life, he transforms his own boy into a bird, one who

flies too high—with disastrous results. It's a cycle of divine justice that takes Icarus away from Daedalus.

After the death of his son, Daedalus has even further adventures. He flies to Sicily and hangs up his wings as a tribute to the god Apollo. But Minos, infuriated that his greatest engineer has escaped, follows him and searches for him among the Sicilians. Minos disguises himself as a mysterious traveler, offering a fortune for anyone who can thread a piece of string through a spiral shell. To any normal mind, this is impossible, but not to Daedalus. He accepts the stranger's challenge and ties the string to the body of an ant, dropping the insect into the body of the shell. As it makes its way out again, the ant threads the string through the innards of the shell. Minos recognizes Daedalus by his skill, but Daedalus has also recognized the king's trap. Before Minos can abduct him and drag him back to Crete, Daedalus and his accomplices sneak into Minos's chambers and pour boiling water into his bath, killing the king instantly. The inventor is finally free to live in peace.

## SUMMARY

King Minos makes the most of Daedalus's ingenuity by forcing him to construct the Labyrinth, but once it is completed the king grows distrustful of the inventor. When Daedalus requests to return to Greece after many years of absence, Minos refuses his request. No one else must know of Minos's secrets. Daedalus realizes that he is a prisoner. Minos's mighty ships control the sea, and there is no other way off the isle of Crete.

Since he has come to Crete, Daedalus has fathered a young son, Icarus. While he and Icarus watch the seagulls whirling in the air above the sea one day, Daedalus realizes that

Minos does not control the air. If he and Icarus want to escape, they must fly. Daedalus makes light, wooden constructions covered with birds' feathers for them to mount on their shoulders. He tests his new invention and finds that he is able to fly through the use of his newly-created wings. He prepares for their departure immediately. Before they take to the skies, Daedalus warns Icarus not to fly too close to the sea or to the sun. If he flies too low, the salt water will weigh down the feathers, and if he flies too high, the hot sun will melt the wax that holds the wings to the frame. Icarus, overcome with excitement, barely listens to these instructions. Father and son take to the skies, but soon Icarus begins to fly far too high. Daedalus yells at his son, but Icarus cannot hear him. As the wax on Icarus's wings begins to melt, the boy realizes the error of his ways. But it is too late. Icarus falls into the ocean and dies. Daedalus continues on to the Greek mainland (Sicily in the original myth) grieving over the loss of his son.

## ESSENTIAL QUESTIONS

- When should you listen to advice?
- What are the dangers of "playing God"?

## CONNECTIONS

**"Landscape with the Fall of Icarus"** is a poem by William Carlos Williams that references a 1558 painting of the same name by Pieter Brueghel the Elder. Both the poem and the painting stress the fact that Icarus's death is inconsequential, and that life will continue in spite of the tragedy that is occurring in the background.

**Ovid's** *Metamorphoses* is the epic poem that is the source for Daedalus and Icarus's story. Reading the original version and comparing it

to this version is a way for students to appreciate the poetic source material.

## ANTICIPATORY QUESTIONS

- When was a time when you did not listen to your parents?
- When you make mistakes are there always second chances?
- When was the first recorded human flight?
- What is the difference between *intelligence* and *wisdom*?

## TEACHABLE TERMS

- **Theme** Because of its cautionary message, this myth is a great way to examine theme. A commonly agreed upon theme is that the inexperienced should listen to the advice of the experienced.
- **Predict** Daedalus and Icarus's conversation concerning the death of the birds on pg. 131 foreshadows Icarus's foolish mistake. This would be a good point to ask students to predict what will happen later in the story.
- **Hyperbole** Icarus uses this term on pg. 133 when he says that he "can touch the sky."
- **Motif** In both myths concerning Daedalus there is a repeating bird motif (many references to birds and flights). Having your students identify this motif would be a good assignment to help them understand the term.

## RECALL QUESTIONS

1. What was Daedalus's greatest creation?
2. Why is Minos holding Daedalus prisoner?
3. How do Daedalus and Icarus escape?
4. What warning does Daedalus give Icarus?
5. What mistake does Icarus make?

# DAEDALUS AND ICARUS

## CAST

**DAEDALUS**  *Renowned Inventor*
**ICARUS**  *His Young Son*
**MINOS**  *King of Crete*
**GUARD**  *Guard of Minos*

**NARRATOR:** Daedalus was known through-out the city-states of Greece as the greatest artificer to ever live. In his day he had made many marvelous inventions—works that even rivaled the works of the gods—but at Crete his *magnum opus* had been realized.

**GUARD:**  *(shouting)* Visitor to the throne! Daedalus the inventor.

**NARRATOR:**  For the past many years, Daedalus had lived on the fortified island of Crete under the watchful eye of King Minos. Minos was wealthy beyond imagination, and

hearing of Daedalus's gifts, he had summoned him to Crete—to take on a special project. Now that project was done, and Daedalus wished to return home to Greece.

**DAEDALUS:** Your majesty, as you know, I have completed the task you gave me. All I ask now is my payment and leave to return to my homeland.

**NARRATOR:** Minos smiled smugly from his golden-horned throne and stroked his beard.

**MINOS:**  *(shrewdly)* Yes, the task is done, and you have done well—but…

**DAEDALUS:** But? There were no *buts* in our agreement! I have made your maze. No man can escape alive—just as you wished! What else can you want from me?

**MINOS:** I have trusted you, Daedalus, with my greatest secret. Will you now betray my trust? Crete is at war with Greece. You think I'm foolish enough to allow you to return there—to sell my secrets?

**DAEDALUS:** What *secrets* would I sell? All of Greece already knows about your wife and her beastly son! They know what walks the corridors of the Labyrinth! It will take more than imprisoning me to keep that quiet!

**MINOS:**  *(laughing)* You are a fool, Daedalus, for taking such a tone with me. But rail all you want. It will do you no good. You came to Crete for gold—for fame—you shall have it. I have not forgotten my end of the bargain.

**DAEDALUS:** I did come for those things, but circumstances have changed! I have a child now. I want him to see my homeland—the land of my ancestors.

**MINOS:** Then I suggest making a device that can peer across the sea because you will never leave Crete! I control the seas! Every ship that docks and sails from this port is mine! No man can escape me!

**DAEDALUS:** Someday you will regret this, Minos.

**MINOS:** *(laughing)* I doubt that!

**NARRATOR:** Still dazed by this news, Daedalus returned to his workshop, built atop the northern cliffs of Crete. As he walked, he gazed out over the sea. Just over the horizon lay Greece. It seemed to be taunting him. It was nearly enough to make the old inventor weep.

**DAEDALUS:** All my genius—all my skill— and yet I am helpless.

**NARRATOR:** Daedalus heard his son's cries as he neared his home.

**ICARUS:** *(happily)* Father! Father!

**DAEDALUS:** How will I tell Icarus? He'll never see the land of his ancestors.

**ICARUS:** Father, what did the king say? Are we going to Greece?

**DAEDALUS:** I'm afraid not, Icarus. We may never leave this island.

**ICARUS:** Never?

**DAEDALUS:** Never.

**NARRATOR:** The next few days brought a terrible melancholy on Daedalus. He gazed listlessly around his cluttered workshop. It was filled with useless wonders and trinkets.

The Labyrinth had been his masterwork, but it had ultimately trapped even him.

**ICARUS:** Father, what's wrong? Why don't you come out to the cliffs with me? Play your pipes! It will make you feel better.

**NARRATOR:** Daedalus looked up and saw his son. He smiled.

**DAEDALUS:** At least we are together, Icarus. Just let me grab my pipes.

**NARRATOR:** Overlooking the sheer drop to the sea, father and son seated themselves on a pair of rocks. Overhead the gulls were soaring in the breeze.

**ICARUS:** Look at the birds, Father! Why can't we fly like them?

**DAEDALUS:** *(laugh)* That is not the way the gods intended it. Oh, but if we could, we would be gone from this cursed island.

**NARRATOR:** After saying these words, the inventor thoughtfully examined the reed pipes in his grasp.

**DAEDALUS:** *(breathlessly)* Is it possible?

**NARRATOR:** He stared at the pattern of the reeds, each one longer than the one before. He looked to the birds wheeling above. He saw the same pattern there in the elegant curvature of their wings.

**ICARUS:** *(yelling)* Look at me, Father! Look at me!

**NARRATOR:** Icarus jumped up from his rock, his arms widespread, mimicking the wheeling of the birds overhead.

**DAEDALUS:**   Quick, Icarus! Back to the house!

**NARRATOR:**   Once there Daedalus dug furiously through the piles of supplies that littered his shop. He pulled forth string—some for him and some for Icarus.

**DAEDALUS:** *(excitedly)* Tie this! Tie the end like this—into a loop.

**ICARUS:** What for, Father?

**DAEDALUS:** To snare the gulls.

**ICARUS:** Why?

**DAEDALUS:** Just do as I say!

**NARRATOR:** Daedalus gleefully knotted a loop in his string.

**DAEDALUS:**   Do you have yours? Good! Now, back to the cliffs!

**NARRATOR:** Back on the cliffs, father and son laid their makeshift snares and baited them for the gulls.

**DAEDALUS:** Easy, son. Wait until they have almost eaten all the bait and suspect nothing and *then* pull the string tight. Only when they take off again will they realize that they are snared.

**NARRATOR:** They caught gull after gull. Daedalus knocked each on the head with a rock and placed the bodies into a large sack at his side. After a while, Daedalus noticed that Icarus was no longer springing his snares.

**DAEDALUS:** What's the matter, son?

**ICARUS:** I'm tired of this game.

**DAEDALUS:** It's not a game, Icarus. This is how we're going to escape this island.

**ICARUS:** I feel sorry for the birds. Why must they die?

**DAEDALUS:** Every creature dies eventually, Icarus. Now is simply their time. See how some of the birds never give our traps a second glance?

**ICARUS:** Yes?

**DAEDALUS:** Those are the *wise* birds. Only the foolish birds, the ones that are too curious for their own good, come close enough for us to catch. We are teaching them a lesson.

**ICARUS:**   But they're dying—just for one little mistake.

**DAEDALUS:** It's the way of the world.

**NARRATOR:**   The sack was bulging now. Daedalus hoisted it over his shoulder and carried it back to their workshop. He heated a great jar of water and boiled every gull body to loosen the feathers.

**DAEDALUS:** After the bodies are boiled, the feathers will pull free—like so. Start plucking! We should have enough feathers here for my plan.

**NARRATOR:** Icarus said nothing. Daedalus worked late into the night, fashioning frames from green limbs that resembled the wings of birds. Using melted wax, he attached the gull feathers to these frames. He built two leather harnesses and attached to these his newly made wings.

When Icarus awoke in the morning, his father now had an impressive wingspan.

**ICARUS:** You're going to fly, Father! You're really going to fly!

**DAEDALUS:** Yes, Icarus. And you will, too.

**NARRATOR:** Only then did Icarus notice a second pair of wings, one much smaller and made for a boy just his size, sitting on the workshop floor.

**ICARUS:** *(excitedly)* Oh, Father!

**DAEDALUS:** But first a test.

**NARRATOR:** They made their way to the cliffside, where the breeze was blowing swiftly out to the sea.

**DAEDALUS:** I will need the up-draft of a fall from the cliff. If I fail, Icarus, never forget your old father.

**NARRATOR:** The boy nodded. Daedalus paced backward from the cliff's edge, gauging the distance carefully. Then with great speed, he ran toward the precipice. When he reached the edge, he jumped forward, out onto the breeze, and plummeted out of sight.

**ICARUS:** Father!

**NARRATOR:** The boy ran to the edge, expecting to see his father's body dashed to pieces on the rocks below.

**DAEDALUS:** Woo-hoo! Woo-hoo!

**NARRATOR:** Daedalus swooped up from the waves, soaring on the breeze.

**ICARUS:** You did it! You really did it!

**DAEDALUS:** Look at me, Icarus! Look at me!

**NARRATOR:** He looped up and around, up over Icarus's head, and with several settling flaps, landed neatly in front of his son.

**ICARUS:** Me next! Me next!

**DAEDALUS:** Of course, son! Of course! We'll leave immediately! No further test is needed. My invention is a success! Wouldn't it be great to see the look on old Minos's face when he realizes we have escaped? Ha-ha! He may control the seas, but no man controls the skies!

**NARRATOR:** Icarus tore back to the workshop and quickly returned with his own miniature set of wings. He began strapping them on.

**ICARUS:** I can't wait to fly like you did, Father! What was it like?

**DAEDALUS:** Exhilarating, son! I felt like one of the gods!

**NARRATOR:** Icarus flapped his own wings for a test and then aimed himself toward the cliff's edge.

**ICARUS:** Here I go!

**DAEDALUS:** Icarus! Wait!

**NARRATOR:** Daedalus lunged forward and seized the boy's arm.

**DAEDALUS:** No! I am an adult, and you are just a boy. Don't rush ahead foolishly before thinking. What I have just done was a calculated flight! There are things I must tell you first.

**ICARUS:** Why? I can't wait to fly!

**DAEDALUS:** Listen to me! If you fly too close to the ocean's spray, the water will wet down your feathers. They will grow too heavy, and you will fall into the ocean and drown. If you fly too high, the heat of the sun will melt the wax that holds the wings together. So, please, son, fly a moderate pitch, or you will be in great danger.

**ICARUS:** No loopty-loops or anything?

**DAEDALUS:** No.

**ICARUS:** I'm not stupid. I watched you. I know what to do now.

**DAEDALUS:** Promise me, Icarus.

**ICARUS:** (*grudgingly*) I promise.

**NARRATOR:** The aged father wrapped his winged arms around his son.

**DAEDALUS:** Now, let us leave this place for good—before Minos's guards spot us here. Icarus, you will go first, but don't fly too far ahead. Head straight north, toward the mainland.

**ICARUS:** Got it!

**NARRATOR:** The youth bolted toward the cliff's edge, wings spread. As soon as he had disappeared over the side, Daedalus began his own take-off. Soon father and son were soaring on the salty sea breeze.

**ICARUS:** Father! This is greater than I ever imagined! Look at this!

**NARRATOR:** Icarus twirled about in the sky.

**DAEDALUS:** Icarus, be careful! This isn't a game! You promised!

**ICARUS:** What? I can't hear you! Hurry up, Father. I'll beat you there if you're not careful!

**NARRATOR:** The old inventor beat his wings furiously to catch up with his son, but Icarus easily outstripped him.

**DAEDALUS:** (*shouting*) Icarus! You're flying too fast—and too high! Icarus!

**ICARUS:** This is great! This must be how the gods feel! I can touch the sky!

**NARRATOR:** Icarus looked back over his shoulder. His father was far below and far behind. Then the boy looked up. The sun was much too close—its heat was bearing down upon him. Sweat was dripping from his brow.

**ICARUS:** (*scared*) Father?

**NARRATOR:** Something hot and sticky was running down both his arms. He flapped them furiously to shake it loose. When he did, feathers flew in all directions. They had come loose instead. To his horror, Icarus began to fall!

**ICARUS:** No! Father!

**DAEDALUS:** (*yelling*) Icarus!

**NARRATOR:** Daedalus saw his son spiraling down toward the sea, a trail of feathers in his wake. He turned his head just as Icarus crashed into the brine.

**DAEDALUS:** (*weeping*) My son. My son.

**NARRATOR:** Time and time again, the old man swooped as low as he dared over the spot where his son had fallen, yet he never saw any trace of the boy. Finally, he gave up hope and, despairing, continued his flight toward Greece.

Many sailors later reported seeing a large bird in the sky that day, a bird with its head hung low, which only barely saved itself from plunging into the sea when the wind brought it low. They said it had the strangest cry—like a man whose heart was breaking.

## DISCUSSION QUESTIONS

1. What is the difference between *wisdom* and *intelligence*?
2. Why is it so hard for children to listen to their parents?
3. Is Daedalus a good father?
4. How could you modernize the story of Daedalus and Icarus?

# THE WINGED HORSE

## TEACHER GUIDE

### BACKGROUND

Pegasus the winged horse is one of Greek mythology's most recognizable characters, yet his rider, the hero Bellerophon, is not. Bellerophon, a minor hero credited with slaying the Chimera, amounts to almost nothing, while his famous horse goes down in history.

Mythology is filled with many mixed-up creatures—centaurs, Minotaurs, satyrs, etc.—but Pegasus is the most intriguing of them all. The Greeks must have wondered: What if the strength of a horse were combined with the swiftness of a bird? There you would have the ultimate weapon—the kind of a weapon that even a hapless hero like Bellerophon could ride to success.

This script-story is a parody of the traditional myth of Pegasus. In the original version Bellerophon is a cookie-cutter hero, brave and bold, who defeats the warrior-women Amazons and the fire-breathing Chimera through the help of his winged steed. This version gives Pegasus credit where credit is due. How far could Bellerophon have gone without Pegasus? Not far.

### SUMMARY

Bellerophon is a prince of Corinth, and his mother, Queen Eurynome, is pressuring him to be a hero. Eurynome tells her son that Poseidon is his true father (which may be a lie) and then hires a famous Corinthian sage, Polyidus, to be Bellerophon's trainer. The wise man tells the queen that Bellerophon is hopeless—he's too weak and lazy to be a hero. The only way Bellerophon could ever become a hero would be if he tamed Pegasus, the winged steed. The only problem with this is that Bellerophon is deathly afraid of horses. In fact, if anyone says the word *horse* around him, he collapses into a fit of fear. Bellerophon's mother tells him that he must face his fears and takes him to the temple of Athena to beg the Goddess of Wisdom for aid. Athena appears to Bellerophon and presents him with a golden bridle to use to tame Pegasus.

Bellerophon journeys to the spring of Pirene, where Pegasus is said to water each night. Bellerophon captures the winged steed using the golden bridle. Pegasus questions the boy as to his motives, and Bellerophon states that he wishes to become a great hero. Pegasus helps train the boy, so that he can defeat Greece's most notorious monster—the Chimera, a fire-breathing creature with elements of a lion, goat, and snake. When faced with the Chimera, Bellerophon lodges a spear with a lump of lead attached to it into the beast's throat. The Chimera's fiery breath causes the lead to melt and suffocates it.

Although Pegasus is almost totally responsible for his success, Bellerophon refuses to acknowledge this and grows more and more prideful. Eventually, he commands Pegasus to fly him to the top of Mount Olympus, where he will demand that Zeus make him a god. On the trip Pegasus bucks Bellerophon from his back—either on purpose or because Zeus caused a gadfly to sting him. Bellerophon is badly wounded from the fall and spends the rest of his life as a cripple.

## ESSENTIAL QUESTIONS

- How can fame or popularity change people?
- What happens when you become too confident?

## CONNECTIONS

**Creature Creation** Mythology is filled with many creatures made from mixed-up animal combinations—centaurs, satyrs, the Minotaur, the Sphinx, the Chimera, and Pegasus. Create an original creature by combining various elements of regular animals into one.

## ANTICIPATORY QUESTIONS

- What is Pegasus?
- How would having a winged horse make someone a better warrior?
- What are some famous monsters from Greek myth that were combinations of real-life animals?
- What is the Chimera?
- What is a parody?
- What are the stages of a typical hero's journey?

## TEACHABLE TERMS

- **Invocation of the Muses** Ancient Greek epic poems begin with an invocation of the muse, a request for inspiration from the art-goddesses as the poet begins the epic work. This script-story begins with an invocation on pg. 137, although the tone is somewhat sarcastic.
- **Parody** This script-story is a parody of the myth of Bellerophon. Although the basic events of the myth are accurate,

humorous touches have been added to make the story more comical.
- **Backstory** On pg. 140 Polyidus mentions that he is going to give a little backstory on Pegasus. Backstory is information from a character's past that is important to the plot.
- **Alliteration** On pg. 142 the phrase "but no fit of fear followed" makes use of alliteration.
- **Anti-hero** Since Bellerophon is the central hero of the story yet lacks heroic qualities, he fits the definition of an anti-hero.
- **Tone** The author's tone toward the events of the story indicates that it is not entirely serious.

## RECALL QUESTIONS

1. Who does Eurynome tell Bellerophon his true father is?
2. What does Athena give to Bellerophon to help him on his quest?
3. What three animals make up the Chimera?
4. What causes the Chimera to suffocate?
5. What place is Bellerophon trying to reach when he is bucked off Pegasus?

# THE WINGED HORSE

## CAST

| | |
|---|---|
| **BELLEROPHON** | *Hopeless Hero* |
| **EURYNOME** | *Mother of Bellerophon* |
| **POLYIDUS** | *Corinthian Wise-Guy* |
| **ATHENA** | *Goddess of Wisdom* |
| **PEGASUS** | *Winged Neigh-Neigh* |
| **CHIMERA** | *Bizarre Monster* |
| **GOAT-HEAD** | *Part of the Chimera* |
| **ZEUS** | *Lord of the Gods* |
| **POSEIDON** | *God of the Seas* |
| **BOY** | *Fan of Bellerophon* |
| **GIRL ONE** | *Admirer of Bellerophon* |
| **GIRL TWO** | *Admirer of Bellerophon* |

**NARRATOR:** O, Muse, sing me the ballad of Bellerophon, that bumbling buffoon—the one who tried to become Greece's greatest hero and ended up falling flat on his face. But mainly tell me about his amazing winged horse that was the reason for his rise—and also his fall.

Bellerophon was a young prince of Corinth. His father, King Glaucus, had died in a tragic accident, wherein he was run over by his own chariot and then devoured by his own horses. Bellerophon's mother, Queen Eurynome, wanted her son to be a great hero. Partially, she had high hopes for him, but mainly she just wanted to get him out of the house.

**EURYNOME:** By Olympus, boy! You don't do anything except sit around here and read these stupid comic books all day!

**BELLEROPHON:** Mother, how many times do I have to tell you? They're called *illustrated scrolls!* And they're *tragic* not *comic.*

**EURYNOME:** Whatever. You're almost eighteen. It's time you made something out of yourself—like a hero!

**BELLEROPHON:** Eh. I don't wanna.

**EURYNOME:** Are you kidding me? Every boy in Greece wants to be a hero! It's a life filled with adventure—rescuing beasts and slaying maidens! *(pause)* Wait. Reverse that.

**BELLEROPHON:** That sounds like work.

**EURYNOME:** So you would rather sit around here and waste your life?

**BELLEROPHON:** Yep. Sounds good to me.

**EURYNOME:** You're going to be a hero, and that's final!

**BELLEROPHON:** Look, Mom. Heroes are all sons of gods. My dad's just an old, dead guy who couldn't drive a chariot. I don't have the right pedigree.

**NARRATOR:** Eurynome realized her son had a point, but that's when her quick wits kicked in.

**EURYNOME:** *(slyly)* Didn't I ever tell you? Your true father *is* actually one of the gods.

**BELLEROPHON:** How convenient. So you cheated on my father with one of the gods?

**EURYNOME:** Exactly! *(catching herself)* I mean, not on purpose. It was an accident.

**BELLEROPHON:** So I'm an accident? Now I'm completely depressed.

**EURYNOME:** Don't you at least want to know which god is your true father?

**BELLEROPHON:** You mean my *alleged* father? Sure. Let me guess. It's probably Hephaestus, the crippled blacksmith god, isn't it?

**EURYNOME:** Definitely not! I do have standards, you know.

**BELLEROPHON:** Then who is it?

**EURYNOME:** It's…uhhh…

**NARRATOR:** Eurynome glanced out toward the sea and thought of Poseidon—powerful, yet unavailable for comment on the matter.

**EURYNOME:** Your true father is Poseidon, God of the Seas!

**BELLEROPHON:** Hmmm. He's not quite as lame as Hephaestus—in either meaning of the word. But I'm pretty sure King Glaucus is my real father. I mean, I look like him. Everybody says I act like him. I have the same blood type as him…

**EURYNOME:** I swear by Poseidon himself that the God of the Sea is your father. If I'm lying, may I never go deep-sea fishing again! Now you're going to be a hero, and that's *final*, young man! But first we need to get you a trainer.

**BELLEROPHON:** What? I have to do training now? This is getting worse and worse!

**NARRATOR:** Queen Eurynome sent for Polyidus, the wise Corinthian sage, who like most wise-guys sold his smarts for money. The queen presented Polyidus to his new hero-in-training.

**POLYIDUS:** The prince? I'm supposed to train the prince? The deal is off! He's hopeless.

**BELLEROPHON:** I agree. I better just stay here and read my illustrated scrolls.

**EURYNOME:** What is so crazy about my son being a hero?

**POLYIDUS:** Well, for starters, look at him. He's way too scrawny to be a strongman.

**BELLEROPHON:** Hey! I resemble that remark!

**POLYIDUS:** And too dimwitted to be a trickster! My queen, how do I put this delicately? *(pause)* Your son is a moron.

EURYNOME: He wants to be a hero!

BELLEROPHON: (grumbling) No, I don't.

POLYIDUS: He should stay here where he's safe and sound. Do you know what happens to would-be heroes? Mutilation! That's what! Do you want him to come back home with a missing leg or a nubby arm?

EURYNOME: He might like a nubby arm!

BELLEROPHON: Actually, I'm fine with the whole arm.

POLYIDUS: My verdict stands. This boy is too pathetic to be a hero. Maybe he should just go into politics.

EURYNOME: So my son is too stupid to be a hero, but he's okay to be a king?

POLYIDUS: Of course. Didn't you ever meet your husband? He was so dumb he was run over by his own chariot. That takes some doing!

EURYNOME: How dare you talk about the boy's father that way!

BELLEROPHON: Uh. I thought Poseidon was my father.

EURYNOME: Butt out!

NARRATOR: The queen grabbed Polyidus by the tunic.

EURYNOME: (forcefully) Look, you old goat. I have raised this boy for the last eighteen years, most of them as a single parent, and if I don't get him out of this house soon, I'm going to snap!

POLYIDUS: Unhand me, my queen! The only way that this kid could *ever* be a hero was if he has some sort of weapon that was so powerful that it enabled him to achieve the impossible. And by "achieve the impossible" I mean "not die immediately."

EURYNOME: That's it! He needs the ultimate weapon—Pegasus!

POLYIDUS: The winged horse?

NARRATOR: At the mention of the word *horse*, Bellerophon's face went deathly white.

BELLEROPHON: (in fright) What did he say? (crying out) Ah!

NARRATOR: The boy curled up into a ball on the floor and continued to scream.

POLYIDUS: Holy Hebe! What is the matter with him now?

EURYNOME: He suffers from severe equinophobia. He is deathly afraid of— (whispering) you-know.

POLYIDUS: You mean, he's afraid of Pegasus? Little girls have pictures of Pegasus hanging on their bedroom walls!

EURYNOME: It's not *just* Pegasus! He is afraid of all…that type of creature. Can you blame him? His father was eaten by his own…you-know-what's.

POLYIDUS: I thought you said Poseidon was his father.

**EURYNOME:** *(ignoring him)* Every time Bellerophon sees one of those creatures or even hears that word, he has a fit.

**POLYIDUS:** Well, you're right, the only thing that can help this boy is Pegasus—and quite a bit of therapy. But Pegasus is no regular horse.

**BELLEROPHON:** *(in extreme terror)* Ahhh! The hooves! The hooves of death!

**EURYNOME:** Don't say that word! Say *neigh-neigh*.

**POLYIDUS:** You can't be serious. *(sigh)* Allow me to give you a little un-asked-for backstory. Pegasus the winged hor—I mean, *neigh-neigh*—was born from the blood of Medusa after she was killed by Perseus, a real hero. Whenever Pegasus strikes his hoof into the ground, a spring arises, and it is only from these springs that he drinks. Pegasus is often sighted at the Spring of Pirene, conveniently located nearby. But the steed is unruly, untamable, and thoroughly uncatchable!

**EURYNOME:** Then how exactly is my son supposed to obtain him?

**POLYIDUS:** Well, that's where actually being a hero comes in handy, isn't it?

**EURYNOME:** But he can't capture a magical horse!

**BELLEROPHON:** *(cry of fright)* Ahhh!

**EURYNOME:** Whoops.

**POLYIDUS:** Usually some god takes pity on heroes and gives them assistance. Maybe your son should ask his "father"—or maybe give the Goddess of Wisdom, Athena, a call. This boy will need all the wisdom he can get. Good day!

**EURYNOME:** Thanks for nothing!

**NARRATOR:** As the sage departed, the queen knelt by her son and took his face into her hands.

**EURYNOME:** Look, son! Get ahold of yourself! Do you know what people are saying about you? They say you're a loser who will never amount to anything! They say you're worthless, brainless, spineless, and hopeless!

**BELLEROPHON:** *(hurt)* Who said those things about me?

**EURYNOME:** Well, I said most of them, but don't you want to prove me wrong? You have to overcome your fears!

**BELLEROPHON:** Do you really think I can do it?

**EURYNOME:** I'm your mother. If I don't believe in you, who will?

**BELLEROPHON:** You didn't really answer the question…

**EURYNOME:** Come on! We have work to do!

**NARRATOR:** Eventually, Bellerophon came around to the idea of being a hero. His mother filled him with all kinds of nonsense—how he could be just like the heroes he read about in his illustrated scrolls—even *without* the strength, skill, and brains they had. All he needed was Pegasus.

**EURYNOME:** To capture Pegasus, you must seek the aid of one of the gods.

**BELLEROPHON:** Then it should be Poseidon. Once I tell him that he is my true father, he will assist me at once.

**EURYNOME:** Ummm. Well, he might not remember you. That was a long time ago, and he has so many children. What about the goddess Athena?

**BELLEROPHON:** She's the animal-lover one, right?

**EURYNOME:** No. Athena is the Goddess of Wisdom.

**BELLEROPHON:** Right! I get all those militant, man-hater goddesses mixed up. Then it's decided. Tonight I do what every great hero must do—cry and beg until the gods come to my aid. I journey to the temple of Artemis!

**EURYNOME:** That's Athena, dear. Now don't offend her. You desperately need her help. She's everything you're not—strong, smart…manly. Just remember! You're not going to take "No!" for an answer.

**BELLEROPHON:** Don't worry, Mother! I can bawl my eyes out with the best of them.

**NARRATOR:** Bellerophon traveled to the temple of Athena and prostrated himself upon the floor.

**BELLEROPHON:** Please, Athena! Help me! Please!

**NARRATOR:** After hours of pitiful sobbing and crying out to the goddess, Bellerophon collapsed in exhaustion.

**ATHENA:** Good grief, not another cry-baby would-be hero! *(sigh)* I better help him. Otherwise, I'll never get any peace and quiet. *(loudly)* Mortal!

**BELLEROPHON:** Ah! Lady Athena! Is it you? I apologize! I fell asleep! Crying really takes it out of me!

**ATHENA:** Mortal, you still slumber. In fact, you still drool all over my marble floor. I am speaking to you through a dream.

**BELLEROPHON:** A dream? Oh no. I'm not having that one where I go to school in my underwear, am I?

**ATHENA:** Silence!

**BELLEROPHON:** Sorry, sir. I mean, ma'am…

**ATHENA:** Don't annoy me, boy! I've come to grant you a boon!

**BELLEROPHON:** I don't understand!

**ATHENA:** I am an all-powerful goddess.

**BELLEROPHON:** I know that. I just don't know what a *boon* is!

**ATHENA:** *(sigh)* What an idiot. Look! I am giving you this golden bridle. See? Shiny thing? You understand that, don't you?

**NARRATOR:** She held aloft a glittering bridle.

**ATHENA:** With it, you may tame Pegasus the winged h—

**BELLEROPHON:** *(loudly)* Don't say it! *(calming)* I apologize, my lady. I have issues.

**ATHENA:** Apparently. Now, if I give you this, you must promise never to come to my temple again or ever try to contact me in any way as long as you live—even if it's an emergency.

**BELLEROPHON:** I promise! I promise!

**NARRATOR:** The goddess lowered the bridle into the boy's eager hands.

**BELLEROPHON:** I have just one question.

**ATHENA:** What is that?

**BELLEROPHON:** I thought you said you were giving me a boon. This is a bridle.

**ATHENA:** Zounds, boy! Be gone before I change my mind!

**NARRATOR:** Seriously second-guessing her decision, the Goddess of Wisdom disappeared, and the boy awoke at once. The golden bridle was still in his hand.

**BELLEROPHON:** Hey! It wasn't a dream!

**NARRATOR:** Bellerophon wiped the drool from his chin and returned to his mother. He showed her the bridle triumphantly.

**BELLEROPHON:** Look! Now I can catch the winged hhhh…the hhhh…

**EURYNOME:** Say it! You must face your fears! Tonight you journey to the Spring of

Pirene to capture Pegasus…the winged *horse*.

**NARRATOR:** Bellerophon cringed at the sound of the word, but no fit of fear followed.

**BELLEROPHON:** I did it! You said *horse*, and I didn't freak out. Wait! I said it, too! I'm cured!

**EURYNOME:** Now, go and capture your steed! At last you have overcome your fears!

**BELLEROPHON:** Can you go with me?

**EURYNOME:** *(sigh)* You are such a mama's boy.

**NARRATOR:** Bellerophon and his mother journeyed to the spring of Pirene.

**EURYNOME:** According to legend, Pegasus kicked this spring into existence with one of his magical hooves.

**BELLEROPHON:** *(frightened)* If his hoof can do that to the ground, imagine what it could do to my skull! Plus, what if Pegasus tries to eat me?

**EURYNOME:** Horses don't eat people.

**BELLEROPHON:** But my father was eaten by his own horses!

**EURYNOME:** He's not your father, remember?

**BELLEROPHON:** Oh yeah. Good point.

**NARRATOR:** They arrived at the spring.

**BELLEROPHON:** (quickly) Well, he's not here. Let's go!

**NARRATOR:** There was a whooshing of wings, and suddenly Pegasus swooped out the night sky. (whooshing of wings and neighing)

**BELLEROPHON:** Argh! (cry of fright)

**EURYNOME:** Courage!

**NARRATOR:** The winged horse settled to the ground and lowered his head to drink from the magical spring.

**EURYNOME:** Go! Use your bridle.

**BELLEROPHON:** I think I wet my tunic just a minute ago. Maybe I should go change first.

**NARRATOR:** The queen shoved her son roughly toward the drinking steed. Bellerophon, his heart racing, tiptoed toward the winged horse. Without raising his head, Pegasus spoke.

**PEGASUS:** I hope you're not trying to capture me. Many men have tried, but all of them have failed.

**BELLEROPHON:** (whimper of fright) Erm. It's talking to me.

**PEGASUS:** Of course, I'm talking. I am an immortal horse. Now read my lips—get lost before I put a hoof through your skull.

**BELLEROPHON:** Okay.

**EURYNOME:** (shouting) Bellerophon! Use the bridle already!

**NARRATOR:** The boy pulled the magical bridle out of his satchel, and Pegasus—mesmerized by its golden sheen—raised his head from the spring. When the goddess Athena bestowed this boon upon Bellerophon, she knew the steed's one weakness—shiny things. Pegasus, mesmerized by the bridle, advanced toward Bellerophon.

**BELLEROPHON:** (nervously) It's getting closer!

**PEGASUS:** (in a daze) Where did you get that pretty thing?

**BELLEROPHON:** Easy! Easy!

**NARRATOR:** Pegasus neared Bellerophon and rubbed his pristinely white muzzle up against the bridle. Bellerophon slipped it over the horse's head, and Pegasus was his.

**BELLEROPHON:** I did it! I did it!

**EURYNOME:** I know, son! I'm just as surprised as you are.

**NARRATOR:** In a single, swift movement Pegasus ducked under the boy's legs and threw him up onto his back.

**BELLEROPHON:** Uh-oh! What's going on? Easy, girl!

**PEGASUS:** Who you calling *girl*?

**NARRATOR:** The steed spread his massive wings and rocketed up into the sky. (Shoom!)

**BELLEROPHON:** Ahhhhhh!

NARRATOR: Eurynome watched as her son disappeared heavenward.

EURYNOME: *(relieved)* Ah. My job is done. My little boy can finally become a great hero. *(pause)* More importantly, I can finally turn his bedroom into that sewing room I've always wanted.

NARRATOR: About an hour later, when Bellerophon finally stopped screaming, Pegasus settled down onto the peak of a high mountain.

PEGASUS: Do you think a girl horse could fly like that?

BELLEROPHON: Sorry. I just assumed. I mean, you are a winged horse. That's kind of girly.

PEGASUS: Says the boy who was terrified of this "girly" winged horse.

BELLEROPHON: Touché.

PEGASUS: Now that you've trapped me with your magical bridle, what is your plan, boy?

BELLEROPHON: Actually I'd prefer it if you called me, "Master."

PEGASUS: Would you prefer walking?

BELLEROPHON: But you're *my* horse now.

PEGASUS: Are you so sure? Maybe *you're my* boy? Now hurry up and tell me what your plan is.

BELLEROPHON: Okay. First I thought we'd form some of kind of typical boy-and-his-horse-bond.

NARRATOR: Pegasus stared at Bellerophon blankly.

PEGASUS: I don't think so.

BELLEROPHON: Well, then my second goal is to become a hero.

PEGASUS: That's almost as improbable— but do-able. If you want to become a hero, that means you will have to slay a fantastical beast of some sort. It's like a hero prerequisite almost.

NARRATOR: Pegasus put a hoof to his mouth thoughtfully.

PEGASUS: Hmmm. Now let's see. Who's left? Medusa lost her head. Thank goodness, or I wouldn't be here. The Sphinx killed herself. She was completely *riddled* with guilt. Get it? Riddle of the Sphinx? She tells riddles.

NARRATOR: Now it was Bellerophon's turn to stare blankly.

PEGASUS: Nevermind. Oh! There is the Chimera! Now that creature is a terror. She has two heads, the head of a lion and a goat, the body of a lion mixed with a goat, and a live snake for a tail.

BELLEROPHON: *(doing mental math)* Add the lion and carry the goat. So it has a total of three heads and two bodies?

PEGASUS: No two heads and one body. One lion head and one goat head.

BELLEROPHON: A goat? That doesn't seem very ferocious.

PEGASUS: You haven't been around goats much. They're mean little boogers. Anyway, to make things worse, the lion-head breathes fire.

BELLEROPHON: Oh! What does the goat-head breathe?

PEGASUS: Oxygen, I guess.

BELLEROPHON: (impressed) Oooh. (pause) But how was such a hideous creature formed?

PEGASUS: A very strange night at the zoo. (pause) No creature deserves death more than the Chimera! Every time we mythical creatures get together, she hogs all the food, tells disgusting jokes, and lights her own flatulence. Plus, she also murders people. She has been plaguing the countryside—killing anyone who journeys near her lair. Tourists mainly. But no one really mourns the death of a tourist.

BELLEROPHON: I don't know. Can I just work up to the man-eating beasts? Maybe start with some meat-eating hamsters or something?

PEGASUS: You better act fast. With all the heroes there are, Greece is running out of monsters.

BELLEROPHON: Then I guess it will have to be the Chi—Chi—what you said.

NARRATOR: Bellerophon raised his sword dramatically.

BELLEROPHON: I swear that I will not rest until I slay—or at least correctly pronounce the name of—this beast. But I'm not exactly the best warrior.

PEGASUS: Can you at least fire a bow and arrow?

BELLEROPHON: Bow? Arrow?

PEGASUS: (sigh) Come on! We have some work to do.

NARRATOR: No one knows why Pegasus took Bellerophon under his wing. Sure, the boy had a magical bridle, but there must have been something more. Pegasus was a smart horse and could have found some way to shake his rider. Perhaps he had a soft spot for the boy and really wanted him to succeed. Maybe he wanted to have some great deed attached to his own name, and he saw Bellerophon as the way to achieve this. Whatever his motive, Pegasus helped train his boy to be a hero.

PEGASUS: All right! At least now you can shoot an arrow in a straight line. Don't even worry about aiming. I'll just point you in the right direction. Now let's kick that Chimera's scaly tail!

NARRATOR: Bellerophon jumped onto Pegasus's back and spurred him on.

BELLEROPHON: Let's go! Yah! Yah!

PEGASUS: Watch it!

NARRATOR: They flew to the lair of the Chimera. The creature happened to be sunning herself upon her bed of bones. She was a monster to be sure with her yellowed and mangy lion-fur covering, her green-tinted goat-udder, and her venom-spewing tail.

**PEGASUS:** Ugh. There she is!

**NARRATOR:** The Chimera's lion-head lifted and snarled at the hovering horse and his rider.

**CHIMERA:** Well, well, well. If it isn't Pegasus—the world's girliest horse.

**PEGASUS:** *(to Bellerophon)* See why she deserves to die? She's always so hateful. *(to the Chimera)* I'm back, Chimera. And this time I brought a warrior with me.

**CHIMERA:** *(fake fright)* Oh, I'm so scared! The sissified horse and his weakling rider are going to shoot me! Help! Help! Ha! What a joke!

**PEGASUS:** Well, at least I'm not some walking freakshow!

**CHIMERA:** Why you—! You'll rue the day you tangled with the Chimera.

**NARRATOR:** The serpentine tail bared its fangs and hissed, the lion-head roared, and the goat-head started munching on some nearby grass. *(snake hissing and lion roaring)* Flames erupted from the Chimera's mouth. *(whooshing of flame)*

**BELLEROPHON:** *(cry of fright)* Ah!

**PEGASUS:** Shoot already!

**NARRATOR:** Pegasus dodged the column of flame, and Bellerophon fumbled with his bow and arrows. At last the boy released a series of shafts. *(twang, twang, twang)* But the Chimera simply incinerated them with her fiery breath. Their charred remains fell helplessly to the ground.

**CHIMERA:** *(loud laughter)* Ha! Nice try! My breath is deadly!

**GOAT-HEAD:** I've been trying to tell you that for years.

**NARRATOR:** The Chimera's goat-head returned to snacking upon the roasted remains of Bellerophon's arrows.

**CHIMERA:** Shut up! *(to Pegasus)* Now come closer, you flying filly! I'm hungry enough to eat a horse!

**NARRATOR:** Pegasus turned to his rider.

**PEGASUS:** If only we had a lump of lead.

**BELLEROPHON:** I have one right here!

**PEGASUS:** What are you doing with that?

**BELLEROPHON:** Well, my mom always told me I was about as useful as a lump of lead. So I found one to see what she was talking about. Turns out a lump of lead is useful after all!

**PEGASUS:** Attach it to the end of your spear. When we pass back over the Chimera, you must hurl that spear directly into her mouth. I'll have to fly low, so watch out for the flames.

**BELLEROPHON:** I don't know if I can.

PEGASUS: Look! You have to do *something* to become a hero. I can't do it all for you. Now let's tame this lion!

BELLEROPHON: Yeah, let's milk this goat! Hmmm. That didn't sound as good as yours.

NARRATOR: Pegasus swooped low over the Chimera.

CHIMERA: Eat flames, horse!

*(whooshing of flame)*

NARRATOR: Bellerophon saw the column of flame coming directly toward him.

PEGASUS: That's it! Say, "Ah!" Now!

NARRATOR: Bellerophon covered his eyes with one hand and hurled the spear with the other. The missile went directly into the Chimera's mouth, lodging the lump of lead into her throat.

CHIMERA: *(gagging sound)*

GOAT-HEAD: Oh no! The lion-head's choking! Does anyone know the Heimlich Maneuver?

NARRATOR: The Chimera's flames were staunched within her throat, and the heat from them caused the lead to melt—sealing shut her throat and suffocating her.

CHIMERA: *(dying sounds)*

NARRATOR: As the lion-head slumped over lifelessly, the goat-head began to moan.

GOAT-HEAD: *(growing weak)* Oh, I tried to tell her that all that tourist-eating would catch up to us one day. *(gasping)* Life is so beautiful…and the grass…so green.

NARRATOR: Death came to the Chimera. The goat-head sank forward, the snake-tail curled into itself, and the scaly goat-udder gave its death-rattle. *(death-rattle of an udder)*

PEGASUS: Ha! Who's a sissified horse, now?

BELLEROPHON: Woo-hoo! I did it! I did it!

PEGASUS: Uh…*we* did it.

BELLEROPHON: Well, I threw the spear.

PEGASUS: Yeah, but I aimed you in the right direction.

BELLEROPHON: True. You were my vehicle. But you're just a horse. When they ask who killed the Chimera, they're not going to say, "Pegasus." They're going to say, "Bellerophon!"

NARRATOR: This event went straight to Bellerophon's head. He started introducing himself as "the slayer of the Chimera."

Somehow the loser-turned-hero became the toast of Greece. All the kings wanted him to visit them and date their daughters. And the hero-jobs just kept coming in. Bellerophon went on adventure after adventure, and thanks to his winged horse, he returned successfully each time. Bellerophon soon became a celebrity.

BOY: Mr. Bellerophon, what's it like being the master of Pegasus?

BELLEROPHON: It's okay, I guess.

BOY: Well, didn't Pegasus help you defeat the Chimera?

BELLEROPHON: Yeah, he was involved—sort of.

PEGASUS: Grrr.

NARRATOR: To Bellerophon's annoyance, when people pressed him for information, they mainly wanted to know more about Pegasus.

BELLEROPHON: Hello, girls. So what would you like to know about me?

GIRL ONE: How fast can Pegasus fly?

GIRL TWO: Does he like apples?

BELLEROPHON: *(to himself)* Grrr. I'm the hero here—not that dumb oat-muncher.

NARRATOR: And so the long-time partners started to have a falling out.

BELLEROPHON: You're stealing my spotlight!

PEGASUS: Nay! Nay!

BELLEROPHON: Does that mean "no," or is that just a sound you're making?

PEGASUS: The first one! What do you mean *your* spotlight? You'd be nothing without me!

BELLEROPHON: Oh yeah!

PEGASUS: Yeah!

BELLEROPHON: You're just jealous because I'm bound for Olympus, and you're not.

PEGASUS: What are you whinnying about?

BELLEROPHON: It happens to all the greatest heroes. They are summoned to Olympus and toasted by the gods. Some of them even become gods themselves. I'm just waiting on the call.

PEGASUS: Don't hold your breath. *(pause)* Or on second thought—do.

NARRATOR: Yet Bellerophon's call from Olympus never came. The gods were snubbing him. He couldn't believe it.

BELLEROPHON: Come on, horse! We're going to fly up to Mount Olympus. I am the mighty—although unconfirmed—son of Poseidon! I deserve a little recognition from the gods.

PEGASUS: Any idiot knows that Zeus won't let you just fly up to the top of Mount Olympus!

BELLEROPHON: Watch me!

PEGASUS: I stand corrected. Any idiot knows that—*except* you. Well, I won't do it! It'll get us both killed.

BELLEROPHON: You're wearing an enchanted bridle, and you'll do what I tell you to do!

PEGASUS: So that's how you want to play this, huh? Fine!

NARRATOR: Pegasus and his rider rocketed upward through the atmosphere.

BELLEROPHON: When I get there, I will demand them to make me a god—or at least give me an island or something!

PEGASUS: (to himself) If you make it that far.

NARRATOR: Up on Mount Olympus the gods watched Bellerophon's approach.

ATHENA: Mortal at twelve o'clock. Approaching fast. Zeus, will you ready your thunderbolt?

ZEUS: He says he's a son of Poseidon.

NARRATOR: All the gods turned to Poseidon. The God of the Sea just shrugged.

POSEIDON: Beats me.

ZEUS: Very well. Down he goes.

NARRATOR: Some say that Zeus sent a gadfly to sting Pegasus—causing him to buck. Others say that Pegasus was just smart and shook his rider on purpose. Either way, all it took was one fling of Pegasus's rump to send Bellerophon sailing out into open air.

BELLEROPHON: (screaming) Ahhhhhhh! (fading away)

PEGASUS: (relieved) Ah. That's better.

NARRATOR: Bellerophon fell all the way to earth. The gods spared his life, in order to teach him a lesson. He landed in an enormous thorn thicket that was just soft enough to keep him from dying but still hard enough to break every bone in his body.

Soon after, Pegasus received the invitation that Bellerophon had been waiting for. The horse was summoned to Mount Olympus, where the gods made him the official bearer of Zeus's thunderbolts and gave him a stable with an eternal supply of oats and apples. There he ate like a horse and lived as free as a bird.

Finally, Zeus placed Pegasus's image in the stars, so that he would be remembered forever.

Meanwhile, Bellerophon spent the rest of his days blind and badly scarred from his fall. Whenever he heard the clip-clop of a hoof or the flutter of a wing, he would cower in fright. And no one said the h-word without him shrieking in fear. To everyone he met, he would ask the same question.

BELLEROPHON: Hello. I am Bellerophon, the slayer of the Chimera. Remember me?

NARRATOR: They would only shake their heads sadly.

BOY: Wait. You're not the one who rode Pegasus, are you?

BELLEROPHON: (coldly) Nevermind.

NARRATOR: In the end, Bellerophon died alone. His cause of death, a deadly wound—to the ego.

## DISCUSSION QUESTIONS

1. How is this version of Bellerophon's story a parody of a typical hero quest?
2. In the original version of the myth, Bellerophon was not an incompetent

hero and Pegasus could not talk. This version is a parody of the original myth. What are some details that alert you to the fact that this is a parody? Explain.

3. How is Bellerophon an example of an anti-hero?

4. Since the Chimera is such a strange monster, the word *chimera* has come to mean "an illusion" or "something that is impossible in reality." What is another example of a chimera?

5. Fame seemed to change Bellerophon's personality. How can fame or popularity change people?

6. What do you think—was Pegasus stung by a gadfly sent by Zeus or did the horse intentionally throw his rider? Explain.

7. Bellerophon has a fall—literally and figuratively. What personality flaw causes Bellerophon's downfall? Explain.

8. Do you feel sorry for Bellerophon? Explain.

# THE CONTEST FOR ATHENS

The very first King of Athens—or the city-state that would come to be called Athens—was a strange, half-human creature named Cecrops. He had the top-half of a man and the bottom-half of a snake. It was said that Cecrops had no father or mother but was born out of the hard earth. By ruling wisely, Cecrops had built up a mighty city-state, yet it did not have a patron god or goddess, a deity to protect and support it—like all the other city-states in Greece had.

Two of the mightiest gods expressed interest in becoming the protector and namesake of Cecrop's city-state. The first was the mighty God of the Sea, Poseidon, and the other was Athena, the Goddess of Wisdom and Battle. They both appeared before the snake-tailed Cecrops and declared themselves to be the perfect god for his city.

"Choose me, Cecrops," said Poseidon. "I have always been a friend of mortals. It was I who created the most magnificent creature ever seen—the horse. I summoned it from the surging breakers of the sea. Its body is as powerful as the ocean currents, and its mane and tail flows like the beautiful sea foam."

"That is impressive," said King Cecrops, curling his snake-tail in excitement.

"Yes, all the mortals were impressed," said Athena. "That is until they realized that it was a completely useless gift."

"What?" spluttered Poseidon. "The horse is the beast most beneficial to man!"

"But not until I showed them how to tame it! Otherwise, it would have run free forever. *I* invented the bridle. Using this tool, man was able to harness the power of the horse—no pun intended. Your gift would have been useless if it weren't for my bridle."

"An excellent point," said Cecrops.

"So tell me—who is the greater friend to mortals—Poseidon or I?"

Poseidon shook his trident menacingly at his divine niece. "You brat, that *invention* was just a worthless piece of leather—an immature attempt to one-up me! I'll never let that happen again!"

"Care to wager on that?" smiled Athena. "I say we have a contest. Whoever gives this city the most useful gift shall be its patron god or goddess. King Cecrops can judge between our gifts."

"A fine idea!" said Cecrops, who was excited by the prospect of what the gods could create.

"Very well," growled Poseidon, "but I will go first."

"May the best goddess win," said Athena coyly.

Poseidon went to the Acropolis, the highest hill of the city. "Behold! Even upon this high point, I summon water to flow forth from the ground. There will forever be a spring flowing here." Sure enough water bubbled up from the ground, and all the mortals murmured in amazement.

"This is a great gift!" said Cecrops, thoroughly impressed. But when the city-dwellers knelt by the pool and tasted the water, they immediately puckered their faces and spat it out. It was salty.

"Foolish Uncle," said Athena, "what good will a salty spring do these people? They only drink fresh water."

Poseidon growled, "Let's see you do any better!"

"Watch and learn," said Athena. She raised her elegant arms, and a tree grew up from the ground. "Behold! The first olive tree!"

Poseidon laughed. "A tree? What good is that?"

"Plenty! The people can harvest its fruit to eat. The oil from the olives can light their lamps and cook their food. They can build their boats and houses from its wood."

All the mortals applauded Athena's gift. It was obviously the more useful of the two.

Cecrops issued his verdict: "Both of your gifts are very kind, but I must say that Athena's gift is more useful."

"Ha! Then this shall be my city," the goddess said. "It shall be named Athens in my honor!"

King Cecrops nodded, and all the people cheered. But Poseidon would not be beaten so easily. He raised his trident and struck the earth—shaking the entire Acropolis violently. "Name this worthless rock pile whatever you want! It will soon be covered by my tides!" At the god's summons the sea rose and covered the plains below. "Rise, waves! Cover this miserable town forever!" He turned to the horrified King Cecrops and his cowering people.

"I suggest you all hold your breath—or grow some gills."

"Uncle, don't be such a sore loser!" Athena cried, but the sea god would not relent. The waters continued to rise, and the frightened city-dwellers sought shelter at the Acropolis. "Fine! If you will not listen to me, I will go to my father!"

Athena flew to Mount Olympus and appealed to her father, Zeus. She explained how she had won the right to be the patron of the city fair and square. So Zeus commanded Poseidon to retract his flood waters.

Poseidon roared in anger, and the ground shook. "Very well! I will not flood this miserable excuse for a city. But I declare that it will always be plagued by a lack of fresh water. You Athenians will find my sea-saltiness seeping into your ground water. When you taste this bitterness, you will regret not choosing me as your god." Then he disappeared dramatically.

Athena addressed the stunned Athenians. "Do not mind him. He is such a baby about these types of things!"

Poseidon's prediction did come partially true. Athens always suffered from a lack of fresh water, but the people never regretted choosing Athena as the protector of their city. She made Athens a bastion of wisdom, a center of learning and innovation. In eternal gratitude the citizens built a massive temple, the Parthenon, dedicated to Athena *Parthenos*, "the maiden goddess."

## DISCUSSION QUESTIONS

1. Why would a god or goddess want a city dedicated to him or her?
2. What does this story show us about Athena? What does it show us about Poseidon? Explain.
3. In another version of the story King Cecrops decides to have the people of the city vote for their patron god. In this election both men and women were allowed to vote. The men all chose Poseidon, and the women all voted for Athena. Since the women outnumbered the men by one person, Athena won the election. In anger the men took the right to vote away from the women. This myth explained why women were not allowed to vote in ancient Athens. Which version of the story do you like better? Explain.

# THE ADVENTURES OF APOLLO

Hera, Queen of Olympus, went into a jealous rage when she found out that the goddess Leto was about to give birth to twins fathered by Zeus. Fearing Hera's wrath, Leto fled from country to country, seeking for a place to deliver her divine twins. But Hera had declared, "No piece of earth will harbor this foul woman, Leto, or it will face my anger!" Since everyone knew just how nasty Hera could be, each place Leto traveled drove her away, although she begged, "Please! I just need a place to give birth to my children!" At last the God of the Seas, Poseidon, took pity on her. "Hera has said that no *land* should harbor you, but there is an island called Delos, which I have just raised from the sea—just a bobbing piece of earth not connected to any land. You may go there to give birth to your children." Leto thanked him, and the sea god whisked her away to the island of Delos.

Leto lay down underneath the only tree on the island, a palm, and gave birth to her twins. Leto's first child was a girl as luminous as the moon. She would one day grow up to be the dark-haired huntress, Artemis. Her second child was a fair-haired boy, Apollo—destined to be the god of light, truth, and music. Soon after this, Zeus appeared upon Delos to visit his new children. He presented each of them with a silver bow and a quiver full of arrows. Then Zeus blessed the island of Delos, and asked Poseidon to secure it to the bottom of the ocean.

As Apollo grew up, he decided to prove himself as one of the finest of the gods. "Mother, since I am young among the gods, I must perform some great deed that will make me worthy of worship."

"There is a terrible beast in the world of men," his mother told him. "It is called Python—a serpent with the strength of the gods. It lives in a deep cave in the side of Mount Parnassus. It terrorizes the mortals who live in the nearby city-state of Delphi."

"Then I have heard enough," Apollo declared. "I must slay it."

Apollo flew to Mount Parnassus and appeared before the cave of Python—his bow and arrows at the ready. "Come forth, earth-dragon!" The serpent came forth, breathing its fiery breath and baring its poisonous fangs, but the god battled it back with his arrows, which were like shafts of light. At last Apollo slew Python, and he dumped the body of the serpent into a deep chasm inside its lair.

"Here I shall make my temple, where people from all over Greece will come to hear the wise words spoken by my prophetess." Apollo appointed a priestess called Pythia to receive his divine messages. He made her a golden, three-legged stool, where she sat over the cleft in the Python's cave. Strange fumes lifted from the crack—rising from the decomposing body of the serpent far below. In a trance-like state, caused by the fumes, Apollo's oracle-prophetess would receive his words. And since Apollo was the God of Truth, the words of the Oracle of Delphi were considered to be as good as gold.

With Python slain and his shrine established, Apollo's reputation among the gods was secured. One day he was boasting of his accomplishments to Eros, the young god of love.

"Yes, it's true," Apollo said. "I slew the Python with my mighty arrows."

"Ha!" said Eros. "My arrows are mightier than yours. I have two types of arrows. One softens the heart and causes intense infatuation. The other hardens the heart and causes indifference."

Apollo laughed haughtily. "Arrows of love? How could you compare those dinky arrows to mine? Why didn't I think of using your *mighty love arrows* on Python? You are a ridiculous little god. Strength is mightier than love."

Angered by these words, Eros swore revenge. "We'll see who has the mightier arrows. Love can bring anyone to their knees."

One day, as Apollo sat watching, a young nymph named Daphne passed by. Eros saw his chance. Into Apollo's heart Eros fired an arrow of love, and into Daphne's heart he fired an arrow of indifference. Apollo was immediately overcome with passion for the young nymph, and he ran down the mountainside toward her shouting. "Yoo-hoo, sweet maiden! I am the god Apollo, slayer of the Python. Will you be my love?"

Thanks to the arrow of Eros, Daphne was instantly repulsed. "No way! Get away from me!"

The nymph ran away, but Apollo, overcome with desire, pursued her. "Wait, maiden! Wait!"

"Leave me alone!" Daphne's disgust drove her on, and Apollo's desire kept him on her heels.

"Please! I will do anything to make you mine! I have defeated Python, and I will defeat you as well!"

Eros watched all this, laughing until his sides ached at the sight of the noble god reduced to a love-struck fool. The chase continued, and although Daphne was swift, Apollo was swifter. She realized that Apollo was going to catch her. As she neared her home, the riverbank where she lived with her father, a river god, she cried out to him, "Father, please save me from this mad god!"

With a final burst of speed Apollo swept Daphne into his arms. "My sweet! At last you are mine!" But as soon as he felt the touch of Daphne's body, it began to change. Her skin roughened into bark, her lovely hair sprouted into leaves, her arms became branches, and her legs rooted themselves into the ground. When the transformation was complete, Daphne was a laurel tree. It was the only way her father could save her from Apollo's love.

Realizing that he had lost Daphne forever, Apollo's heart broke. "Oh, Eros, you are right. Your arrows are more powerful than mine. I will bear this deep wound forever." Then Apollo called out to the tree, "Laurel, who was once a maiden I loved, I will make you my sacred tree. Your leaves will crown the heads of mighty men. You will be a symbol of my greatness forever. At least in this way, you will be mine." At these words the tree seemed to bow its head in acknowledgement of Apollo's honor, and the god went sadly away.

## DISCUSSION QUESTIONS

1. What lessons did Apollo learn on his adventures?
2. Do you feel sorry for Apollo? Do you feel sorry for Daphne? Explain.
3. In ancient Greece laurel wreaths were placed on the heads of winners in athletic and poetic contests. The modern word *laureate* means one who has made an achievement in art or science. The phrase "resting on your laurels" means being content with your past successes and making no attempt to improve upon them. How are these traditions connected to the myth?

# UNDERWORLD FIND·IT

## CAN YOU FIND ALL OF THESE ITEMS IN THE PICTURE?

- Argo
- Bats (3)
- Bow and Arrows
- Calydonian Boar
- Cattle
- Chained Titans (2)
- Charon
- Chimera
- Crows (2)
- Flying Ram
- Flying Sandals (2)
- Ghosts (6)
- Giant Snake
- Girdle of Aphrodite
- Golden Fleece
- Gopher

- Gray Sisters (3)
- Hades
- Harpy
- Heads of Cerberus (3)
- Helmet of Invisibility
- Heracles
- Hermes
- Homer
- Icarus
- King Midas
- Medusa
- Minos, Judge of the Dead
- Minotaur
- Missing Eyeball
- Narcissus

- Orpheus
- Pegasus Symbol
- Persephone
- Pie
- Severed Heads (2)
- Skulls (12)
- Sphinx
- Spider
- Thunderbolt of Zeus
- Tiny Snake
- Tiresias
- Toad
- Tree of Dreams
- Trident of Poseidon
- Worm

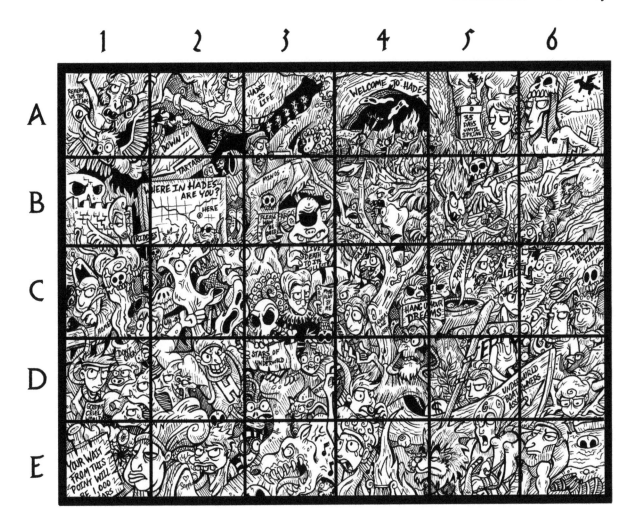

## UNDERWORLD FIND·IT ANSWER KEY

Argo, **B3**

Bats, **A2, D3**

Bow and Arrows, **D3-4**

Calydonian Boar, **C4**

Cattle, **C5-6**

Chained Titans, **A1-2**

Charon, **D4-5**

Chimera, **E4-5**

Crows, **B4, D6**

Flying Ram, **A3**

Flying Sandals, **A2, C6**

Ghosts, **A4, A5-B5, C2**

Giant Snake, **B4**

Girdle of Aphrodite, **B2**

Golden Fleece, **C3**

Gopher, **A3**

Gray Sisters, **C4-C5**

Hades, **A6**

Harpy, **B5**

Heads of Cerberus, **B4, C2, E3**

Helmet of Invis., **C1**

Heracles, **D2**

Hermes, **A4**

Homer, **C1**

Icarus, **A1**

King Midas, **C6**

Medusa, **D3**

Minos, **A-B3**

Minotaur, **C2-3**

Missing Eyeball, **E4**

Narcissus, **D6**

Orpheus, **E4**

Pegasus Symbol, **A6**

Persephone, **A5**

Pie, **C2**

Severed Heads, **D3, D5**

Skulls, **A6, A6, B1, B3, B5, C1, C3, C3, C6, D2, E3, E6**

Sphinx, **B1**

Spider, **E1**

Thunderbolt of Zeus, **A6**

Tiny Snake, **D5**

Tiresias, **B2**

Toad, **E3**

Tree of Dreams, **B4-C4-D4**

Trident, **C-D6**

Worm, **C4**

# TEMPLE TROUBLE

**Introduction to the Game:** You are the ruler of a nameless city-state in ancient Greece, and you want your city to be the richest in the land. You know that the way city-states become wealthy is by selling off their surplus grain after the harvest. The only way to get the grain to grow is to receive the blessing of the gods of Olympus, and the main way to get their favor is to build temples to them. But the gods are a fickle bunch. There are so many of them, and they're all so jealous of each other. In order to appease them all and keep from feeling their wrath, you will have to build many different temples! Welcome to Temple Trouble!

**Gameplay:** You decide how many temples to build to each god or goddess. Each time you build a temple to one of the gods, he or she gives you an immediate reward (e.g. money, an increase in bushels of grain, an increase in sale prices for your grain, etc.). When you reach the end of the game, any god or goddess who does *not* have at least one temple will strike you with a curse—exacting a punishment on your city-state. You must weigh your options carefully. Can you risk upsetting some of the gods if it means building more temples to others? Herein lies the strategy of the game.

**Object of the Game:** Make your city-state the richest in Greece. Money is made primarily through stockpiling grain and selling it at the end of the game.

**Number of Players:** 2-30 (Each player competes against all other players to see who will have the most money at the end of the game.)

**Game Setup:** Each player needs the following items:
1. A copy of the "Temple Trouble" game-sheet (pgs. 162-163)
2. A copy of the tally sheet (pg. 164)
3. A writing utensil
4. A calculator (optional)

**Game-Sheet:** This sheet is located on pgs. 162-163. It gives you information on the major gods and goddesses. Next to each Olympian is a reward and a punishment.
- **Rewards:** Each time you build a temple to a certain god or goddess, you are rewarded. For example, if you build a temple to Ares, he rewards you with $30 to add to your building funds. (Note: This reward is the same amount each time you build a temple to the god or

goddess. The reward amount does *not* increase or decrease based on the total number of temples you have built to a certain god or goddess.)

- **Punishments:** If you reach the end of the game and you have *not* built at least one temple to a certain god or goddess, he or she will punish you. This punishment happens *only once* at the end of the game. (For example, you did not build a temple to Hera. At the end of the game, she will strike you with the listed punishment.)

**Tally Sheet:** The tally sheet is on pg. 164.

1. Players use the tally sheet to keep track of four numerical totals.
    a. **Bushels of grain:** This is the amount of grain your city-state produces.
    b. **Building funds ($):** This money is for you to use to construct temples.
    c. **Number of citizens:** This is the number of people living in your city-state. This may increase or decrease based upon the reward or punishment of the gods.
    d. **Sale price per surplus bushel of grain:** At the end of the game, every citizen in your city-state uses a bushel of grain. Any leftover bushels will be considered surplus bushels. Then you can sell these surplus bushels for a hefty profit.
2. Players should begin with the following totals recorded on their tally sheet:
    a. Bushels of grain = 400
    b. Building funds ($) = $500
    c. Number of citizens = 200
    d. Sale price per surplus bushel of grain = $10
3. Changes to any of these totals should be recorded immediately on the tally sheet.
4. When your building funds reach $0, the game is over.

**Building Temples**

1. Decide which god or goddess you wish to build a temple.
2. The cost of each temple must be deducted immediately from the building funds.
    a. Each temple costs $25
    b. For example, you decide that your first temple will be built to Athena. You subtract $25 from your building funds ($), and make a tally mark for the goddess Athena on your game-sheet.
3. Use the tally sheet to keep track of every temple you build to each god or goddess. (Remember: If a god or goddess does not have a temple by the end of the game, he or she will punish you.)
4. Once you have built a temple, you *immediately* receive the reward that the god or goddess promises. For example, for each temple you build to Athena, she gives you $50. This $50 should be added to your building funds ($).
5. Temples can affect four things:
    a. Your number of bushels of grain
    b. Your number of citizens
    c. Your amount of building funds ($)
    d. The amount of money you receive for surplus bushels of grain at the end of the game
6. **Important:** A maximum of *five* temples can be built to each god or goddess. (For example, if you have built five temples to Hera, you must choose another Olympian.)

**Ending the Game**

1. When your building funds ($) reach zero (or you cannot build any more temples), the game is over.

    a. **Note:** The game can be ended and a final score calculated at any time the player chooses, but it is usually most advantageous to build temples until all building funds are spent.

2. Using the game-sheet, follow these steps to determine your final score:

    a. **Exact the Gods' Punishments:** Apply the punishment of any god or goddess who did not receive at least one temple.

    b. **Every Citizen Uses a Bushel of Grain:** Subtract your number of citizens (first column of the tally sheet) from your bushels of grain (second column). This number is your total bushels of surplus grain.

    c. **Selling Off Surplus Bushels:** Now multiply the bushels of surplus grain by the sale price of surplus bushels of grain (fourth column).

    d. **Totaling the City-State's Profit from the Grain:** This total is the amount of profit the city-state receives from the surplus grain. This is also your final score for the game.

    e. **Remaining building funds:** Add any remaining building funds to your profit/score.

    f. **Determining the Winner:** Compare your score to that of other players to see who has won.

# TEMPLE TROUBLE: AN ANCIENT GREEK TEMPLE-BUILDING GAME

| NAME | REWARD | PUNISHMENT |
|---|---|---|
| **ARES** God of War | You defeat the city-states who challenge you in battle. You win new wealth through military victories.<br><br>**Effect:** +25 drachmas ($) | You stink it up on the battlefield. You suffer military defeats and lose cropland.<br><br>**Effect:** -25 bushels of grain |
| **APHRODITE** Goddess of Love | Your citizens fall in love with their work, and industry increases.<br><br>**Effect:** +10 bushels of grain | Your citizens fall in love with each other, and the population increases.<br><br>**Effect:** +10 to number of citizens |
| **ZEUS** Lord of the Gods | The amount of rainfall increases, and your fields produce more grain.<br><br>**Effect:** +15 bushels of grain | A lightning storm damages your city-state and burns the surrounding fields.<br><br>**Effect:** -50 bushels of grain |
| **HERA** Queen of the Gods | The marriages of your citizens are strengthened, increasing their happiness and work ethic—not to mention the rate of childbirth.<br>**Effect:** +5 to number of citizens<br>+5 bushels of grain | The married women of your city grow unhappy. They stage a rebellion, stealing from the treasury and the grain supplies. Also childbirth rates increase.<br>**Effect:** -40 bushels of grain<br>+20 to number of citizens |
| **HERMES** Messenger God and God of Commerce | Trade between your city-state and the other city-states of Greece is increased.<br><br>**Effect:** +12 to surplus grain sale price | Trade between the city-states is slowed.<br><br>**Effect:** -5 to surplus grain sale price |
| **HEPHAESTUS** God of Fire and the Forge | The metal factories in your city-state become more profitable.<br><br>**Effect:** +30 drachmas ($) | The workers in your metal factories lose their desire to work hard.<br><br>**Effect:** -10 bushels of grain |
| **HEBE** Goddess of Youth | Your citizens feel more youthful and energetic; therefore, they work harder.<br><br>**Effect:** +10 bushels of grain | Your citizens feel older, complain of back pain, and work more slowly.<br><br>**Effect:** -5 bushels of grain |
| **HADES** Lord of the Underworld | The cold grip of death seizes some of your more unprofitable citizens.<br><br>**Effect:** -5 from number of citizens + 25 bushels of grain | Some of your laziest former citizens return from the Underworld and infect the other workers.<br><br>**Effect:** +15 number of citizens -10 bushels of grain |
| **DEMETER** Goddess of Agriculture | Demeter is pleased. Your fields prosper, and your grain supply increases.<br>**Effect:** +50 bushels of grain | Demeter's mood changes, and your fields wither.<br><br>**Effect:** -50 bushels of grain |

| | | |
|---|---|---|
| **PERSEPHONE** Goddess of Springtime | Persephone pays her mother, Demeter, a surprise visit. Conditions grow more spring-like. Your grain output increases.<br><br>**Effect:** +25 bushels of grain | Persephone refuses to visit her mother (or even give her a call). Conditions grow hostile. Your grain output decreases.<br><br>**Effect:** -35 bushels of grain |
| **APOLLO** God of Light, Truth, and the Arts | Drama, art, and music increase in your city-state. Your citizens are entertained at night, so they work harder during the day.<br>**Effect:** +35 bushels of grain | Your city is filled by bad art and re-run plays. Your citizens are *not* amused and refuse to work.<br><br>**Effect:** -15 bushels of grain |
| **ARTEMIS** Goddess of the Hunt | Your citizens are more successful in hunting wild game. They eat more meat and less grain.<br><br>**Effect:** +25 bushels of grain | Your citizens can't kill any wild game. Out of frustration over their lack of meat, they eat more grain.<br><br>**Effect:** -35 bushels of grain |
| **HESTIA** Goddess of the Home | Your citizens have happier home lives. The rate of childbirth increases, as does the amount of happiness tax paid by each household.<br>**Effect:** +5 to number of citizens +25 drachmas ($) | Some of your citizens love their homes so much they become afraid of the outside world. Because they don't show up in the fields, grain output decreases.<br><br>**Effect:** -10 bushels of grain |
| **POSEIDON** God of the Seas | Sea travel grows safer, and your city-state starts trading more with ports across the seas.<br>**Effect:** +10 to surplus grain sale price | Storms destroy part of your trading ships. Trade is decreased.<br><br>**Effect:** -7 to surplus grain sale price |
| **ATHENA** Goddess of Wisdom | Your citizens learn how to work smarter instead of harder. Industry in the city is increased.<br>**Effect:** +50 drachmas ($) | Your citizens become dumber. Worker accidents increase. Industry and field production decreases.<br>**Effect:** -20 bushels of grain |

# FINAL SCORE CALCULATOR

When your building funds reach $0 or are so low you cannot build more temples, the game is over. Any gods or goddess who did not receive a temple will punish you. Inflict these punishments now. Then calculate your final score using the system below.

1. Bushels of grain − number of citizens = # of surplus bushels of grain
2. # of surplus bushels of grain x sale price per surplus bushel = Final score ($)

FINAL SCORE: _____

| Number of Citizens | Bushels of Grain | Building Funds ($) | Sale Price Per Surplus Bushel of Grain |
|---|---|---|---|
| 200 | 400 | 500 | 10 |
| | | | |

| TEMPLE TALLY MARKS | Ares | Aphrodite | Zeus |
|---|---|---|---|
| Hera | Hermes | Hephaestus | Hebe |
| Hades | Demeter | Persephone | Apollo |
| Artemis | Hestia | Poseidon | Athena |

# GLOSSARY OF IMPORTANT NAMES

**Achilles** Greatest Greek warrior in the Trojan War, son of Thetis the sea nymph, trained by Chiron the centaur, died by taking one of Paris's arrows in the heel

**Aeneas** Trojan son of Aphrodite, after the sack of Troy set out on his own quest to start a new city-state based on the legacy of Troy

**Aeolus** Lord of the winds

**Agamemnon** Ruler of Mycenae, brother of Menelaus, leader of the united Greek armies, slain by his wife, Clytemnestra

**Ajax** Greek chieftain who committed suicide during the Trojan War

**Alecto** (see "Furies")

**Andromache** Wife of Hector, taken into captivity after the Trojan War by Pyrrhus, the son of Achilles

**Aphrodite** (Roman name: Venus) Goddess of love and beauty, born from the foam of the sea, sister of Zeus, wife of Hephaestus, lover of Ares, mother of Eros and Aeneas

**Apollo** (Roman name: Phoebus Apollo) God of light and truth, twin brother to Artemis, son of Zeus, gifted in poetry and the playing of the lyre, his oracle in Delphi was the most popular in Greece

**Arachne** Weaver, transformed by Athena into the first spider

**Ares** (Roman name: Mars) God of war, son of Zeus

**Argus** One-hundred-eyed henchman of Hera

**Ariadne** Daughter of Minos, helper of Theseus

**Artemis** (Roman name: Diana) Goddess of wild things, goddess of the moon, twin sister to Apollo, daughter of Zeus, virgin goddess

**Astyanax** Infant son of Hector and Andromache, during the sack of Troy flung from the walls of the city to his death

**Atalanta** Heroine of ancient Greece, known for her nearly superhuman speed, helped to kill the giant boar of Calydon, joined Jason on his quest for the Golden Fleece

**Athena** (Roman name: Minerva) Goddess of wisdom, goddess of handicrafts, protector of the city, daughter of Zeus, inventor of the bridle, patroness of Athens, leader of the virgin goddesses

**Atlas** The titan who is forced to forever bear the weight of the sky

**Bellerophon** Hero of ancient Greece, tamer of Pegasus, slayer of the Chimera

**Calypso** Sea nymph, lover of Odysseus

**Cassandra** Sister of Hector and Paris, prophetess, taken as a concubine by Agamemnon after the fall of Troy

**Centaur** Half-man, half-horse creature known for its wild and violent tendencies

**Cerberus** Three-headed hell-hound that prevents entrance into the Underworld

**Charon** Aged boatman who ferries souls across the River Styx in the Underworld

**Charybdis** Gigantic whirlpool, notorious for sucking ships down to their destruction

**Chimera** Fearsome creature, part-lion, part-goat, part-snake, defeated by Bellerophon

**Chiron** Wise centaur, renowned as a trainer of heroes, raised Jason up from a child, trainer of Achilles

**Circe** Famous witch, transforms the men of Odysseus into pigs

**Cronus** (Roman name: Saturn) Titan father of the first gods, devours his children to prevent them from overthrowing him

**Cyclops** (plural: Cyclopes) Large beings that have only one eye, said to be the sons of Poseidon

**Daedalus** Famous Athenian inventor, designer of the Labyrinth

**Demeter** (Roman name: Ceres) Goddess of the harvest and nature, mother of Persephone

**Deucalion** Mortal who along with his wife, Pyrrha, built a boat to escape the great flood

**Dido** Queen of Carthage, lover of Aeneas

**Diomedes** Famed warrior of the Greeks, during the Trojan War earned the distinction of physically harming two gods

**Dionysus** (Roman name: Bacchus) God of wine, the youngest of the gods

**Dryad** Tree nymph

**Electra** Daughter of Agamemnon and Clytemnestra

**Eos** (Roman name: Aurora) Goddess of the dawn

**Epimetheus** Titan, dimwitted brother of Prometheus

**Eris** Goddess of discord

**Eros** (Roman name: Cupid) Son of Aphrodite, shoots arrows that cause extreme infatuation

**Fates** Three ancient beings that control the lives of all living things, one spins out the thread of life, one measures out its length, one cuts the thread at the time of death

**Furies** Three foul spirits who torture those who commit offensive crimes

**Gaea** Spirit of the earth, "Mother Earth"

**Giants** Large monsters born from the blood of Uranus, attempt to climb to Olympus

**Gorgon** (see "Medusa")

**Gray Women** Three old hags who all share a single eyeball

**Hades** (Roman name: Pluto) Ruler of the Underworld and the dead

**Harpy** Evil creature, head of a woman, body of a bird, repugnant stench

**Hebe** Goddess of youth, cupbearer of the gods

**Hector** Greatest prince of Troy, defended his brother Paris against the Greeks

**Hecuba** Queen of Troy, wife of Priam, taken into slavery after the fall of Troy, stoned to death by the men of Odysseus

**Helen** Most beautiful woman in the world, daughter of Zeus, wife of Menelaus, given back to Menelaus after the fall of Troy

**Helios** God of the sun, drives a fiery chariot across the sky each day

**Hephaestus** (Roman name: Vulcan) God of fire and the forge, only ugly god, husband of Aphrodite, son of Zeus

**Hera** (Roman name: Juno) Queen of Olympus, protector of marriage, jealous wife of Zeus, busied herself making life miserable for Zeus's many mistresses and illegitimate children

**Heracles** (Roman name: Hercules) Mightiest Greek hero, endowed with superhuman strength, mortal enemy of Hera

**Hermes** (Roman name: Mercury) Messenger god of Olympus, god of commerce, guides souls down to the Underworld after death, master thief, inventor of the lyre, wears winged sandals upon his feet and a winged cap upon his head, carries a magical wand bearing the image of spread wings and intertwined serpents

**Hippomenes** Swift warrior, husband of Atalanta

**Icarus** Son of Daedalus, died while attempting human flight

**Iphigenia** Daughter of Agamemnon and Clytemnestra, offered as a human sacrifice to appease the anger of Artemis

**Iris** Goddess of the rainbow, secondary messenger of the gods

**Iulus** Young son of Aeneas

**Jason** Leader of the Argonauts, trained by Chiron, husband of Medea

**Medea** Witch, wife of Jason, murdered her young sons

**Medusa** Snake-haired gorgon, possessed the power to turn men into stone if they met her gaze

**Meleager** Famous warrior, admirer of Atalanta

**Menelaus** Brother of Agamemnon, ruler of Sparta, husband of Helen

**Midas** Foolish king who wished for everything he touched to turn to gold

**Minos** King of Crete, keeper of the Minotaur

**Minotaur** Half-man, half-bull creature, kept by King Minos in the Labyrinth

**Mnemosyne** Goddess of memory, mother of the nine muses

**Muses** Nine immortal beings who inspire every form of art

**Myrmidons** Fighting men of Achilles, their race is said to have been created from ants

**Naiad** Water nymph

**Narcissus** Handsome boy who falls in love with his own reflection

**Nemesis** Goddess of retribution

**Nestor** Oldest Greek chieftain who fought in the Trojan War, known for his great wisdom

**Nymph** Female nature spirit (see "Dryad" and "Naiad")

**Ocean** Punished titan, the body of water which surrounds the known world

**Odysseus** (Roman name: Ulysses) King of Ithaca, vowed to protect the honor of Helen with the other kings of Greece, formed the idea of the Trojan Horse, wandered ten years at sea to reach his home after the fall of Troy

**Oedipus** King of Thebes, murdered his father and married his mother

**Olympus** Home of the gods

**Oracle** One who speaks the wisdom of the gods, traditionally the priestess of a god or goddess's temple

**Orestes** Son of Agamemnon and Clytemnestra, avenges the murder of his father

**Orpheus** Famed musician, descended into the Underworld to rescue his lost love, accompanied Jason on his quest for the Golden Fleece

**Pan** Satyr, god of shepherds

**Pandora** First woman, opens a jar filled with evils sent to her by Zeus

**Paris** Exiled prince of Troy, lover of Helen, son of Priam, judged the beauty contest of the goddesses, killed by Prince Philoctetes in the Trojan War

**Patroclus** Beloved friend of Achilles, his death caused Achilles to re-enter the Trojan War

**Pegasus** Famed winged horse, ridden by Bellerophon

**Penelope** Queen of Ithaca, wife of Odysseus

**Persephone** (Roman name: Proserpine) Goddess of spring, queen of the Underworld

**Perseus** Hero, slayer of Medusa, founded the city-state Mycenae, married to the princess Andromeda

**Phaethon** Mortal son of Helios, asked to drive his father's chariot, caused natural disasters all across the world

**Philoctetes** Prince who bore the bow and arrows of Heracles, abandoned by the Greeks on the island of Lemnos for ten years

**Phineus** Prophet cursed by Zeus, plagued by the Harpies, helps the Argonauts on their quest

**Polyphemus** Famous Cyclops, tricked by Odysseus (Ulysses) and blinded by his men

**Poseidon** (Roman name: Neptune) God of the sea, brother of Zeus, giver of the horse to man, carries a trident (a three-pronged spear)

**Priam** Elderly king of Troy, defended his son Paris against the Greeks, killed by the son of Achilles during the sack of Troy

**Prometheus** Titan who stole fire from the gods and gave it to man

**Proteus** Shape-shifting creature, known as "the old man of the sea"

**Pyrrhus** Red-haired son of Achilles, sired by Achilles during his stay at the court of Lycomedes, brought to Troy by Odysseus

**Rhadamanthus** Mortal king who judges the dead in the Underworld

**Rhea** Titan, mother of the first gods

**Satyr** Half-goat, half-man creature

**Scylla** Many-headed monster rooted to a rock in the middle of the ocean, notorious for sinking ships

**Selene** Goddess of the moon, drives her silvery chariot across the sky each night

**Silenus** Satyr, foster-father and tutor of Dionysus

**Sisyphus** Mortal king punished in the Underworld, must roll a boulder up a hill for eternity

**Sphinx** Creature with the head of a woman, the body of a lion, the wings of an eagle, and the tail of a snake, great teller of riddles, defeated by Oedipus

**Tantalus** Mortal king punished in the Underworld, cannot drink from the water at his feet or eat of the fruit that hangs just out of his reach

**Tartarus** The deepest part of the Underworld, where many of the titans were chained

**Telemachus** Prince of Ithaca, son of Odysseus

**Thanatos** God of death, releases mortal souls from their bodies

**Theseus** Famous Greek hero, slayer of the Minotaur

**Thetis** Sea nymph, mother of Achilles, wife of Peleus

**Tiresias** Blind prophet of Thebes, lived for seven generations of men

**Troy** City of legend, located on the shores of Asia Minor, destroyed by the Greeks

**Uranus** "Father Heaven," deity of the sky, castrated by his son Cronus

**Zephyr** The west wind

**Zeus** (Roman name: Jupiter, Jove) Ruler of the gods, wielder of the mighty thunderbolt, father of many heroes

# PRONUNCIATION GUIDE

| | | | |
|---|---|---|---|
| Achates | (UH-KĀ-TEEZ) | Briseis | (BRIH-SEE-US) |
| Acheron | (ACK-UH-RUN) | Cadmus | (KAD-MUS) |
| Achilles | (UH-KIL-EEZ) | Calchas | (KAL-KUS) |
| Acrisius | (UH-KRIH-SEE-US) | Calliope | (KUH-LĪ-Ō-PEE) |
| Actaeon | (ACT-EE-ON) | Calydon | (KAL-IH-DUN) |
| Æetes | (EE-UH-TEEZ) | Calypso | (KUH-LIP-SŌ) |
| Aegeus | (EE-GEE-US) | Carthage | (KAR-THIJ) |
| Aegina | (EE-JĪ-NUH) | Cassandra | (KUH-SAN-DRUH) |
| Aeneas | (EE-NEE-US) | Castor | (KAS-TER) |
| Aeneid | (EE-NEE-ID) | Caucasus | (KAW-KĀ-SUS) |
| Aeolus | (EE-Ō-LUS) | Cecrops | (SEE-KROPS) |
| Aethra | (EE-THRUH) | Centaur | (SIN-TAWR) |
| Agamemnon | (AG-UH-MEM-NON) | Cerberus | (SER-BUR-US) |
| Alcema | (AL-SEE-MUH) | Charon | (KAH-RUN) |
| Alcinous | (AL-SIN-YOO-US) | Charybdis | (KUH-RIB-DIS) |
| Alcmene | (ALK-MEE-NEE) | Chimera | (KĪ-MEE-RUH) |
| Alecto | (UH-LEK-TŌ) | Chiron | (KĪ-RUN) |
| Amata | (UH-MĀ-TUH) | Chryseis | (KRĪ-SEE-ISS) |
| Amphitryon | (AM-FIT-TREE-UN) | Circe | (SER-SEE) |
| Anchises | (AN-KĪ-ZEEZ) | Clio | (KLEE-Ō) |
| Androgeos | (AN-DRO-GEE-US) | Clymene | (KLĪ-MEE-NEE) |
| Andromache | (AN-DRAH-MUH-KEE) | Clytemnestra | (KLĪ-TIM-NES-TRUH) |
| Andromeda | (AN-DRAH-MEE-DUH) | Colchis | (KŌL-KIS) |
| Antigone | (AN-TIG-UH-NEE) | Corinth | (KŌR-INTH) |
| Antinous | (AN-TEN-YOO-US) | Creon | (KREE-ON) |
| Aphrodite | (AF-RŌ-DĪ-TEE) | Cronus | (KRŌ-NUS) |
| Apollo | (UH-PAW-LŌ) | Cumae | (KOO-MEE) |
| Arachne | (UH-RAK-NEE) | Cupid | (KEW-PID) |
| Arcadia | (AR-KĀ-DEE-UH) | Cyclopes | (SĪ-KLOP-EEZ) |
| Ares | (AIR-EEZ) | Cyclops | (SĪ-KLOPZ) |
| Argos | (AR-GŌS) | Daedalus | (DĀ-DUH-LUS) |
| Argus | (AR-GUS) | Danaë | (DUH-NĀ-EE) |
| Ariadne | (AIR-EE-AHD-NEE) | Deidamia | (DEE-UH-DAH-MEE-UH) |
| Artemis | (AR-TUH-MIS) | Delos | (DEE-LŌS) |
| Asterion | (AS-TEER-EE-UN) | Delphi | (DEL-FĪ) |
| Astyanax | (UH-STĪ-UH-NAX) | Demeter | (DEE-MEE-TER) |
| Atalanta | (AT-UH-LAN-TUH) | Deucalion | (DOO-KĀ-LEE-UN) |
| Athena | (UH-THEE-NUH) | Dido | (DĪ-DŌ) |
| Atlas | (AT-LUS) | Diomedes | (DĪ-Ō-MEE-DEEZ) |
| Atreus | (UH-TRĀ-OOS) | Dionysus | (DĪ-Ō-NĪ-SUS) |
| Augeas | (AWG-EE-US) | Dryad | (DRĪ-AD) |
| Aulis | (Ō-LIS) | Electra | (EE-LEK-TRUH) |
| Bacchus | (BAHK-US) | Eos | (EE-AHS) |
| Battus | (BAT-US) | Epaphus | (EH-PUH-FUS) |
| Bellerophon | (BEH-LEHR-UH-FUN) | Epeios | (EE-PĀ-OS) |
| Bia | (BĪ-UH) | Ephialtes | (EH-FEE-UHL-TEEZ) |

| | | | |
|---|---|---|---|
| Epimetheus | (EP-IH-MEE-THEE-US) | Kithairon | (KIH-THĪ-RUN) |
| Eris | (EH-RUS) | Knossos | (NAW-SUS) |
| Eros | (EE-ROS) | Kratos | (KRĀ-TŌS) |
| Eumaeus | (YOO-MĀ-US) | Lacedaemon | (LAH-SEE-DEE-MUN) |
| Europa | (YOO-RŌ-PUH) | Laertes | (LĀ-ER-TEEZ) |
| Eurycleia | (YOOR-IH-KLEE-UH) | Laius | (LĀ-US) |
| Eurydice | (YOO-RIH-DIH-SEE) | Laocoön | (LĀ-Ō-KOO-UN) |
| Eurylochus | (YOO-RIL-UH-KUS) | Latinus | (LUH-TĪ-NUS) |
| Eurymachus | (YOO-RIM-UH-KUS) | Latium | (LĀ-SHI-UM) |
| Eurynome | (YOO-RIH-NUH-MEE) | Leda | (LEE-DUH) |
| Eurystheus | (YOO-RIS-THEE-US) | Lemnos | (LEM-NUS) |
| Gaea | (GĪ-UH) | Lethe | (LEE-THEE) |
| Geryon | (JEER-EE-UN) | Leto | (LEE-TŌ) |
| Glaucus | (GLAW-KUS) | Lycaon | (LĪ-KĀ-UN) |
| Gorgon | (GOR-GUN) | Lycomedes | (LĪ-KŌ-MEE-DEEZ) |
| Hades | (HĀ-DEEZ) | Lycus | (LĪ-KUS) |
| Harpies | (HAR-PEEZ) | Lyre | (LĪ-ER) |
| Hebe | (HEE-BEE) | Maenad | (MEE-NAD) |
| Hector | (HEK-TER) | Maron | (MAH-RUN) |
| Hecuba | (HEK-YOO-BUH) | Medea | (MEE-DEE-UH) |
| Helenus | (HEL-UH-NUS) | Medus | (MEH-DUS) |
| Helios | (HEE-LEE-ŌS) | Medusa | (MEH-DOO-SUH) |
| Hephaestus | (HEE-FES-TUS) | Meleager | (MEH-LEE-UH-JER) |
| Hera | (HEH-RUH) | Memnon | (MEM-NUN) |
| Heracles | (HEH-RUH-KLEEZ) | Menelaus | (MEN-UH-LĀ-US) |
| Hercules | (HER-KYOO-LEEZ) | Mentes | (MEN-TEEZ) |
| Hermes | (HER-MEEZ) | Mercury | (MER-KYOO-REE) |
| Hermione | (HER-MĪ-Ō-NEE) | Midas | (MĪ-DUS) |
| Hesperides | (HES-PER-Ī-DEES) | Minerva | (MIH-NER-VUH) |
| Hippolyta | (HIH-PAW-LIH-TUH) | Minos | (MĪ-NUS) |
| Hippomenes | (HIH-PAWM-UH-NEEZ) | Minotaur | (MĪ-NŌ-TAR) |
| Hypsipyle | (HIP-SIP-UH-LEE) | Mnemosyne | (NEE-MAWZ-IH-NEE) |
| Iasus | (Ī-Ā-SUS) | Mycenae | (MĪ-SEE-NEE) |
| Icarius | (IH-KAR-EE-US) | Myrmidon | (MER-MIH-DON) |
| Icarus | (IH-KAR-US) | Naiad | (NĪ-AD) |
| Iliad | (IH-LEE-AD) | Narcissus | (NAR-SIS-US) |
| Ilium | (IH-LEE-UM) | Nausicaa | (NAW-SEE-KUH) |
| Ino | (Ī-NŌ) | Nemean | (NEE-MEE-UN) |
| Io | (Ī-O) | Neoptolemus | (NEE-Ō-TOL-EE-MUS) |
| Iolaus | (Ī-Ō-LĀ-US) | Neptune | (NEP-TOON) |
| Iolcus | (Ī-UL-KUS) | Niobe | (NĪ-Ō-BEE) |
| Iphigenia | (IF-UH-JUH-NĪ-UH) | Odysseus | (Ō-DIS-EE-US) |
| Iris | (Ī-RIS) | Oedipus | (ED-IH-PUS) |
| Ithaca | (ITH-UH-KUH) | Oeta | (EE-TUH) |
| Iulus | (YOO-LUS) | Ogygia | (Ō-JIH-JEE-UH) |
| Janus | (JĀ-NUS) | Orestes | (Ō-RES-TEEZ) |
| Jocasta | (YŌ-KAS-TUH) | Orpheus | (OR-FEE-US) |
| Juno | (JOO-NŌ) | Otus | (Ō-TUS) |
| Jupiter | (JOO-PIH-TUR) | Ovid | (Ō-VID) |

| | | | |
|---|---|---|---|
| Palamedes | (PAL-UH-MEE-DEEZ) | Pylos | (PĪ-LŌS) |
| Pallas | (PAL-US) | Pyrrha | (PEER-UH) |
| Pandarus | (PAN-DĀR-US) | Pyrrhus | (PEER-US) |
| Pandora | (PAN-DOR-UH) | Remus | (REE-MUS) |
| Parnassus | (PAR-NAH-SUS) | Rhea | (REE-UH) |
| Pasiphae | (PAS-IH-FĀ-EE) | Romulus | (ROM-YOO-LUS) |
| Patroclus | (PAH-TRŌ-KLUS) | Satyr | (SĀ-TER) |
| Peleus | (PEE-LEE-US) | Sciron | (SKĪ-RUN) |
| Pelias | (PEE-LEE-US) | Scorpio | (SKOR-PEE-Ō) |
| Penelope | (PEH-NEL-Ō-PEE) | Scylla | (SIL-UH) |
| Penthesilea | (PEN-THES-UH-LEE-UH) | Scyros | (SKĪ-RUS) |
| Perigune | (PER-IH-GOO-NEE) | Selene | (SEE-LEE-NEE) |
| Persephone | (PER-SEF-UH-NEE) | Silenus | (SUH-LĪ-NUS) |
| Perseus | (PER-SEE-US) | Sinis | (SĪ-NUS) |
| Phaeacia | (FĀ-EE-SHUH) | Sinon | (SĪ-NON) |
| Phaethon | (FĀ-UH-THUN) | Sisyphus | (SIH-SIH-FUS) |
| Philoctetes | (FIL-OK-TEE-TEEZ) | Styx | (STIKS) |
| Phineus | (FIN-EE-US) | Tantalus | (TAN-TUH-LUS) |
| Phoebe | (FEE-BEE) | Tartarus | (TAR-TUH-RUS) |
| Phoebus | (FEE-BUS) | Taurus | (TAW-RUS) |
| Phrygia | (FRIH-GEE-UH) | Telemachus | (TUH-LEM-UH-KUS) |
| Pirene | (PĪ-REE-NEE) | Thalia | (THUH-LĪ-UH) |
| Pisistratus | (PIH-SIH-STRAH-TUS) | Thanatos | (THAN-UH-TŌS) |
| Pittheus | (PITH-EE-US) | Thebes | (THEEBZ) |
| Plautus | (PLAW-TUS) | Themis | (THEE-MUS) |
| Pluto | (PLOO-TŌ) | Theseus | (THEE-SEE-US) |
| Polites | (PŌ-LĪ-TEEZ) | Thessaly | (THEHS-UH-LEE) |
| Polyidus | (PŌ-LEE-Ī-DUS) | Thetis | (THEE-TIS) |
| Polyphemus | (PŌ-LEE-FEE-MUS) | Tiresias | (TĪ-REE-SEE-US) |
| Polyxena | (POL-EK-ZEE-NUH) | Tiryns | (TEER-UNZ) |
| Poseidon | (PŌ-SĪ-DUN) | Troezen | (TREE-ZUN) |
| Priam | (PRĪ-UM) | Troilus | (TROY-LUS) |
| Procrustes | (PRŌ-KRUS-TEEZ) | Tyndareus | (TIN-DARE-EE-US) |
| Prometheus | (PRŌ-MEE-THEE-US) | Uranus | (YOO-RUN-US) |
| Proserpine | (PRŌ-SER-PEEN-UH) | Zeus | (ZOOS) |
| Proteus | (PRŌ-TEE-US) | | |

## ABOUT THE AUTHOR

Zachary "Zak" Hamby is a teacher of English in rural Missouri, where he has taught mythology for many years. In mythology he has seen the ability of ancient stories to capture the imaginations of young people today. For this reason he has created a variety of teaching materials (including textbooks, posters, and websites) that focus specifically on the teaching of mythology to young people. He is the author of two book series, the *Reaching Olympus* series and the *Mythology for Teens* series. He is also a professional illustrator. His wife (and editor), Rachel, is an English teacher as well. They reside in the beautiful Ozark hills with their two children.

For more information and products including textbooks, posters, and electronic content visit his website **www.mythologyteacher.com**

Contact him by email at **hambypublishing@gmail.com**

CPSIA information can be obtained
at www.ICGtesting.com
Printed in the USA
BVHW06s1948110518
515764BV00007B/91/P

9 780982 704905